3²⁰

HUBERT H. HUMPHREY
Champion of Human Rights

Men of Achievement Series

HUBERT H. HUMPHREY
Champion of Human Rights

by
GLADYS ZEHNPFENNIG

Publishers
T. S. DENISON & COMPANY, INC.
Minneapolis

27345

Dedication:

To Grace Tully

whose candlelight

has warmed our spirits.

Foreword

The skinny, vibrant-voiced young leader of the Minnesota delegation leaped to national fame at the Democratic Convention in 1948 with the most stirring civil rights appeal since the days of Abraham Lincoln. Hubert Horatio Humphrey, who had already achieved stature as the crusading mayor of Minneapolis, was following the dictates of his conscience at the risk of becoming a political "shooting star" in the space of those few minutes.

Humphrey is an exuberant, high-spirited patriot with a progressive, humanitarian philosophy and a firm belief in government of, by, and for all the people. The drama and suspense of politics, the tumultuous cheers of victory or the leaden-gray silence of defeat—to these he seems born, as much as any man can be born to a certain destiny.

Why would an average American boy from a small town on the South Dakota prairies dare to ask so much of life, and why does he encourage other bright young people to interest themselves in politics as "a distinguished and honorable profession?" How did he get there—this man who was a pharmacist in an agricultural community during the depression, a college "drop-out" when money was scarce, an apartment house janitor, and even a part-time sandwich peddler on the campus of Louisiana State University?

The story of Hubert Humphrey is the story of a man in action, a man who looked to the doors ahead and speeded toward them with bubbling wit and enthusiasm. He was the young genius behind the merger of the Democratic and Farmer-Labor parties in Minnesota—a political phenomenon that has carried other energetic young candidates to top offices in the state and nation. As the first Democrat to be elected to the Senate from Minnesota in ninety years, he was never at a loss for words because he always did his "legislative homework" with zest and dedication.

There were periods of frustration and grim disappointment, but Humphrey was often stimulated by a vision of the Greatest American Dream of all. It came, on a night of dazzling glory in Atlantic City, when President Lyndon B. Johnson tantalized the suspense-charged Democratic Convention with his description of "the best-equipped man in this nation to be President if something happened to the President." At last he gave the delegates and the country the name of Hubert Horatio Humphrey, who would become the first man from the Upper Midwest ever to achieve one of the two highest executive offices in the land.

Hubert Humphrey, the speaker, has often overshadowed Hubert Humphrey, the legislator. Every American should be informed about Senator Humphrey's persistent promotion of the Food-for-Peace, Medicare, Civil Rights and Peace Corps programs. He has fought fiercely for legislation that has touched the life of almost every American—the farmer, the small businessman, the elementary and college student, the worker in the factory and the victim of poverty and discrimination. He has become recognized as an authority on everything from farm and business problems to international relations and space exploration.

As the "Evangelist for the Great Society," Vice President Humphrey talks of his country in terms of people. He is ambitious for his countrymen—and not only for its little people who are struggling to become bigger people. He also speaks with glowing admiration of the dynamics of modern big business leadership and refers to the American free enterprise system as "humanitarian capitalism."

Included in the biography is the full text of the young Minneapolis mayor's challenging Civil Rights speech at the 1948 Democratic Convention. Other highlights deal with the Minnesota Senator's eight-hour "talkathon" with Premier Khrushchev, his affectionate regard for President Kennedy and President Johnson, his interest in young people, and his deep commitment to the war against poverty, illiteracy and oppression everywhere in the world.

The author of this biography was born in South Dakota and later lived in Minnesota during the years when Hubert Humphrey was winning his way from the lower rungs to the heights of the political ladder. Now as a resident of Winchester, Virginia, she has had access to sources of information at the Library of Congress and the Capitol in Washington.

Contents

Chapter One

A Breathless Eagerness

"I see, in the America of tomorrow, the true spiritual and cultural capital of the world. It will be heir to man's loftiest hopes and achievements. It will be a land of many races and religions, of peoples cosmopolitan and understanding of each other—yet each cherishing unique traditions. It will be a land such as never existed before, and it will vibrate with the creativity of unleashed talents of millions . . ." Hubert H. Humphrey in "The Cause Is Humanity."

* * * *

A young lad, in 1920, could "mosey along" through goldenrod and weed patches where random grasshoppers flipped into the air and a rabbit might be glimpsed fleeing through the coarse foliage. In the cropped grass of prairie pasture lands, a gopher might dive frantically into his hole. There are remembrances of a lively land—of hot blue skies, of pelting rains, of fantastic blizzards.

Between that time and now, the face of the northern prairie would change. The grasshoppers would no longer skip high as though in friendly greeting, the skies would rain dust on wilting cornfields, and many of the bright expectations of the future would curdle in the throes of a gigantic depression.

Between that time and now, there would be hardship and heartache, recovery and progress. And one fine day the people of the northern prairie could look toward the great dome of the nation's capitol and feel proud that a native son had achieved one of the most honorable and powerful offices in the world.

Hubert Horatio Humphrey represents the triumph of that northern prairie country—a region of sweeping pasture lands, of fertile acres of wheat and alfalfa, of corn that is knee high by the Fourth of July.

Every now and then, an average-appearing youngster will grow up to bring a burst of historical immortality to his native state. Even though Humphrey achieved national fame as a spunky mayor of Minneapolis and Honorable Member of the United States Senate from Minnesota, South Dakota shares the pride and distinction. When the thirty-eighth Vice President of the United States reminisces about his boyhood, he talks glowingly of Doland, South Dakota.

Other distinguished statesmen from the Upper Midwest have served in Congress and the Cabinet, and some of them have set their sights toward higher goals —but Hubert Humphrey's election to the nation's number two position is a "first." Particularly significant is the fact that South Dakota—a traditionally Republican state—gave the Johnson-Humphrey ticket a comfortable margin in the 1964 election. In 1960, the winner's name was Richard Nixon.

Midwesterners marvel at the Humphrey "miracle." They say, "You've got to give him credit—he certainly didn't start out with more than anybody else!" Or did he? It is apparent that he was born with a silver tongue, instead of a silver spoon, in his mouth.

Young Hubert's birthplace was the small town of Wallace, South Dakota, an almost deserted village now. When the future Vice President of the United States made his appearance there, on May 27, 1911, he undoubtedly announced his arrival with oratorical gusto. Whether or not it had anything to do with his success, he had managed to be born in one of the most delightful months of the prairie country year. The grass is green, the lilacs are magnificent, and school children search the pastures for "May Flowers"—the American Pasque Flower that is the official state flower of South Dakota. Almost forgotten are the below-zero temperatures of winter and the lingering slush of March and April. The hot winds of August seem far in the future.

Humphrey's lifelong interest in small businessmen was a grass roots affair. Rather than "to any mansion born," he was "to the drugstore born." The family living quarters were located above his father's drugstore. Before the town of Wallace made much impression on two-year-old Hubert, his father moved the family and his business to Doland, another small town farther west in the prairie state. There, Hubert and his older brother Ralph, and two younger sisters, Fern and Frances, spent the years of their youth. Every now and then they were taken back to Wallace to visit on the farm of their maternal grandparents, and to enjoy reunions with a host of relatives with wonderful Norwegian names.

The mother of the family, Christine Sannes Humphrey, was blessed with the hardy Scandinavian ancestry of many South Dakotans. Born in Kristiansand, Norway, she was endowed by nature with the ability to keep a home both tidy and comfortable for a family of bubbling extroverts. Frances, the younger daughter, recalls that their mother would make up little poems for them. "She also read us Dickens and the classics."

Ever since he was a small boy, Hubert Jr.'s interest in people has involved him in their joys and despairs, their dreams of glory and their hopes for the future. Much of the stimulation and inspiration for this attitude can be traced to his father, a very unusual gentleman who didn't believe in corporal punishment. As Frances so eloquently put it, "Father's discipline was not to spank but to look at us as if he didn't know us for a week and that silent treatment was enough."

Hubert spent a good deal of his young life working in Dad Humphrey's drugstore. He grew up watching his father operate as a useful citizen, a rural pharmacist with modern ideas about dispensing prescriptions, miscellaneous merchandise, and light lunches—all under one roof—in the interests of keeping a thriving business going.

There was one unique difference; Hubert Sr. also dispensed his own brands of philosophical and practical wisdom. Talkative, well-informed, filled with patriotic idealism, Dad Humphrey was one of Doland's two intellectual leaders. The other was the local Methodist minister who had gone to Harvard and could hold up his own end of the conversation. The talkers and listeners would often gather in the Humphrey drugstore until all hours of the night.

The elder Humphrey's ancestors came to South Dakota by way of New England and far-western territory. One forebear fought in the Revolutionary War, but Dad Humphrey was born near the attractive town of Albany, Oregon.

Hubert Humphrey Sr., who worked his way up through a succession of "shoestring" drugstores in South Dakota, was a man of deep social awareness. Loving his country, he could see beyond its shortcomings to its magnificent potential. He was an optimistic booster for America and the future of democracy. He was not afraid to be different—he was a liberal Democrat at a time when most South Dakotans considered it "nicer" to be conservative Republicans.

There is something quite conservative about most of the Dakota terrain, and the people have deep ties with the soil. Once described as "wilderness country unfit for human habitation," the pioneers who broke the soil found good earth there. Mostly, South Dakota is level prairie land—hundreds of square miles of it.

Sometimes visitors drive westward out of their shadowed city canyons in New York and Chicago and complain that the prairie is flat and monotonous, with only a sprinkling of identical small towns, except for Brookings, Huron and Pierre.

To the people who live in them, there is nothing

godforsaken about the small towns of South Dakota. "Where else would anybody want to live?" the local businessmen and farmers will ask. In the summer, their eyes will measure the near-by wheat and corn fields. When it's twenty below zero, they'll look toward the towering red grain elevators over by the railroad tracks. "This is the breadbasket of the nation!" they'll tell the heathen from outside.

Many modern South Dakotans have been other places and seen other things, and they are famous for saying that it feels good to get back home again. Quite a bit of the world has come to South Dakota. Gradually the state has become dotted with airports.

When the Humphrey children were growing up, the state was just beginning to pave the major highways, and people felt good if they had "gravel roads." During spring thaws and heavy rains, the dirt roads often turned to masses of rich black pudding. That is the way many of Hubert Humphrey's contemporaries recall it.

There are "predust bowl" words to describe the land that Norwegian settlers found on the prairies of South Dakota. In Ole Rolvaag's pioneer classic, "Giants in the Earth," Per Hansa ecstatically contemplates his "one hundred and sixty acres of the best land in the world. . . . Such soil! Only to sink the plow into it, to turn over the sod—and there was a field ready for seeding. . . . And this was not just ordinary soil, fit for barley, and oats, and potatoes, and hay, and that sort of thing; indeed, it had been meant for much finer and daintier uses; it was the soil for wheat, the king of all grains!"

Hubert Humphrey remembers his small town childhood and youth with pleasure because he lived each day with a breathless eagerness that is still part of his personality. He has never tried to run away from the nickname of "Pinky" that someone pinned on him. Because of his national prominence today, some research has been done on the subject. One school of thought insists that his mother used to dress him in Buster Brown suits with pink trimmings. Some of his boyhood contemporaries maintain that he got the nickname because his face was peppered with pinkish freckles, and others recall that the boy sunburned easily.

Another theory might be supported by the northern winter weather. There are no pinker cheeks in the world than those of a paper boy who goes loping along his route with a below-zero gale sweeping down from Canada. "Pinky" Humphrey first started delivering papers when he was seven years old, and he didn't stop until he was sixteen. Somewhere along the line, the ambitious young monopolist should have tangled with a "trust buster." Humphrey recalls triumphantly that he bought out all the other paper boys in town.

Doland was a small place, and young Hubert certainly knew almost everyone in it. When customers came into the drugstore, he could greet them by name. Like all paper boys, he knew when anyone moved in or out of town and learned at an early age to keep track of a wide variety of information.

Doland townspeople remember the young businessman as "talkative, aggressive, and energetic." If he

ever slowed down to a walk, there is no record of it.
He galloped—he dashed—he jogged—he trotted. He
acted as though the days held promises of many open
doors, and he had to race through each one before it
slammed shut.

The younger Humphrey daughter remembers her
famous brother as " 'small and spindly' when he was
little." When she saw him wrestling with the other
boys, she always flew into the fracas too—even though
he didn't need her help. He liked her spirit so well
that he trained her to be a track champion. At the age
of ten, little Frances won the fifty-yard dash in the
state contest.

In addition to cornering the newspaper market and
working at the drugstore, young Hubert gradually became involved in just about every activity—including
the musical groups—in the local school. He seems to
have been born with a huge distaste for waste of time
and talent, even of minor talent. He wasn't the star of
the team, but he draped his scrawny frame in a football
uniform and is remembered primarily for his "scrappi-
ness" on the field. He knew the rules and he played
hard. He also threw himself into basketball and baseball, and he was a dauntless distance man on the track
team—even when he was outdistanced.

If Pinky did not help to fill the trophy case at Doland High with athletic cups, he at least was still charg-
ing ahead at the final bell and the last inch. The school
was small and they needed every bit of brawn they
could get, but young Humphrey was probably the
"skinniest" four-letter-man in the countryside.

Perhaps his intuition told Dad Humphrey's second son that it is part of the Great American Dream that a future statesman or tycoon should once have been a barefoot boy. A former Doland High School superintendent, Guy Cook, recalls that Hubert and one of his friends sometimes came to school barefoot—"but there was no objection."

It was not poverty that caused Hubert to go without shoes. The Humphrey family lived in the type of big square white house that is associated with middle-class prosperity in the Upper Midwest, and Mrs. Humphrey even had a "hired girl" to help with the housework. Whenever Hubert Humphrey refers to his childhood home in Doland, there is affection in his voice. He loved that house with its wide front porch, its comfortable rooms, its inviting dining room table.

An upstairs bedroom in that house was also the scene of one of Pinky's most miserable experiences. Those were the years before "miracle drugs," when dreaded flu epidemics would sweep the countryside and pneumonia was often fatal. In almost every family, there are memories of talking in hushed voices and tiptoeing from room to room for days, of sitting in prayerful anguish beside a white bed and waiting for the "crisis." After he had recovered from pneumonia, little Hubert learned that he had been very close to death. A devoted family friend had driven through the icy prairie night to Minneapolis to bring him the new type of medicine that saved him. Not until many years later would he discover that he had been left with a slight amount of lung damage, a condition that didn't slow him down at all.

The boy bounced back to the business of living again, of taking a whopping interest in the life that he had come close to missing. He was not the type of youngster who would complain that he had nothing to do. He kept himself busy trying to do justice to all the hours of the day.

In the memories of his childhood, he would thrill again to the rip-roaring melodramas and "serials" at the Doland movie theater, for those were the days of Hoot Gibson and Pearl White and Tom Mix. He would sit again at his small desk in a succession of classrooms. He would go to Scout meetings and work his way through all the projects until he became a Life Scout. He would accompany his family every Sunday to Methodist church services in Doland and would participate in the young people's religious and social activities. In Doland, the good habits of a lifetime would be formed.

This does not mean that a halo hovered over Pinky's freckled face. He had all the normal arguments and squabbles with his brothers and sisters—and even more, perhaps, because the Humphreys are irrepressible individualists.

In "This Is Humphrey," Michael Amrine tells of the time when brother Ralph used his inventive talents to assemble the first radio in Doland. "He and Hubert would snuggle under the covers at night wearing earphones, and when their mother poked her head in to see if they were asleep they would appear to be lost in dreamland. Actually they were shaking with silent giggles as they listened to broadcasts from stations as far away as Kansas City, St. Joe, Missouri, and Minneapolis."

It is a good time to remember, those years of growing up in South Dakota. The recent death of Clyde Beatty rang a bell in the minds of grownups who had been young three and four decades ago. Sioux Falls and Watertown might be more likely to have the Ringling Brothers, but in the small towns the youngsters shivered with delight to see the gaudy Clyde Beatty Circus posters that heralded the impending arrival of clowns and elephants and snarling jungle beasts. It was almost like waiting for Christmas, once they put up those posters. In Doland, Hubert Humphrey did not only want to see the circus. He became involved in it, watering the elephants and doing odd jobs to earn his admission tickets.

Hilarious pranks appealed to young Hubert's impish sense of humor. A former classmate, Mrs. Les Decker of Huron, laughed as she told of the "fowl deed" she and Hubert perpetrated during a community sale at Doland. They stealthily opened several crates of live chickens—and then made a quick getaway and went into hiding for hours.

Chapter Two

Calm Before the Storm

In the vast prairie country, where the sky and the horizon stretch into infinity, the emptiness begs to be filled with noises and special thoughts.

Some boys like to "holler into the wind," to challenge the bland voids of silence. When Hubert hollered, his young voice must have been a forerunner of the "sonic boom." On his route, he yelled the name of each paper as he sent it flying toward the customer's door. Townspeople recall that he could be heard for blocks when he stood on Main Street selling Twin Cities papers. This, he has said, showed he had pride in his product; it was good advertising!

The boy did spend some moments in silent contemplation when he measured the gleam of the sun on the shining railroad tracks stretching onward and outward across the level prairie toward the beckoning horizon. Any direction you might some day choose to go, there was a whole lot of continent waiting, east and west, and north and south. Depending on where you started to draw your two diagonal lines, you could come out with Pierre—or maybe even Doland—at the exact center of the North American continent.

The boy wasted few precious moments in stationary daydreaming, because there were so many immediate things to do. In addition to his participation in all the other activities at Doland High, he was discovering that words—backed up by the power to assemble and apply knowledge — could make a star debater of a young man.

His father had already brought much of the world beyond the horizon into the comfortable Humphrey home in Doland. The personality and ethical standards of Hubert Humphrey Sr. would influence his son through all the years that both would live.

Dad Humphrey made his own impact on the community in which he was one of the leading and most articulate citizens. He is remembered as bighearted, genial, and devoted to the interests of a progressive American society.

Most important of all, the senior Humphrey was a man who enjoyed reading, often aloud, on a variety of intellectual levels—including the poems of Edgar A. Guest which used to appear regularly in many South Dakota papers. E. A. Guest might suffer by comparison with Robert Frost, but he was a great optimist about human nature. So was Dad Humphrey.

The Vice President remembers his father as an unusually good human being, a man who believed that ". . . in a country so blessed with natural resources, men should be able to make a decent living from their own labor. He wanted all people to walk proudly, in dignity, as he did. He was incapable of prejudice for reason of color or creed." Rather than recalling his father as "a loner or a rebel against the times," he sees him in retrospect as "a product of all that had gone before—a child of the freedom long developing in the nation, of the American humane spirit."

Dad Humphrey was not "a rebel against the times," but he was unique in an area that still retained some of the grimness of Ole Rolvaag's "Giants in the Earth." The Dakota farmer had long ago set the fashion for prodigious hard labor, pitting his energy against soil that sometimes seemed to fight back, squaring hunched shoulders against the constant threat of tornadoes, grasshopper invasions, and "dry spells."

"Elbow grease" was considered more righteous than a whole lot of "book reading." When a farmer was out in the fields from early till late, he didn't get in the habit of talking or reading much. He liked a good sermon from the minister in church on Sunday, but he was a bit suspicious of anyone else who "ran off at the mouth too much." He had a solid set of values: work hard, save your money, vote the Republican ticket, and be cordial to your neighbor but keep your nose out of his business.

Once in awhile there would be a South Dakotan like Dad Humphrey who would subscribe wholeheartedly to the convictions about hard work and thrift—but whose expansive imagination could not be contained in a vessel of ordinary proportions. From all accounts, Hubert Humphrey Sr. had a protective feeling about his neighbors. If people had trouble, he would not immediately conclude that they were lazy or hadn't saved their money—or hadn't voted the straight Republican ticket.

In a recent Washington speech, Dad Humphrey's namesake told how his father had become a Democrat, even though he had been reared in a strong Republican family. The elder Humphrey had been living in Elk River, Minnesota many years before. One day he went down to Minneapolis to hear William Jennings Bryan speak—"and that wasn't hard to do, because you could hear William Jennings Bryan a mile away!" Dad Humphrey didn't subscribe to all of Bryan's policies, but he liked the progressive spirit and the dynamic personality of the Silver-Tongued Orator from Nebraska. He believed he was breaking a trail for the social reformers who would follow him.

Dad Humphrey must have been good company for the Methodist minister who had been to Harvard and for anyone else who cared about discussing the major issues of the day. Young Hubert was an eager listener during informal debates that often were held in the Humphrey parlor after church services on Sunday nights, with his mother keeping the coffee cups filled and passing plates of homemade cinnamon rolls. Since "coming events cast their shadows before," it is not surprising to learn that Hubert Jr. contributed some "precocious" remarks to the conversation. When he was ten, he was already familiar with Woodrow Wilson's Fourteen-Point program for world peace.

Dad Humphrey was a teacher by nature, and young Pinky soaked up knowledge like a sponge. The entire

Humphrey family found drama and excitement in the writings of Thomas Paine, Benjamin Franklin, Thomas Jefferson, and anything related to Woodrow Wilson. When it came to Elbert Hubbard, they went far beyond the school requirements of "A Message to Garcia."

Perhaps that is the measure of Dad Humphrey's priceless legacy—that he should inspire his children by example to reach far out beyond the intellectual boundaries that are accepted as necessary. It was not enough merely to see that his youngsters were fed, clothed and sent to school to get an education. The Humphrey children grew up discussing great events and national and international politics, even during meals. This was a family involvement.

In any forum, Dad Humphrey always had a substantial supply of "talking material" in his head. As recently as last year, State Representative Ralph Woodring told some of his fellow South Dakota legislators, "I remember him well. He was always talking politics in his drugstore."

Whenever he speaks of his childhood, Hubert recalls the period when his father fought a lonely but furious battle against the impersonal forces of a huge corporation. Dad Humphrey had taken personal satisfaction in the power and light company that Doland had built for itself, and he believed that the rest of the town should want to safeguard the ownership of their local utility. To him it was not "socialism"—it was a form of proud municipal independence.

Young Hubert managed to be close enough to the city council meetings to weigh the blandishments of the "city slickers" who wanted to buy the Doland power plant against his father's indignant arguments in favor of municipal ownership. With his finger in the dike, Hubert Sr. valiantly tried to hold back a flood and nobody came to his rescue. Even in defeat, the elder Humphrey won some points. He slowed down the power company juggernaut and staged a debate that some Doland folks would remember for half a century. The lengthy struggle gave his son a feeling of identity with great economic issues, and he hasn't forgotten that the power company never did make good on some of its promises.

The reform spirit of President Woodrow Wilson's administration was still strong in the land, even after Warren G. Harding became President in 1920, followed by Calvin Coolidge in 1924. Young Hubert Humphrey went into high school in 1926 knowing about such adult subjects as the Federal Trade Commission Act, the Federal Child-Labor Law, the Clayton Anti-Trust Act, the Farm Loan Act, and the act which established the Federal Reserve System. The Wilson epoch had been a period of spectacular transformation. Amendments to the Constitution had provided for direct election of Senators, had produced Prohibition, and had given women the vote—all of which would decisively alter the literature and the talking habits of the nation for many years to come.

Pinky Humphrey, with his mind filled with historical philosophy and attuned to the new political age as well, was ready to absorb any new information that came his way. The radio was beginning to bring "instant news" from everywhere, stimulating his imagination and extending the feeling of "world citizenship" that he had gained from contact with President Wilson's Fourteen Points—that crucial League of Nations program that had been rejected by the Harding administration.

It is no wonder that Hubert excelled most in activities that involved words-words-words. The skinny, restless student played the baritone horn in the high school band, gave a rip-roaring performance in the title role of "Captain Applejack" in his senior year, and continued to be active in sports, but he reached the sublime heights of teen-age achievement as a bright student and a persuasive public speaker.

After following in his father's book-loving steps through most of his childhood, studying held no terrors for him. Between natural talent and previous practice, he was able to memorize his assignments with one reading. There was no question of being slipshod about his school work. "I was expected to be a good student," he says. With straight A's all through high school except for one B in Latin, he wasn't a disappointment.

It might be said that Hubert was an enthusiastic participant in everything he tried to do, but debating and oratory were at the top of the list. To stand in front of an audience and let the words come pouring out, to blend logic with wit, to assemble facts and reach triumphant conclusions — this was ambrosia to young Hubert Horatio Humphrey. He had the honor of captaining the three-man debate team that went to Vermillion for the state tournament in 1928.

It was fitting that Hubert's side should be debating in favor of the McNary-Haugen Bill, designed to re-

lieve the economic distress of the American farmer
who was bogged down by low prices and large surpluses, a condition that was aggravated by the Ford-
ney-McCumber protective tariff in 1922 and the
Hawley Smoot Act of 1930. If Humphrey had still been
debating at Doland High after 1930, he could have
scored some points by insisting that those two bills
helped to stagnate the economy on both sides of the
ocean, and he would have been right. Forty other nations greeted the Hawley Smoot Act with higher tariffs of their own against goods from the United States.

Even though they did not quite win the state title,
it was remarkable that a debate team from a town the
size of Doland could reach the state tournament at all.
Undoubtedly they were doing their dedicated best with
an unpopular topic; the McNary-Haugen Bill had been
vetoed by Calvin Coolidge.

Hubert was a "natural" for oratory; and he and
his partner, Lewis Terpstra, did quite well. However,
Hubert scored his highest triumph when he coached
his young sister, Frances, in "declamatory." Much to
her big brother's satisfaction, her declamation won the
state tournament.

To most of us who started high school in South Dakota in 1926, life seemed fairly uncomplicated. There
was a hush of peace and tranquility over the prairie
towns. World War I was only a shadowy blur left over
from childhood.

Once in awhile there were some "banana wars" in
"remote" Latin American areas, but they didn't count.
It was only a case of "The natives are restless tonight,"

and nobody asked what they were restless about. In their modest requests for assistance, church missionaries would send back reports from China, from India; people were starving to death in the streets of Asia. In China, impoverished parents were dropping their girl babies into the Yangtze. Wouldn't it be awful to live in a country like that? But it was so far away, so unreal.

Although there weren't many wealthy people, the middle-class structure was strong in the prairie towns and on the farms. There were people who felt the bone-deep ache of hard times and misery, but they usually tightened their belts and tried to survive somehow, in an inconspicuous state of semimalnutrition.

Perhaps no generation has ever grown up in so green a valley as that verdant stretch of years seemed to be. Hubert Humphrey has spoken with warmth of the pleasant, friendly atmosphere in his home town. There were occasional accidents and tragedies, but generally there was a feeling of preserving the status quo and looking ahead to one kind of a solid future or another. This was a generation that did not have to grow up in the shadows of war, either hot or cold.

What else could happen? Dad Humphrey seemed to feel that the nation should be girding its loins for something. As one of a handful of liberals in Doland, he dwelt on questions that were considered to be "better left alone."

Any Humphrey biographer is bound to be as fascinated with Hubert Sr. as with Hubert Jr. Both father and son agreed that the farm country needed the

McNary-Haugen Bill, before the surplus problem drove the price of grain any lower. They agreed that something should be done about reducing those protective tariffs that were choking off a healthy exchange of trade between the United States and Europe—and protecting the American farmer right out of business.

Even though his ideas sometimes seemed "radical" for those days, Hubert Humphrey Sr. was elected mayor of Doland for a term. In small towns, this is much like winning a popularity contest. While they might not agree with him very often, his neighbors respected the intellectual prowess behind Dad Humphrey's arguments. To apply a typical South Dakotan colloquialism, he was "a darned smart fellow, that Humphrey!"

Dad Humphrey was a businessman with some revolutionary ideas about merchandising that sometimes were a flop, but he thought that this was the American ideal—to keep experimenting, to keep exercising individual initiative.

Perhaps Dad Humphrey visualized an era in which there might be something resembling a "great society." In his "better world of the future," banks would be solid institutions, and bankers would serve the community instead of playing "God" to it. Farmers and small businessmen could get the long-range assistance they needed without having to pay such exorbitant interest rates—which often merely slowed down the eventual foreclosure or bankruptcy proceedings. Now, audiences laugh uproariously at melodramas in which the mustachioed banker threatens to foreclose the mortgage unless the farmer's beautiful daughter will marry him. When Dad Humphrey was a boy, that theme was more of a tragedy than a comedy.

Hubert's father put his money in one of the two banks in Doland—at least one too many for so small a town—even though he always felt rather distrustful about banks and bankers. In those days they were in the same category with the old stock market organization, before the establishment of the Security and Exchange Commission in 1934. Until some safeguards were put on local banks by the establishment of the Federal Reserve System in 1914, neither bankers nor their depositors were protected at all during the panics of 1893 and 1907. Hubert Humphrey Sr. had thought a lot about the way a whole community could go bankrupt overnight. He must have been clairvoyant. The Federal Reserve System would not be strong enough to protect the depositors when one of the banks in Doland closed its doors in 1927. It would not be strong enough to save the beloved big white Humphrey home, with its spacious basement that was large enough for romping and tinkering around, and its hardwood floors, and two bathrooms.

Last year, when Hubert Humphrey mentioned that family home on the CBS feature, "Memories of My Childhood," there was still a note of regret in his voice. If he never enters that house again, it will always live clearly in his memory. His thoughts will pace from room to room. He will remember the healthy discussions and arguments at the dining room table, the fine selection of books in his father's library—even the boost he got from putting on his first pair of long trousers, back when boys wore knee-length knickers until they were teen-agers. He will remember the year when he practiced his piano lessons with more discipline than musical talent in the comfortable living room. He will remember rolling out of bed, day after day, in the room he shared with Ralph—in winter's icy darkness and summer's early sunlight—knowing there were stacks of papers waiting to be delivered.

The tide of the 1929 debacle was already launching "feelers" along the weakening shoreline of the American economy. There would be a bank failure here and there, a rash of farm mortgage foreclosures, some businesses "going broke."

In 1927 when the bank in which Hubert Humphrey Sr. and a good many other Doland citizens had their money closed its doors, Hubert's father salvaged as many assets as he could and took his business to the other bank. Banks were an American institution, and Dad Humphrey was too much of a modern businessman to stash his cash away in a mattress. Perhaps that would have been the wisest course, because the other bank went broke within a month.

The strain of that tragedy was almost unbearable for the Humphrey family, even though they did get five thousand dollars for that fine big house—at a time when wages of one hundred dollars a month were considered very respectable. To Hubert it had been much more than a place to eat and sleep. It was "our wonderful home and our whole world."

Their next home was adequate enough—smaller and just as clean. The word "clean" often enters the story of the Humphrey family. They liked a sparkling

clean home, a sparkling clean drugstore where you
didn't need to blow the dust off the merchandise before you handed it to a customer.

With the new small home as their base of activities, the Humphrey family tried to pick up the pieces
and keep going. They were resolved not to lose the
drugstore, and Dad Humphrey's fine credit rating
helped to keep merchandise on the shelves and medicines in the prescription room. For years, Dad Humphrey had been carrying a good many customers on
his "charge account" books. With both banks closed
and cash so scarce, Humphrey's drugstore just "for-
gave" the items on those books. That was all a part of
a more prosperous past, when people could put their
money in the bank and get it out again. True to the
family creed, the Humphreys did not mourn for themselves alone. Everybody was having it "tough." If they
could just hang on—until times got better!

At least they didn't need to hire any clerks in the
drugstore. All the Humphrey children worked there,
from the time they were "knee-high to grasshoppers."

Those were the years when Green Rivers and
cherry phosphates were popular at the soda fountain.
The "candy kitchen" and the drugstore had taken the
place of the pre-1918 saloon, and millions of American
children were growing up without having seen a glass
of beer. There were rumors of the wild and woolly
"Flapper Age" from farther east, and South Dakota
young people copied the clothes of that era and some
of its zany language. Doland got a long-distance view
of the highjinks from copies of "College Humor" in the

magazine rack at Humphrey's Drugstore, and from movies featuring Clara Bow as the "It" girl.

The "Flapper Age" did make a decisive impact on South Dakota social life. First there was the "flea hop" and then came the Charleston and all the lively variation of the two-step that would keep the crowded dance floors of South Dakota in an uproar for years. Young Hubert Humphrey not only loved to dance—he quickly won a reputation as one of the "smoothest." Among the girls, that counted even more than his being a star debater.

In the spring of 1929, the Humphrey family listened proudly as Hubert delivered the valedictory address of his graduating class at Doland High. The young man had done what was "expected" of him—and much, much more. With his aggressive attitude and winning personality, surely he was headed straight for a bright future.

Chapter Three

"Don't Laugh at Me, Muriel"

Rainfall was becoming scarce, and farmers were doing their "sky-squinting" with anxious eyes. Midwesterners were already beginning to feel the pinch of tight money in September 1929.

In the Twenties the percentage of rural students who "went away to college" was not very high, even in prosperous farm families. "Pa" was usually putting his money into another "eighty" to leave to his children, and they would continue to stay close to the soil that was heart and soul of the family.

It is obvious that Dad Humphrey had a middle-class professional attitude. It was natural that Ralph should be in college with expectations of studying law, but the older brother stayed home to manage the drugstore in 1929 so Hubert could have his chance. Profits were too slim to keep both boys in college at once, with some Doland farmers already having to swap eggs and poultry for drug products. It has been noted that Ralph had always had a talent for the drugstore business—an operation that probably furnished a wider variety of challenges than the practice of law, especially in the late Twenties.

When Hubert Jr. chose to go to the University of Minnesota, high on the bluffs above the mighty Mississippi, he may have been reaching out again across the vast level prairies—as he had in his boyhood—toward that mysterious horizon in the distance.

Hubert had seen the Twin Cities only once before, on a brief trip with his father and Ralph. Compared with Sioux Falls, the largest city in South Dakota, Minneapolis and St. Paul were huge, teeming metropolises. Bumptious, bouncing with enterprise, they resembled Eastern cities with their tall buildings crowding narrow downtown streets thronged with traffic.

By 1929, a St. Paul boy named Francis Scott Key Fitzgerald had gone to Princeton — casting wistful backward glances at the Summit Avenue "high society" he had never known—and had become famous as the literary high priest of the "jazz age."

A homely fellow named Sinclair "Red" Lewis from up in Sauk Centre was reaching the point where he would be awarded the Nobel Prize for Literature in 1930, mainly because of "Main Street" and "Babbitt." In intellectually sophisticated circles, Lewis' satires were being hailed as a call-to-arms against small-town mediocrity and stagnation of the human spirit.

Hubert Humphrey, arriving at the University of Minnesota in 1929, was not worrying about becoming another Fitzgerald or Lewis. It took plenty of guts and gumption just to survive as a student. Hubert had received fifty dollars from a generous uncle, Dr. Harry

B. Humphrey, who was with the Department of Agriculture in Washington, D. C. The young man enjoyed school as much as ever, but it's a wonder he had time to attend classes. Almost like polar explorers, the freshman from Doland and ten other hopeful scholars were "roughing it" in an unheated attic in Minneapolis. Hubert could get thawed out when he tended the furnace, and he also did household chores in exchange for his room and board. He was able to earn some cash, too, by working part-time in Swoboda's old campus drugstore for fifteen cents an hour.

Hubert had just begun his second year at the University when the reverberations of the stock market crash started thundering their message of doom all across the countryside. Instead of giving up and going home when the money situation got painful, many college students showed how resourceful they could be. Hubert would have been capable of dogged persistence through four years of college, if his father had not asked him to come home during his sophomore year.

Home would no longer be Doland. By that time, Dad Humphrey had faced the fact that the drugstore business was scraping bottom and that their beloved home town would be a poor place to be stranded if business got any worse.

Ralph had gone back to college and would be able to finish his senior year. Hubert helped his father get credit for five thousand dollars' worth of drugstore products in Minneapolis and then he went home to help the family move to Huron, about thirty-five miles south of Doland, where a new Humphrey's Drugstore would be located.

The Humphreys knew how to pick up the pieces. They smiled optimistically and welcomed the Huron ladies to the grand opening with fresh roses.

Huron, which was about twenty times the size of Doland, is a progressive, famous little city in South Dakota. In 1931, it was on a major highway, its streets were paved, and it even boasted a college—Huron College, founded in 1883. The Humphreys would always remember Doland with affection but there were some compensations in Huron, including the State Fair.

There was also a terrific amount of competition. Huron needed another drugstore like a dog needs fleas, especially during those depression years. It was obvious that Humphrey's Drugstore would need to emphasize a "specialty" to succeed, so the firm rolled up its sleeves and set out to make special customers of the farmers. Dad Humphrey had known South Dakota farmers all his life and had appreciated their courage and sympathized with their difficulties.

Michael Amrine, in "This Is Humphrey," told at length about the pig sign that has become legendary. When the Humphreys began concentrating on veterinarian products and services, they were given a sign depicting a life-sized pig of no particular charm, but they recognized that it would serve as a beacon to the farmers so they hung it out. Quite a few years later, when the Humphreys remodeled the store front, "The boys thought they were a little too sophisticated to hang out the sign again." But the farm customers kept noticing that the old pig was missing, and they seemed worried that the store was "taking on airs" and might even set up a perfume counter next to the front door.

They were reassured when Hubert put up the sign again. Being the "farmers' friend" came first.

When Hubert came home from the University of Minnesota, he hardly had time for wistful, wishful thinking about going back to college. His father was still very education-minded; Frances, after a year at Huron College, went east to live with Uncle Harry Humphrey and attend George Washington University in the nation's capital. Dad Humphrey, feeling a surge of hope after the election of Franklin D. Roosevelt in 1932, "scraped together" a few hundred dollars to send Hubert to the Denver College of Pharmacy where he crammed a two-year course into his eager young brain in about five months.

Hubert liked the school and appreciated the encouragement he got there, even though his frenzied pace kept him in class from early morning until ten at night on week-days, with additional lectures on Saturdays. Since chemistry was his favorite subject, his future interest in science had a solid foundation. He admired the exactness of the scientific approach to problem-solving.

It was evident that his "vacation" from school had not dulled the young man's hunger for knowledge, because his father later discovered that Hubert had memorized the names of all the drugs, including their Latin derivatives and dosages, listed in the Pharmacopoeia —a feat that is rare among practicing pharmacists.

It felt good to see that framed diploma hanging above the prescription counter in Humphrey's Drugstore in the late spring of 1933. It was fortunate that

Hubert had time to take a deep breath that summer; by fall, deep breathing would be more difficult.

That was the summer Hubert met an attractive Huron College student named Muriel Buck at a dance at the Elks' Hall. Depression or no depression, South Dakota kept right on dancing, especially when the tune was "Tiger Rag." There were regular dances and college dances and barn dances and wedding dances. It was worth driving quite far if the orchestra happened to be called "Lawrence Welk and His Novelty Band." Lawrence sometimes strolled informally among the dancers on the floor, flashing that friendly smile as he played his accordion. After the last dreamy notes of "Good Night, Ladies" faded away, the seven or eight members of the band might travel all night and stay up to play some early morning tunes over WNAX at Yankton.

Those were the years when radio was becoming the giant of the entertainment and advertising world. In Huron, both Dad Humphrey and Hubert poured their eloquence into the microphone, amusing their unseen audience with poetry, words of wisdom and advertisements calculated to bring their customers hurrying to Humphrey's, "Huron's Leading Druggist"— operating under the sign of the pig.

Dad Humphrey recognized that the whole country was trying to pull itself up by its bootstraps. It was a precarious decade in history, when forces alien to American democracy might have taken over. The middle class, bulwark of rational democracy, was fighting for survival. It was a good sign that Americans kept right on trying to develop radio networks and build

better cars—even though the stock market had collapsed like a paper rainbow, and the drouth era made
those years of surplus crops seem ridiculously healthy.

Pheasant hunting in South Dakota wasn't the national sport it would later become; residents of "The
Sunshine State" would merely go out to get themselves
a few of the colorful ring-necked birds that had been
imported from China. One day in November 1933,
when Hubert Humphrey was out in the country with
his gun, he saw the distant horizon darkening. As many
moisture-starved South Dakotans did, he thought this
might be a prelude to a heavy rainstorm. He kept an
eye on the eerie purplish shadow that was beginning
to obliterate the sun, as he hurried toward home.

The rains did not come; instead, the dust came.
There would be at least one dust storm a week, for
more than a year, and then they began to taper off.
Nobody got used to them. That dust had a gritty con-
sistency and flavor all its own, and the bad taste comes
back whenever anyone mentions "Dust Bowl." It was
worse in regions farther west, but much of South Dakota was on the dismal edge of it. Perhaps the winters
were bleakest when the dust clouds carried only a few
puny snowflakes as they swept along icy streets and
roads.

It was a time when the surviving Indians might
have said to the white man, "You took the prairie away
from us; now the Great Spirit is blowing it out of
your hands."

The energetic pioneers had fought a successful battle to rid the land of natural vegetation, but their victory had turned against them. For many years, wheat-

growing farmers in the West had wrested as many crops as possible from weary Mother Nature, with no thought of soil conservation measures. When prolonged drouth had dried out the land and the crops, the soil lay barren for the wind to carry—even as far east as the Atlantic.

Catastrophe was moving in a series of sequences. There were always some grasshoppers jumping harmlessly around in weed patches and cornfields. When vegetation became scarce, they turned into migratory locusts, stripping many fields of every edible morsel that the drouth had not already withered. Farmers would grit their teeth and say, "If we can just save the cows and pigs we've got left!" But the hay in the hayloft was almost gone and there was nothing but stubble in the pasture for the cows to eat, and it looked as if the pigs might be getting the cholera.

When he wasn't working in the store, Hubert was dashing around the farm country with his father in their old Ford, peddling veterinary medicines and vaccinating hogs. They saw honest, hard-working farmers facing ruin for want of a little "marginal assistance" to tide them over. Hubert would never forget the haggard faces of those men, trying to crack jokes about the way their hogs objected to having needles stuck into them. He saw how deeply they cared about their farms. No matter how bad things looked, a part of them would die if they had to let go of these animals, this barn, this farmhouse, and those acres stretching out toward the horizon. Many years later, Hubert would note with respect that "the small farmer clings to his land fiercely."

Even though President Franklin D. Roosevelt had started out slowly, Dad Humphrey had faith in the basic philosophy of the Democrat who would head the nation during that time of hardship and peril.

Some people considered Dad Humphrey quite "bullheaded" about his politics and some other things, but he certainly never was dull and he had much more than his share of vision. "F.D.R.," who had taken office after what Dad Humphrey considered twelve years of Republican frustration, would become the hero of a vast majority of depression-sick Americans with his New Deal program of assistance for the "little people" —the small businessmen who were losing their businesses, the small farmers who were losing their farms, and the millions of small wage earners who no longer had wages or jobs.

Eastern millionaires, finding themselves bankrupt after the stock market crash, had jumped out of skyscraper windows in desperation, but there are still people who think that the problems would have "straightened themselves out." More than three decades later, it is easy for some solid citizens to forget that they ever worked for a WPA check—and were happy to get it—or received relief food for their families from the "government." As in any huge program of the New Deal type, there were some abuses; but for the countless millions of people who desperately needed help, it was nothing short of a Godsend. Dad Humphrey saw those WPA checks coming into the stores, and he knew they were giving the rock-bottom economy the boost it absolutely had to have. That was the period when many businesses, large and small, began to show noticeable profits.

Feeling as he did about the old-time banking system—and Hubert had grown up to feel the same way—Dad Humphrey might have been standing at F.D.R.'s shoulder nodding approval as the President outlined legislation to make banking as foolproof as possible. If bank deposits had been insured in 1927, the Humphreys might not have lost their home in Doland.

There would always be one special reason why Hubert Jr. could rejoice about that move to Huron in 1931. That was where he had met Muriel Buck, and she sometimes dropped into the drugstore with her girl friends for lunch or a cool drink at the soda fountain. It must be assumed that she received preferential service from a smiling young man who delivered her sandwiches with a flourish and sometimes entertained her with rapid-fire conversation.

A girl with a middle-class Presbyterian background, Muriel was a native of Huron and had studied piano at Huron College. She had kept books for her father, until his once-prosperous produce company became one of the depression casualties. Later, Mr. Buck built a tourist resort at Bigstone Lake. From all accounts, the Buck family—especially Muriel and her two brothers, Merle and Gordon—were very fond of Bigstone Lake.

Old friends in Huron remember that Muriel was very much as she is now—"quiet, beautifully groomed, a bit shy, capable and thoughtful." She was popular, and many a classmate remembers sitting on the steps of the Buck home at the top of ski hill visiting with her. Evidently she was always a "good listener." She was very well liked in school and dated for all the school functions.

"Bucky" and Hubert started "going steady" sometime in 1934, and the romance seems to have made an unforgettable impact. One of Muriel's co-workers recalls that Hubert's girl would come into the office in the morning saying, "Pinky's the best dancer in town!"

Frances Humphrey had arrived in Washington before Hubert had a glimpse of the city, and had lived for awhile with their uncle, Dr. Harry Humphrey. Hubert—traveling on a shoestring—managed to go east for his sister's graduation from George Washington University in 1935. He stayed with his uncle, and the two of them discussed national politics for hours. As chief of Plant Industry with the Department of Agriculture for many years, Dr. Humphrey knew his Washington—and loved it anyway. Watching administrations come and go, he had seen through the red tape and the eternal jostling for political and social status to the hard core of healthy democracy underneath. Hubert was eager to be thrilled about that trip to "D. C." and Uncle Harry sent his natural enthusiasm soaring.

When most Americans visit the gallery in the Senate and the House, their feeling of identification is not as personal as Hubert's was. It helped to have Uncle Harry tell him that others had gotten there, and he could too—"with hard work, study and the right principles."

It is evident that Muriel Buck cherished her letters

from Pinky because one of them has now become famous. Her fiance was in Washington, after a strenuous day-and-night bus trip, without enough money for room and board if he hadn't been able to stay with Uncle Harry, and yet he could write a letter as filled with vision and high hopes as this one:

This trip has impressed one thing on my mind; need of an education, alert mind, clean living and a bit of culture which undoubtedly will come with age and learning.

I don't necessarily mean more college. I need to do more reading, more writing, more thinking if I want to fulfill my dream of being someone in this world. Maybe I seem foolish to have such vain hopes and plans, but Bucky, I can see how someday if you and I just apply ourselves and make up our minds to work for bigger things, how we can someday live here in Washington.

I intend to set my aim at Congress. Don't laugh at me, Muriel. Maybe it does sound egotistical and beyond reason but I do know others have succeeded. Why haven't I a chance?

That letter should serve as an incentive to bright young people who are deeply interested in politics but feel that the cause is hopeless unless they have a "mintful" of money and a powerful group of backers behind them.

Perhaps the sharing of a dream drew Hubert and Muriel even closer together when he returned home, because she was a "practical dreamer" too. She didn't laugh at him or consider his ambitions foolish. They were an attractive young couple, on or off the dance floor. Hubert was almost six feet tall, and Bucky was five-feet-three.

Muriel had learned the household arts of sewing and cooking. Her father would be pleasantly surprised to know that his favorite beef soup ranks right up there with Pedernales River chili, in the latest edition of the Congressional Cookbook. Hubert Horatio Humphrey also loves that savory dish, and that may be the secret of his success. "His soup gives him his vim and vigor," says his spouse.

The years would prove that Muriel had deep, quiet reserves of character and determination. Legends are now being built up around everything she has done and said. When their friends insist that Hubert could not have gotten so far without her, she may laugh ruefully as she remembers that Hubert ran into a poor "jaywalking" cow on the way home from their wonderful honeymoon trip to Minneapolis and had trouble getting as far as Huron without being towed. It might have been an omen of some of the roadblocks ahead.

Hubert and Muriel had not rushed into wedlock like a house afire. For almost two years before the wedding on September 3, 1936, they recognized that the shadow of the depression still lay heavy over the land, but being together made their hearts feel lighter. In the words of a popular dance tune of that era, it was a time for "drifting and dreaming"—while keeping alert for a glimmer of light through those falling shadows.

A former Huron girl, Edith Smith—now Mrs. Rudolph Lee of Peoria, Illinois—remembers the Humphrey family well. When Edith was in the bank at Huron, she used to wait on Dad Humphrey and Hubert, and she is one of those who noticed the special kinship of spirit between father and son. She recalls the way

Pinky "would push the front door open, dash into the lobby (just like today—a man on the go), with a great big smile and always something to say."

In a recent illustrated story about the Vice President in "Look" magazine, Edith noticed the handsome portrait of President Roosevelt on the wall in the Vice President's Executive Building office. The picture reminded her of some playful shenanigans that occurred when the Humphreys were newlyweds and the "office gang" paid them a visit. Knowing about Hubert's great respect for F.D.R., the visitors were not surprised to see a picture of the New Deal President on the bedroom wall. "They thought it would be great to hide it, so under the bed it went." With a mischievous glint in their eyes, they awaited Hubert's reaction. Muriel later reported that, when they returned home, H.H.H. just knew someone had broken into the place because the precious picture was gone from the wall.

Settling down in a three-room bungalow in Huron, the young couple soon became involved in the business routine and in Scouting and civic activities and social life with their friends.

When they were alone in the evening Hubert didn't just kick off his shoes and say, "Ho-hum, another day, another dollar." He hadn't forgotten his dream about that world out beyond the horizon, and it was a blessing to know that Muriel kept understanding what he meant. It had been necessary to scrimp on wedding details just to afford that honeymoon in Minneapolis, but that didn't keep them from playing "wishing games" about a trip to Europe.

As a youngster and as a man, there was in Hubert Humphrey that special quality of yearning to speed ahead—to see all there was to see, to learn all there was to learn, to waste no precious time getting through those tantalizing doors before they slammed shut. He undoubtedly suffered periods of bleak misgiving, but his mind kept churning restlessly as though aware of invisible hands beckoning him back to "the halls of ivy." It was fine to be a good druggist who knew the pharmacopoeia by heart. It was fine to know about the farm situation and the difficulties of the small businessman. It was fine to be an authority on rural life and politics in South Dakota, but he wanted to broaden his field of knowledge. In the back of his mind was a picture of that magnificent monument to democracy, the United States Capitol in Washington, D. C.

A few years before, he had thought he might be a pharmacist all his life, but he knew he was also a politician at heart. He was his father's son. The year of Hubert's marriage was also a year when the Humphrey household was bouncing with even more than the usual political excitement. Dad Humphrey was running for the South Dakota House of Representatives, and Beadle County gave him its blessing.

Dad Humphrey and Hubert, in 1937, were of one mind about the young man's future. He should have his chance to see what he could do with himself, outside the drugstore business. The old phrase, "If I get back to college . . ." was being amended to "When I get back to college . . ."

Dad Humphrey, Ralph and sister Fern probably could handle the drugstore all right, now that the economy was improving under New Deal stimulus. If not, Hubert and Muriel could always come back.

Although they have never broken "the old home ties," they would not live permanently in South Dakota again. Minnesota would have a valid educational and political claim on Hubert Horatio Humphrey, starting in 1937, when he was twenty-seven years old. He went back to finish getting his degree at the University of Minnesota. South Dakota had given him the boots. Minnesota gave him the bootstraps and invited him to lift himself.

Chapter Four

Scholar in a Hurry

The Twin Cities, in the mid-'30s, represented a political, industrial, social and cultural cross section of all the human temperaments that might be gathered together in one progressive metropolitan area. The main campus of the University of Minnesota, over on the Minneapolis end of University Avenue, often served as a "sounding board" for a variety of political causes.

Collegiate unrest was not unknown at that time. In 1935 a former North Dakota boy named Eric Sevareid was graduated from the University of Minnesota and went to work on the Minneapolis papers. Today, as he wears the mantle of his distinguished mentor, the late Edward R. Murrow, he has been heard to say on television that he was something of a rebel during his university days. For better or for worse, the passing years have made him less sympathetic with campus rebellions.

When the Humphreys arrived at the University of Minnesota in 1937, Minnesota Republicans were about to indulge themselves in the great American pastime of investigating the party that was doomed to go out of power in 1938. It would be a full-dress affair, with all the dramatic props and a full cast of subpoenaed characters. To anyone following the action closely, it would seem as though the GOP had been working on the script for all the frustrating years since the Farmer-Labor Party had captured the Governor's chair in 1930. The Republicans sounded as though they were exorcising the devil, while the Farmer-Laborites went right ahead with their plans to propose the late Governor Floyd B. Olson for political sainthood.

Standing on the distant sidelines, a skinny, unpretentious political science student at the University took a deep breath of atmosphere that was throbbing with political vitality. What a battlefield for him to study!

At that time, the Farmer-Labor and Democratic parties in Minnesota were separate groups. In fact, the 1918 Farmer-Laborites had sought to team up with the Republicans, but it probably wouldn't have been logical. In "Minnesota Heritage," Governor Karl F. Rolvaag lists the "reforming forces" that have invigorated the party he now represents. "The Grange, the Farmer's Alliance, the Greenbackers, the People's party and the Populist movement, the Anti-Monopolists, the Progressives, the Knights of Labor, the Federation of Labor, the Nonpartisan League, the Farmer-Labor Party, the CIO, and the Farmers Union have all left their impact on the Democratic Farmer-Labor Party."

Governor Rolvaag notes that "In these movements there have been many outspoken leaders and strong personalities." Going back as far as Ignatius Donnelly, "The Sage of Nininger," Rolvaag lists some targets toward which the progressive-protest groups have directed "their wrath and attention" during the past century: the railroads, Wall Street, the trusts and combines, money policies, the Minneapolis Grain Exchange, tight farm credit, land speculation, war profits, the steel trusts, long work days and low wages, safety laws for workers, workmen's compensations and unemployment insurance, taxes, education, and farm-to-market roads, conservation, and iron ore."

Val Bjornson, a progressive Republican who is so highly respected that the opposition keeps crossing the ballot to elect him State Treasurer, agrees with Governor Rolvaag that issues and principles have produced a "crisscross voting pattern." Mr. Bjornson noted, in the political section of "Minnesota Heritage": "Despite the fact that Republicans have held the executive reins for seventy-eight out of Minnesota's first hundred years, voters of the state have long been described as 'political mavericks.' It is likely true that no state equals Minnesota's consistent record of inconsistent voting."

Hubert Humphrey got the picture. Here was resiliency, vitality, and atmosphere of challenge that appeared to be charged with electricity. It seemed as though everyone around the University had a political philosophy to promote or defend.

Hubert, with eyes shining and words flowing energetically, reveled in a stimulating exchange of knowledge and opinion that sometimes lasted far into the night. These were not debates that would end when time was called—they were more like "serial stories" that were continued until the next bull session.

There is no doubt that Hubert talked a good deal— and enjoyed every syllable of it—when he was making a point, or maybe two, or even three. He also studied, and listened to lectures and read books by the dozen. There was so much to learn, here in this huge citadel of knowledge! Would he ever make a dent in all of it? The finger was beckoning more urgently from the next open door. "Hurry, Hubert, hurry!"

Hubert hurried, from lecture hall to library to part-time work in drugstores and to any other odd jobs he could find. Muriel sped along beside him, pulling more than her own slight weight. She found herself an office job to help support them and keep Hubert in school.

It is a question whether the bristling political climate in Minnesota produced the highly talented political science faculty, or whether the instructors produced much of the progressive stimulation. Hubert Humphrey found himself listening to men who inspired him, who aroused an even greater respect for political endeavor than he had felt before. Among them was Dr. William Anderson, head of the department—a fact worth noting at a time when many American college students complain that the most prestigious faculty members are only "window dressing" as far as under-graduate contact is concerned.

Humphrey found himself in the middle of a new political group, socializing outside the classroom. He plunged into discussions with professors and other students who had already achieved some status as political theorists, and he was no "shy violet" about stating his opinions and backing them up with all the facts he was packing away in his mind for future reference.

Hubert considered the study of history in depth a fascinating, stimulating part of his education in political science, and he did his "homework" thoroughly. He knew that yesterday's history can furnish valuable clues for tomorrow's social and political progress. Political science was vague in some areas and precise in others. It started with the people around you and fanned out through all the years and generations of mankind. A politician with a social conscience would never ask "for whom the bell tolls."

During those undergraduate years at the University, Hubert formed friendships that would not be taken lightly. Professor Evron M. Kirkpatrick would later become a campaign advisor. Dr. William Kubicek and Fred Kottke, medical research students at that time, would become actively involved in state politics.

Back in the late '30s there was also a young football player named Orville Freeman. Later, on some of the rare occasions when Hubert and Muriel went out for a few hours of recreation, it was Orville who was their "baby sitter." Freeman, a law student, was reluctant about politics at first; it was Hubert Humphrey who convinced him that this was the road he should take. If either of them had been able to look ahead to the 1950's and 1960's, Orville probably would have been the most astonished of the two.

It wasn't that Hubert was puffed up with self-confidence about an empty seat marked "Humphrey" that might be waiting for him in some legislative chamber. When a man is barely able to finance his way through college, all the lofty pinnacles seem as remote as the peaks of Mt. Everest.

When Hubert Horatio Humphrey received his Bachelor of Arts degree from the University of Minnesota in 1939, he was wearing a Phi Beta Kappa key and was graduated magna cum laude—overwhelming proof of his ability as a scholar.

That year—1939—is a good one to remember in measuring the progress of the unknown "young man in a hurry" who, at that point, was not loaded with material advantages. Baby Nancy was born on February 27, so he had become a father. He was more mature than most of his classmates—by about eight years. It was ten years since he had received his high school diploma, six years since he had gone to the Denver College of Pharmacy. But, in or out of school, he had never stopped studying and drawing conclusions that sparkled in his joyfully retentive mind.

Humphrey eagerly accepted a teaching fellowship at the University of Louisiana and moved his small family south to Baton Rouge. There appears to be a pattern to the territory Hubert was covering. He had gone slightly to the east when he went to the University of Minnesota and he had also managed to get to Washington, D. C. Denver was quite "a far piece" to the west. In 1939-1940, he would see something of life in the South. The world "beyond the horizon" still fascinated the boy from the prairies of South Dakota.

With those discerning eyes of his, he would notice differences and similarities between the Northern and Southern cultures in his native land. He had seen some Negroes living in slums in the Twin Cities and being subjected to discrimination and unreasoning hatred, but he had also seen Negro students on the University campus and Negro adults holding down responsible positions. He had seen them voting and walking with dignity. In tracing the history of the labor movement in the North, he had been shocked at the treatment of the workers during the Haymarket Riot in Chicago in 1886. In Louisiana he saw strikers being threatened with machine guns by state police.

Humphrey did not run up and down the streets in Baton Rouge shouting that this was the Twentieth Century in the United States of America! He had a good sense of proportion; he knew there was room for improvement in the North as well as the South. Still, he filed all his impressions away in his mind for future reference.

He and Muriel settled down in the alien academic community and immediately made friends. They enjoyed the Southern hospitality and congenial company of an enlightened group of professors and students which included Russell Long, son of the Senator Huey Long whose stormy political career had ended in a dramatic assassination in 1935. Hubert arrived in time to study some of the post-Huey Long turmoil in Louisiana, where the heirs of the mighty "Kingfish" were still jockeying for control of his "empire."

With the baby keeping her at home, Muriel helped out on the family exchequer by making stacks of sandwiches which her husband sold on the campus for ten cents apiece.

In addition to teaching and functioning as a sandwich salesman, Humphrey was studying for his Master's Degree at Louisiana State University. One of his instructors later was asked if Hubert hadn't talked too much. "Yes," he replied, "but you have to remember he learns so much while he is talking." The Minnesotan was achieving a reputation as a very loquacious gentleman who was also a mastermind in the field of political theory.

For his thesis, Humphrey chose a topic close to his heart: "The Philosophy of the New Deal." It was more of an idealistic commentary than an unbiased scrutiny, and some of the ideas may have been closer to Hubert's heart than to F.D.R.'s. "The Philosophy of the New Deal" reflected Humphrey's personal involvement in the hardships of the depression and the harassments of drouth, dust storms and flying grasshoppers. It revealed his growing commitment to the type of liberalism that "calls for a man to help himself insofar as he is able, but for Government action to meet problems insoluble by the individual."

He was not exactly against big business and big money, but he was opposed to greediness in the market place. It was important, he believed, "to preserve the capitalistic system, with no desire to destroy individual liberty, but rather to adjust personal freedom with the social good." Humphrey saw the New Deal as heralding a new era of social values. "If the depression of the early 1930's gave America the New Deal, the New

Deal gave America a revitalization of democracy. The new administration opened its political ears to the multitudinous demands of the people . . ."

After some good-humored ribbing from a board of academic inquisitors, Humphrey received his Master's Degree from Louisiana State University in 1940, and he and Muriel and Nancy returned to Minneapolis. That was the spring when their young friend, Orville Freeman, received his B.A. from the University of Minnesota—also magna cum laude and with a Phi Beta Kappa key.

Humphrey had already been told that he had all the attributes necessary to a political careerist—the knowledge and ability to discuss issues from every angle, an engaging personality, and enough bouncing enthusiasm to convince people that their cause was his cause.

It is possible to study political science and get an advanced degree in the subject, but you can't just go out and apply for a job. The open doors are limited. Considering most of the dictionary definitions for "politician," you would almost expect them to be located at the dead ends of alleys where you would need to knock three times and say, "Joe sent me." The United States is proud of her mature statesmen, but it is a fact that they usually have served an apprentice-ship as "politicians"—a term that is viewed more with apprehension than respect. A "fearless" Congressman often has learned the lessons of fearlessness as a lowly grass roots politician.

As a student and as a teacher of political history,

Humphrey learned that even the most dedicated leader must take the punishment with the glory, the scowls with the loud hurrahs. He knew what to expect, before he ever got into it.

If he could have afforded to stay in school in 1941, Hubert would have tried for a law degree. He could have gone back into the drugstore business almost anywhere and made a success of it with his flair for salesmanship. As a journalist, he would never have missed a deadline, and he could have qualified as a full-time radio newscaster and commentator.

The University of Minnesota welcomed Hubert back with the offer of a teaching position in the political science department. Teaching was talking, and Hubert liked that. However, it is not ethical for a classroom lecturer to stump for his private political philosophy, and Assistant Professor Humphrey observed the rules.

With a moral and spiritual commitment to the New Deal Program, Humphrey kept an eye out for a opportunity to become an active participant. When it came, it proved to be of incalculable significance. It was still 1941 when he rushed through the next open door to become a member of the administrative staff of the Works Projects Administration, a New Deal program that President Roosevelt had established at the height of the depression in 1935. Originally called the Works Progress Administration, it had reached into every blighted little town and depressed area to provide employment for eight-and-one-half million Americans at various periods of grim necessity.

The opposition party called it "artificial prosperity"—a term calculated to make Dad Humphrey and Hubert retort, "You call THIS artificial? How about that boom-and-bust prosperity of 1929?"

People who were getting along all right described the WPA as a refuge for the lazy and incompetent, but the grateful "shovel men" went ahead with a program of building and improving more than 644,000 miles of roads, 750 airports, 24,000 miles of sewage lines, and 120,000 public buildings—including libraries, schools, and municipal, state and federal buildings.

The WPA's adult education program provided employment for more than 44,000 teachers and instruction for more than 1,700,000 persons. Through the assistance of the NYA—National Youth Administration—thousands of young people were able to finish their educations. There was a gigantic school lunch program and sponsorship of a variety of cultural activities. Betty MacDonald, the author of "The Egg and I," wrote of attending one of the writing classes in Seattle. During World War II, the still-functioning machinery of the WPA swung into the business of establishing nurseries for children of women employed in defense jobs and the training of workers for skilled jobs in war industries.

There was the usual number of "human nature abuses" of the WPA program. Occasionally people got "government food" when they didn't need it, and sometimes workmen leaned on their shovels a bit too long. WPA officials were swamped with criticism from self-appointed prophets of doom.

When the WPA was terminated in 1943, it had operated for seven years at a cost of about ten billion dollars. Since wages were only at a subsistence level, the money was pumped right back into the economy and often ended up in the pockets and cash registers of the very people who complained most about Roosevelt's "pump-priming."

Perhaps the grim horrors of poverty during the depression were brought home most forcefully to Humphrey during his years in Minneapolis. He saw the pitiful misery and disease of old age on the spittle-stained streets of Washington Avenue, near the main depot, where flop-house dormitories served as "home" for aged derelicts whose "dining room" was the nearest soup kitchen. Even in the poorest rural farmhouse, there was usually a place for Grandpa next to the warm kitchen stove.

Whatever their past had been, the drifters on the big city's Skid Row had no present, and no future except death. Some passersby shuddered with repugnance and crossed to the other side of the street, and others would shake their heads and wonder what could be done for those desolate souls.

Looking back, it seems as though those were the days when there started to be something "subversive" about being humane. Humphrey would occasionally be advised against revealing his natural sympathy for the underprivileged, for the objects of misfortune and the victims of prejudice. It wasn't considered "good political tactics."

Humphrey had viewed one face of the depression

in South Dakota. In the large metropolitan areas of Minneapolis and St. Paul, there would be honest citizens who had almost starved for want of jobs—not because they lacked skills or education, but because they belonged to racial and religious minorities.

Historians have written of Communist infiltration on the "far left" in Minnesota. Humphrey, on his way up, would willingly denounce any groups tainted with the scent of Communism, but he would never forget that it is desperation and defeat that help to destroy a man's faith in his government—especially during a depression. It would have to be more than a matter of fighting Communism; it would also have to be a fight against poverty and discrimination and economic injustice—the prime breeding grounds of subversives.

Little is heard about Communistic influences in Minnesota today. Labor, business, industry and education have united in a solid front that has produced a large, reasonably-happy middle class. Undoubtedly some of the old "radicals" were among the Twin Citians who wept unashamedly in the streets when they heard that Franklin Delano Roosevelt was dead. Undoubtedly some of them had sons and grandsons who would be fighting the Communists in Korea and Vietnam.

Humphrey had some interesting experiences with another group of people who were temporarily considered "a poor investment"—thirty thousand of them. When he was with the War Production Training and Re-employment Program of the WPA, he helped to establish vocational schools all over the state. The thirty thousand diplomas, all personally inscribed with his signature, are "collectors' items" now.

In "War On Poverty," Hubert Humphrey told a heartwarming story about one of those "graduates." A few years after the program was concluded, a man came up to Humphrey at his church and told him, "You got me off the relief rolls up in Stearns County and put me into a vocational training school. The Government paid me $60 or $70 a month. I know there were an awful lot of people who were saying this was a waste of money. But I would like to tell you something. I am now the supervisor out at Honeywell."

Honeywell, near Minneapolis, is a large industrial electronics plant that played a major role in defense production.

The man told Humphrey he had a boy who had just finished forty missions in the Air Force, and two others who were in the Navy. He concluded with these words, "I just want to ask you one question: Do you think the Government wasted its money on me?"

Chapter Five

The Door to the Mayor's Office

President Roosevelt's New Deal Program was becoming a hallmark of the Democratic Party, and Hubert Humphrey felt at home with the challenges it presented. By 1943, he had been appointed assistant regional director of the War Manpower Commission.

There are many excellent small colleges in the adjoining city of St. Paul, and Hubert Humphrey also began to serve as a visiting professor of political science at Macalester that year.

Another notable feature of 1943 was an enticing door that swung shut before Humphrey could quite get through it. Urged by friends and supporters who believed in his political future, he decided to plunge bravely into the Minneapolis mayoralty race. The opposition candidate, Mayor Marvin Kline, was firmly entrenched in that office.

Most Minneapolitans considered Mayor Kline as satisfactory as a mayor needed to be. And here came Hubert Humphrey, a man who was practically unknown to most of the people in his adopted city!

The aspiring young politician, with the assistance of a handful of loyal colleagues, set out to make Minneapolis aware that a young man named Hubert Humphrey was ready to serve their great city with vigor and dedication. He could easily point to some improvements that would benefit the citizens of the metropolis.

Operating with every scarce penny that the "campaign committee" could scrape up, the Humphrey boosters could afford to print only one piece of campaign literature, and Humphrey even distributed copies in person at odd hours of the day and night.

In addition to other obvious qualifications, the campaign "flyer" revealed that Mr. Humphrey spent an admirable part of each Lord's Day in the proper places. Every Sunday morning he conducted an adult study class at the First Congregational Church, and on Sunday nights he lectured at the Hennepin Avenue Methodist Church on a program series called "The University of Life."

Hubert and his group of happy young warriors were exuberant about his prospects, and there was no lack of encouragement from Dad Humphrey's direction out in Huron. Young Mrs. Humphrey took a keen interest in the political hopes of her husband, ringing doorbells and campaigning by phone for him.

Humphrey had learned the arts of salesmanship in a highly competitive business. During that 1943 campaign, when he dashed all over the city delivering one stirring speech after another, he often referred to himself in the third person to make his name known and recognized. "Humphrey believes that his program will be good for Minneapolis . . ." and "Humphrey will help you to improve this situation . . ." He was running on a "do-something" platform.

To a majority of people, Mayor Kline's re-election seemed a foregone conclusion, and Humphrey's candidacy made little impact in the outside world. When the votes were counted, however, the results were quite astonishing. Humphrey had lost by less than five thousand votes in the tenth largest city in the United States. Somehow Humphrey, and the people who had faith in him, had gotten his message across to almost half the voting population of Minneapolis. He had drawn his strongest support from labor groups.

The heady hours of hope were past, and Humphrey was left staring at a closed door that seemed to be inscribed with an awesome figure—$1,300. Even though they had pared expenses to the limit, this was the deficit for campaign expenditures.

The Humphreys assumed full responsibility for the debt—a large sum to save out of a small income. In addition to political science lectures at Macalester, Humphrey was a news analyst on WTCN five nights a week, a part-time druggist, and an apartment house "maintenance man."

In his janitorial capacity, he was working for an apartment house manager named Muriel Humphrey who had made the arrangements. While her husband was taking care of loose plaster and other odd jobs, Muriel cleaned the apartment house halls and even mowed the lawn. In addition to everything else, she had to keep track of four-year-old Nancy and one-year-old Hubert Humphrey III, who is better known as "Skip."

After every penny had been repaid and life was a bit easier for the Humphreys, Muriel was asked if she had been anxious about getting that campaign debt paid off. "I would have taken in washing," she replied. That is a typical South Dakota answer and is based on an abiding spirit of idealism. Mothers in that part of the country have been heard to vow, "I would scrub floors and take in washing to help my children get through college," and they mean other people's floors and other people's washing. It is part of the pioneer tradition.

Humphrey was very much aware that World War II was going on. He had grown up in Doland with the famous McNickle "aces." According to a story in the Minneapolis Star Journal for September 3, 1943, one of the McNickle twins, Lieut. Col. Marvin McNickle, reported in a letter to his mother that his brother, Lieut. Col. Melvin McNickle, failed to return to his bombing base in England after a mission over Europe. Several pilots had seen men parachuting from planes "and he hoped Melvin might be one of them." Front page news, that day, was the launching of the Italian invasion from Sicily.

Humphrey's close friend, Orville Freeman, was fighting the good fight as a Marine officer in the bloody South Pacific. Harold Stassen had resigned as Governor of Minnesota to become a naval officer. Although he was a married man with a family, Humphrey turned a deaf ear to suggestions that he run for governor or any other office. He was determined to serve his country as an active fighting man, but he kept running into frustrations.

At first he had been "frozen" into his teaching job at Macalester because he was conducting some classes for Air Force Reserve officers. After he had been released from those duties, he tried to get into the Navy first, and then the Army. He had always considered himself an extremely healthy man, able to dash around and gobble up huge stacks of work on four or five hours of sleep a night. Suddenly he was transported back in memory to that quiet room in the big house in Doland where he had struggled as a small boy to throw off the dread pneumonia virus. The service doctors found that he had been left with a small amount of lung calcification. There was also some indication of a hernia. Since nothing had ever slowed him down, Humphrey pooh-poohed the idea that he wasn't as healthy as a horse.

After being classified and reclassified, he even got his hands on a uniform at Fort Snelling, but his classification was abruptly changed from 1-A to 2-A. Undoubtedly no man tried harder or argued more vehemently for war service than Humphrey did, and it is considered a shabby political trick to ask what he was doing during World War II.

At the same time, Humphrey knew that he was being considered part of the state political picture. He had realized he was moving ahead when the late Gideon Seymour, executive editor of the Minneapolis Star Journal and Herald Tribune, asked him in 1943 if he might be interested in running for office under the Republican banner.

The estimable Mr. Seymour favored a more progressive, liberal Republican party, and Hubert Humphrey must have been dazzled to realize that he could have the backing of the strongest, best-organized political party in the state—especially when he was busy fixing clogged drains and repairing electrical wiring in that apartment house. The country might like to have a picture of Humphrey's face when he told Mr. Seymour it would break his father's heart if he didn't stay with the liberals.

Actually, it would be difficult to peg Humphrey's political position in Minnesota at that time, because most of the liberals were opposing each other as either Democrats or Farmer-Laborites. Before 1943 there had been some casual discussion about fusing the two parties, if they could resolve their historic differences. Separately, they had been easy to beat because they were fighting each other. More discussion was not enough for Hubert Horatio Humphrey. The situation called for another frugal trip to Washington and a search for some influential open doors. Today it is almost funny to contemplate the run-around he got, as he commuted from Uncle Harry's house in Cabin John to the portals of the mighty in the heart of the nation's capitol.

He had announced his impending arrival with several letters that had suffered the fate of much mail that goes pouring into the yawning bureaucratic hopper. Postmaster General Frank C. Walker, the national

Democratic Party chairman, had put up no "Welcome, Humphrey" banners, and no bands were playing in his honor. Not in 1943. He was treated as such an absolute nobody that he might have wondered if he had given Gideon Seymour the right answer.

For several days Humphrey fretted and fumed as he kept a lonely vigil in the outer offices of prominent officials. At last, when he was ready to go back to Minneapolis in disgust, he remembered to call an old friend of the family, Mr. Cecil Howes, for a last-minute chat. The friendly exchange of amenities progressed to the point where Hubert told Mr. Howes about the almost-successful mayoralty campaign and his high hopes for a party merger.

Looking back, a Humphrey biographer might wonder what would have happened if H.H.H. hadn't made that casual phone call. Mr. Howes had been an assistant postmaster general, and he knew how to open doors that appeared sealed to ordinary citizens. In a few minutes, Hubert found himself riding with Mr. Howes to Postmaster General Walker's office.

Humphrey, at the age of thirty-three, was facing one of the major challenges of his career when he went home to Minnesota. Exhilarated by the encouragement and assistance he immediately started receiving from the upper echelons of the National Democratic Committee, he set to work convincing the leaders of the Minnesota Democratic and Farmer-Labor parties that their differences could be adjusted and that a strong, united party could emerge to make itself felt at the polls in Minnesota.

Such a project would take a maximum of persuading, cajoling and fence-mending. The divergent viewpoints in the two parties ranged all the way from conservative to downright radical. Humphrey was glad that he had run for mayor as a nonpartisan. He could not be accused of playing favorites with any faction in the merger. Here Humphrey revealed his talents for laying out a large-scale program—for organizing and harmonizing diverse elements, for delegating power and authority. Among his most valuable assets was an ability to reject pettiness. He kept his eye on the main goal and refused to be argued up any blind alleys. His passionate appeals were so stimulating that his listeners could almost see the victory road ahead for a progressive phenomenon that would soon be known as the Democratic Farmer-Labor Party of Minnesota, or DFL.

In "Minnesota Heritage," Governor Karl F. Rolvaag refers to Humphrey as the "guiding genius" of the fusion, as well as "an orator with the uncanny ability to educate his audiences." That Humphrey was well qualified to lead is evident: "Endowed with a sensitive and perceptive mind, and tireless energy, he has attracted to the young party a host of aggressive labor and farm leaders and was able to merge their efforts with those of the students, professors, intellectuals, as well as the veteran campaigners of the Democratic and Farmer-Labor parties."

Humphrey was the "key man" of the Minnesota DFL delegation at the Democratic National Convention in Chicago in 1944. Although he had been an admirer of Vice President Henry A. Wallace for many years, Humphrey became convinced at the convention that Wallace had shifted too far away from his "moderate liberal" position. At that time he was not too impressed with Harry Truman either, and even joined the ADA in a statement favoring the drafting of someone like General Eisenhower or General MacArthur—for the Democratic Vice Presidency, of course.

After the decision was made, the Minnesota DFL backed Roosevelt and Truman, and Humphrey stumped the state to help bring victory to the two men at the top of the Democratic ticket. Franklin D. Roosevelt was elected to an unprecedented fourth term which he would not finish serving. When he died on April 12, 1945, Harry Truman became President of the United States.

In 1945 Humphrey was back on the campaign trail on his own behalf, facing Mayor Kline again. At the risk of criticism from leading conservatives, Gideon Seymour threw the weight of the powerful Minneapolis Star Journal and Tribune behind the young crusader who had already begun speaking for human rights. Humphrey received editorial cheers for "his savage attack on the conditions which breed the scandalous anti-Semitism which has come into the open in Minneapolis." In his speeches and radio addresses, the young candidate appealed to the best that was in his fellow citizens by calling for "a unified community program based upon recognition of the true ideals of democracy, wherein every person is accepted as a human being with dignity and worth, regardless of race, color or creed."

At the age of thirty-four, Hubert Humphrey became mayor of Minneapolis by the greatest plurality in the history of the city—more than 31,000 votes. Undoubtedly he was also the most active, during the two terms he served. He took the job seriously, seeing things that needed to be done and getting down to business on them. It would not be a "one-man" administration. He appointed committees and survey groups to investigate each area of concern, and then joined them in seeking solutions. The mayor's office was nonpartisan, and Humphrey tapped conservatives as well as liberals for committee chairmanships.

That he got off to a "flying start" in his first year as mayor is evident from the fact that he was awarded both the 1945 Junior Association Chamber of Commerce Award for the Outstanding Minneapolitan and the 1945 Junior Chamber Award for the Outstanding Minnesotan.

Minneapolis had been developing a reputation as a "wide-open city." Chicago underworld characters had often considered both of the Twin Cities good places to "hide out while the heat was on," and racketeers and other questionable characters had infiltrated the entertainment and night club business. Mayor Humphrey appointed an FBI-trained chief of police, Ed Ryan, who has since received national recognition as the top law enforcement officer of Hennepin County in which Minneapolis is located.

"Cleaning up the city" meant more to His Honor than clamping down on liquor stores and unsavory night clubs. The mayor's office embarked on an intensive slum cleanup program. There were other huge projects to provide housing for returning veterans.

One of the veterans was a Marine officer who had served the Corps from 1941 to 1945, progressing from Second Lieutenant to Major. Orville Freeman had been so badly wounded in the jaw, during the battle of Bougainville in the Solomon Islands, that he had to spend months learning to talk again. Mayor Humphrey felt that this was a man who was familiar with Veterans' Affairs, so he put him in charge of them. While he was serving in that office, Freeman continued to study law and was admitted to the Minnesota Bar in 1947.

The friends with whom he had discussed and debated politics in many a University "bull session"— the men who had looked into a crystal ball and told Humphrey they saw a shining political future for him, and who had worked with him in defeat and victory— were still in his "corner." They would continue to serve the DFL Party, often more for love than money, through the years ahead. Professors Herb McClosky and Evron Kirkpatrick continued to be Humphrey advisors. Dr. William Kubicek held offices in the state party. Dr. Arthur J. Naftalin, who might be described as a remarkable publicity man as well as a political scientist, was associated with Humphrey and Freeman since the early days. Almost everyone knows what happened to Orville Freeman. Another indispensable "regular" was William Simms, H.H.H.'s first campaign manager. These and other staunch supporters, including Max N. Kampelman, attorney and political science expert, later added strength to the party by building

up a reservoir of advisory talent. Mr. Kampelman, who
is associated with a private law firm in Washington,
still is Mr. Humphrey's good friend and personal attorney.

In any evaluation of his years as Mayor of Minneapolis, from 1945 through 1948, Humphrey's greatest
achievements were in the fields of law enforcement,
antidiscrimination legislation, and labor relations.
Closest to his heart, perhaps, was his moral aversion
to racial and religious prejudice. Michael Amrine, in
"This Is Humphrey," tells a humorous anecdote about
a veteran policeman who was heard advising a new
member of the force, "And don't arrest too many Negroes, the mayor doesn't like it."

Humphrey was far ahead of his time, and he did
not banish all intolerance from Minneapolis—but he
was visualizing an era in American history when racial
and religious discrimination would be considered "so-
cially unacceptable." Humphrey was the first mayor
in the country to achieve passage of a Fair Employment
Practices Act, and the mayor's Council on Human Relations pressured the real estate agents to remove re-
strictive clauses from housing deeds. Humphrey has
always been positive that there are answers to human
problems, if you look at them in the clear light of good
conscience and moral conviction.

The labor vote had been important to Hubert Humphrey from the start, but he did not permit it to sway
his judgment except when he agreed with its goals.
Perhaps the best comment on that subject may be
found in the doctoral thesis of Charles E. Gilbert who

worked on Humphrey's staff for a year and a half while he wrote "Problems of a Senator: A Study in Legislative Behavior." Dr. Gilbert quoted Gideon Seymour as having said that Hubert Humphrey is "not labor's man" . . . "that Humphrey was, if anything, too rigidly guided by principle, and that I would find he was not anybody's man."

There were about twenty strikes in Minneapolis during that turbulent period when unions were trying to establish status and identity. Recalling all he had learned about the harsh struggles of the working man throughout history, and still carrying a mental picture of the "police state action" against those strikers in Mississippi, Mayor Humphrey did not call out the police to wave tommy guns around. He worked day and night at arbitration tables. There were some critical periods, but there were no Haymarket Riots in Minneapolis.

When it came to strikes that would threaten human health and welfare, Humphrey gave the unions fair warning that he would be against them one hundred per cent.

The activities and utterances of Mayor Hubert Humphrey of Minneapolis were being considered newsworthy by The New York Times in 1947. On March 4, it was noted that he was at Atlantic City telling the Convention of American School Administrators that educators had to take some responsibility for dodging "controversial issues" in the classroom. "Between 1920 and 1930," he said, "American educational leaders bowed subserviently to the disciplines of 'isolationism, protectivism, high tariff, and in many quarters, racial intolerance.' . . . Our schools must be more attuned to the needs of democracy." He emphasized that "something must be done" about providing adequate salaries for teachers.

Early in 1947, The Minneapolis Tribune reported receiving information that three shots had been fired at Mayor Humphrey when he returned from a political meeting. Usually Mr. Humphrey's driver, Patrolman Vern Bartholomew, accompanied the Mayor to the door, but that night he ran up to unlock it alone. Later the Mayor went outside to investigate, but could find no trace of the sinister visitor. Perhaps Humphrey was thinking ruefully to himself, "This is the price a mayor must pay if he is determined to clean up a city." Since his election in July 1945, the Mayor had received many threats against his life. That was the reason he usually had a policeman at the wheel of his car.

Almost twenty years ago, liberal opposition to the Taft-Hartley Law was as vociferous as it is today. On June 21, at the Cleveland Convention of the International Ladies Garment Workers, AFL, The New York Times reported that "tumultuous demonstrations" had greeted President Truman's veto of the Taft-Hartley Labor Bill the day before. (The House promptly overrode the veto 331-83.) Humphrey was at the Cleveland convention, urging liberals to organize politically for a "dynamic fight against reaction." He endorsed a peacetime European Recovery Program such as Secretary of State George C. Marshall had advocated earlier that month at Harvard.

The New York Times referred to Mayor Humphrey of Minneapolis as "a leader in Americans for Democratic Action"—a subject which has been a bone of contention since that time. Although he chooses not to be described as an intellectual and even seemed awed by the "high-powered brains" of the ADA founders, Humphrey is no laggard when it comes to matching gray matter with anyone. He denies being a prolific reader, but he obviously did not absorb all the facts and figures and historical data on an incredible array of subjects through some vague process of osmosis.

There were several reasons why Humphrey would be attracted to an "intellectual debating society" of ADA's caliber. During his boyhood, young Hubert had been fascinated with the discussions in the drugstore, and in the Humphrey living room after Epworth League meetings on Sunday nights. He knew that it is much easier to find yes-men in a group of extremists than in a group of well-informed intellectuals. The ADA was a stimulating forum for the young debater from Doland, South Dakota.

Much of the criticism against the ADA has been based on the fact that its members have always taken a strong stand on human rights, bolstered by a scholarly faith in the "ultimate decency" of the great human family. Depending upon the way mankind behaves, this philosophy may become much more popular before the end of the Twentieth Century.

Charles Gilbert explained that the Minnesota ADA, which Humphrey helped to found in 1946, was "strictly an anti-Communist organization, and, in fact, it disbanded in 1949 after the struggle had been won and its 'raison d'etre' had evaporated." In 1949 Humphrey felt honored to serve as national chairman of ADA.

There is no denying the presence of some Communists and "fellow travelers" in the state as late as 1948. Robert Esbjornson, in "A Christian in Politics: Luther W. Youngdahl," wrote this description of a union disturbance that caused Governor Youngdahl some anxiety: "The strikers belonged to the United Packing House Workers of America, CIO. The union was not in a very strong position. Organized in 1943, it was not wealthy. It was torn by an inner dissention involving its right-wing, a few Communists, its 'go-slow' faction and the 'hotheads.' "

Michael Amrine declared that, "Humphrey is the only major American political figure who has personally tangled in political combat with Communists determined to defeat him and his friends."

The extent of Communist participation in the young DFL party remains problematic, and Humphrey understood that it was not always possible to turn off sympathy for a brave World War II ally as though it were a faucet. After the war, it came as a shock to many Americans to realize that the U.S.S.R. was still hell-bent on world domination—and that the United States was included in the pattern. In Minnesota they went to work and weeded out the "dissident, disruptive, left-wing elements," as Governor Rolvaag describes the negative forces in the old Farmer-Labor party. Undoubtedly some bitterness was aroused, but the DFL party was strengthened by a new surge of healthy unity.

Humphrey's confrontation with Communism in Minnesota would some day be of value on an international scale. His knowledge of the extreme-leftist point of view would give him an insight such as few Americans possess.

From all the evidence, Humphrey's democratic positivism leaves no room for negativism. He seems dedicated to the proposition that extremism—to the far left or to the far right—is negative. It is a device for abusing and shattering, not for building. It rejoices in tearing apart, not in putting together. It sits in a dark cellar and plots obstacles to human progress.

The ebb tides of war washed other problems into the mayor's office. An Associated Press story in The New York Times for November 23, 1947, reveals Humphrey's indignation against illegal profiteering. He had asked the Department of Justice to send F.B.I. men to investigate reports of "hoarding and black marketing of critical building materials." He was convinced that persistent rumors had a basis in fact. "There's hardly a square inch of warehouse space available in Minneapolis today. Something must be in them."

By 1948 Humphrey had proved himself a remarkable organizer, a nonpartisan diplomat in countless areas, an early champion in the new surge toward human rights, a vocal foe of slum housing and gangsterism, and a whirlwind speaker on the national platform circuit. Most of all, he had shown that a mayor's job could—and should—be more than a status symbol or a chair-warming proposition.

The Humphreys had moved into a home of their

own, a square, three-bedroom stucco house that is typical of middle-class Minneapolis. During some of those years as a young mother at home, Mrs. Humphrey earned a small personal income testing Betty Crocker cake and biscuit mixes for General Mills.

With her husband's heavy speaking schedule and multiple conferences on everything from beautifying the parks to battling philosophies alien to democracy, Muriel could understand why he was seldom able to be at home with his family. In 1948, there were four lively, attractive children in the Humphrey household. Two more sons, Robert and baby Douglas, had joined Nancy and "Skipper." Mrs. Hubert Humphrey was a busy, conscientious mother, with a "born knack" for cooking, sewing and housekeeping.

Muriel Humphrey's record speaks for itself. She is vibrantly interested in learning something new every day. Like her husband, she took pride in working with her hands as well as her brain during the "lean years." Her respect for thriftiness, combined with an artistic flair for fashion designing, kept her involved in one splendid "sewing production" after another.

During the years of their early struggles, Muriel shopped for materials for the children's clothing and spent long evenings at the sewing machine. Even then, it was a delight for her to see the attractive garments she could make from bargain remnants. When she could afford finer fabrics, her adeptness with tailors' tacks and linings and button-hole stitching gave her a warm feeling of creative accomplishment. While His

Honor was out "mayoring," the First Lady of Minneapolis was doing a superb job of taking care of the children and entertaining herself with a practical, fascinating hobby that would some day make her the delight of the homemaking magazines. The life she had led would cause millions of other American wives and mothers to feel that Muriel Humphrey is a "kindred soul."

Whether they agree with her husband's politics or not, it is impossible to find anyone who doesn't admire Muriel Humphrey. The enthusiasm ranges all the way from "She's a doll!" to "She's terrifically intelligent!"

Chapter Six

From Civil Rights to Senate—1948

In 1948, Mayor Humphrey began to glimpse some colossal doors standing wide open in the distance. He had applied his talents vigorously in the cause of good government in Minneapolis, and he had continued to receive the support of progressive Republicans, as well as the DFL and the National Democratic Committee.

As Humphrey, Freeman and Company prepared to lead the Minnesota DFL delegates to the 1948 Democratic Convention, they could look back on several gains—even though they hadn't exactly overwhelmed the Republicans. William Gallegher and Frank Starkey had been elected Congressmen in 1944 but were defeated in 1946. There was rejoicing about John Blatnik's election to the House of Representatives in 1946. The party was feeling unified and hopeful in 1948, but the Republicans would have a strong ticket.

Before Hubert Humphrey left that convention in 1948, he would come face to face with his principles. The healing of the breach between the Democratic and Farmer-Labor parties had been a political miracle.

Now he would find himself choosing between going along with the dictates of political expediency, or wrenching a large chunk out of the Democratic party. The latter road might lead him straight back to the drugstore or the classroom, and that wouldn't be so bad. He would be able to live with his conscience. As Dr. Gilbert so aptly put it, "His conscience can give him terrible trouble when he is not sure he has kept faith with it."

Humphrey was barely thirty-eight, and he was already considered a promising liberal "comer" in national Democratic circles. With one false move, he might hear the irrevocable slamming of illustrious doors. He could serve in Minnesota politics and wait for another convention in a more favorable year, when it wasn't so vital for the Democrats to present a united front against a candidate as popular as Thomas E. Dewey of New York.

The Minnesotan, however, was facing a national test of his "positivism" in the field of human rights. The first sparks of the Civil War had begun crackling almost one hundred years before, and the words that cried out to be spoken could make Humphrey seem as inflammatory in the eyes of the South as old John Brown of Osawatomie.

Humphrey tried to be as conciliatory as possible, in an effort to keep the Southern delegates from walking out of that Philadelphia convention, but the Minnesota delegation had pledged itself to a strong civil rights plank in the platform. A "watered down" version might please the Deep South, but it would have little significance.

In and out of the interminable platform committee meetings Humphrey debated the issue, with himself as well as with other influential party leaders. Both Dad Humphrey and Ralph were there, spurring him on and telling him they knew he would do the right thing.

Humphrey was not underestimating the mid-century surge of moral dedication to civil rights, among leading clergymen, businessmen and educators—as well as "intellectuals" in general. On the other hand he had made friends in the South, especially during his year at Louisiana State University, and he longed to find a compromise that would please everyone.

At last he faced the fact that no "bland" compromise would lubricate the wheels of civil rights justice. There is a time in history when a breakthrough is demanded; Humphrey had to "try this one for size," come what may.

Never had "the importance of being eloquent" been of greater consequence in Humphrey's career. The speech he prepared, with so much soul-searching, echoed through the convention hall and poured out through radios into the countryside. Housewives paused in their ironing or looked up from bathing the baby—motorists turned quizzical glances toward their car radios—shoppers slowed thoughtfully near loudspeakers in the streets. They were hearing an appeal that would slash through the apathy of too many tragic decades and would challenge the course of history in the years ahead:

"I realize that I am dealing with a charged issue— with an issue which has been confused by emotionalism on all sides. I realize that there are those here—friends and colleagues of mine, many of them—who feel as deeply as I do about this issue and who are yet in complete disagreement with me.

"My respect and admiration for these men and their views was great when I came here.

"It is now far greater because of the sincerity, the courtesy and the forthrightness with which they have argued in our discussions.

"Because of this very respect—because of my profound belief that we have a challenging task to do here —because good conscience demands it—I feel I must rise at this time to support this report—a report that spells out our democracy, a report that the people will understand and enthusiastically acclaim.

"Let me say at the outset that this proposal is made with no single region, no single class, no single racial or religious group in mind.

"All regions and all states have shared in the precious heritage of American freedom. All states and all regions have at least some infringements of that freedom—all people, all groups have been the victims of discrimination.

"The masterly statement of our keynote speaker, the distinguished United States Senator from Kentucky, Alben Barkley, made that point with great force. Speaking of the founder of our party, Thomas Jefferson, he said:

" 'He did not proclaim that all white, or black, or red, or yellow men are equal; that all Christian or Jewish men are equal; that all Protestant and Catholic men are equal; that all rich or poor men are equal; that all good or bad men are equal.

" 'What he declared was that all men are equal; and the equality which he proclaimed was equality in the right to enjoy the blessings of free government in which they may participate and to which they have given their consent.'

"We are here as Democrats. But more important, as Americans—and I firmly believe that as men concerned with our country's future, we must specify in our platform the guarantees which I have mentioned.

"Yes, this is far more than a party matter. Every citizen has a stake in the emergence of the United States as the leader of the free world. That world is being challenged by the world of slavery. For us to play our part effectively, we must be in a morally sound position.

"We cannot use a double standard for measuring our own and other people's policies. Our demands for democratic practices in other lands will be no more effective than the guarantees of those practiced in our own country.

"We are God-fearing men and women. We place our faith in the brotherhood of man under the fatherhood of God.

"I do not believe that there can be any compromise of the guarantees of civil rights which I have mentioned.

"In spite of my desire for unanimous agreement on the platform there are some matters which I think must be stated without qualification. There can be no hedging—no watering down.

"There are those who say to you—we are rushing this issue of civil rights. I say we are 172 years late.

"There are those who say—this issue of civil rights is an infringement on states' rights. The time has arrived for the Democratic party to get out of the shadow of states' rights and walk forthrightly into the bright sunshine of human rights.

"People—human beings—this is the issue of the twentieth century. People — all kinds and sorts of people—look to America for leadership—for help—for guidance.

"My friends—my fellow Democrats—I ask you for a calm consideration of our historic opportunity. Let us forget the evil passions, the blindness of the past. In these times of world economic, political, and spiritual—above all, spiritual—crisis, we cannot—we must not, turn from the path so plainly before us.

"That path has already led us through many valleys of the shadow of death. Now is the time to recall those who were left on that path of American freedom.

"For all of us here, for the millions who have sent us, for the whole two billion members of the human family—our land is now, more than ever, the last best hope on earth. I know that we can—I know that we shall—begin here the fuller and richer realization of that hope—that promise of a land where all men are free and equal, and each man uses his freedom wisely and well."

In those few short minutes, Hubert Humphrey became a man with a national destiny. As the last words rang out, most of the delegates leaped to their feet, cheering lustily as they followed Paul Douglas of Illinois in a rafter-shaking demonstration up and down the crowded aisles of convention hall. The endorsement for Humphrey's civil rights amendment to the party platform had been won.

Delegations from the Southern states, as everyone had feared, leaped to their feet, too, and marched out in a state of painful indignation—right into a pelting rainstorm. It might be said that Humphrey "formed" a new party, but he did not belong to it. The States' Rights Democrats, better known as the "Dixiecrats," chose Senator J. Strom Thurmond as their candidate for President, with the subsequent loss to the Democratic Party of the electoral votes of Alabama, Louisiana, Mississippi, South Carolina and Tennessee.

The cavernous old Minneapolis depot echoed to the music of brass bands and the cheers of loyal supporters when the Minnesota delegation returned home. University students "demonstrated" with signs proclaiming: "Humphrey, Champion of Human Rights!"

The depot celebration received its share of attention in the Minneapolis papers and on the radio. Such boisterous displays of emotion were viewed with smug complacency by the opposition party. All that noise— including all that "tongue-wagging" by Humphrey— would do the DFL no good. Dewey would win, and the rest of the country would follow. Many liberal Republicans, who admired Humphrey as a crusading nonpartisan mayor of Minneapolis, shrugged impatiently

when he spoke of Harry Truman as the man who would
not be moving out of the White House. Harry Truman
didn't have a chance—all the wise men said.

Some Humphrey fans had already referred to him
in hushed voices as a future senatorial prospect, and
a few even said it out loud. The reaction to his civil
rights speech was encouraging, and undoubtedly he
was ahead of many candidates who are known only in
their home country. He had achieved status as a
speaker on national platforms, he had run those first
two "shoestring" trips to Washington up to many more
and had even spoken before Congress on municipal
reforms, and his radio voice was becoming almost as
familiar as Jack Benny's.

Still, in retrospect, it seemed that Humphrey was
sprinting toward some doors that tradition had already
locked and bolted. Minnesota had not sent a Democrat
to the United States Senate since 1858—ninety years
before. There seemed to be an unwritten law that the
Senate was the Republicans' private preserve. It would
be expensive to run and calamitous to be defeated, but
that old dream was still prodding him on. Humphrey
filed for the Senate race against the junior incumbent,
Joseph Ball.

Just as Marvin Kline had been considered a satisfactory mayor of Minneapolis, Minnesota had gotten
used to the idea of Joe Ball as a Senator. On two of the
major campaign issues, Humphrey and Ball were definitely on opposite sides of the fence. Senator Ball had
voted "yes" for the Taft-Hartley Law and "no" for the
Marshall Plan. Humphrey took a firm grip on those

two issues and a number of lesser ones—and away he went!

The new candidate started off talking like a "blue streak," and there were some unkind remarks like, "I'll bet he talks all night in his sleep." Humphrey had a great deal to say to the people of the state. He had to tell the farmers that he had been a country-town boy and had vaccinated more hogs than he could count and that he understood their problems and knew that farm families weren't getting the rewards and credit they deserved for laboring long and hard to feed the country. He wanted them to know the other side of Humphrey—the side that had not been mayor of the largest city in the state.

The words poured out, warmed by a naturally friendly feeling toward people. He told them all—the city workers and businessmen, the farmers, the small-town folks—that Humphrey cared about their welfare. His cheery, unsophisticated approach added a lot of new friends to the many who had already rallied around him. His main campaign topics were the repeal of the Taft-Hartley Law, reasonable farm price supports, the importance of the United Nations as mankind's hope of salvation, and civil rights legislation; but he could discuss almost anything in terms of human progress and often did—at length.

Humphrey's campaign mileage ran to about thirty thousand miles, and his "verbal mileage" is incalculable. Often he was just leaving one town when he was due at another, but he told one of his drivers that he would rather be "the Hubert Humphrey who got there late than the late Hubert Humphrey." There were large and small audiences all over the state. Whenever Humphrey saw a new face, he was likely to deliver a speech and hand out some campaign literature. He ate hot dogs and potato salad and drank pop with the rest of "the folks" at more than fifty county fairs. On one occasion he persuaded the Master Showman of the Midwest, Jay Gould, to delay his next performance by explaining that "A political speaker hasn't a ghost of a chance against a lineup of beautiful hula-hula girls."

Since he was not shirking his job as mayor of Minneapolis, H.H.H. was working "double shifts" almost every day. He appeared to thrive on it, looking and sounding fresh when he should have been staggering with weariness.

Humphrey could talk faster and harder than Joseph Ball on the campaign circuit, and he loved to wade into a crowd and make friends and influence people. How was he doing? Humphrey seemed too much of an extrovert to people who disagreed with his policies and preferred Joe Ball's slow, careful way of speaking. The DFL candidate needed to swing a lot of voters over to his side, and sometimes he was "running scared."

On election night, Hubert Humphrey learned that he had gone hurtling through the widest portals he had ever contemplated in his mind—by a margin of almost 243,000 votes!

In 1935 he had written to his fiancee in Huron, South Dakota, to tell her he was setting his aim at Congress. Now it was 1948, the year of magnificent achievement. He had done a tremendous amount of living in that period of time, but it had actually been only thirteen years—from the drugstore to the mighty Senate Chamber in Washington, D. C. The most remarkable part of the phenomenon was the fact that he had started out with no more wealth or prestige than millions of other Americans.

The 1948 Congressional triumph of the DFL Party in Minnesota was not limited to Hubert H. Humphrey. Eugene McCarthy, a tall attractive instructor from St. Thomas College in St. Paul, was elected to the House of Representatives. Roy Wier and Fred Marshall were elected to the House for the first time, and John Blatnik was re-elected.

On the national ticket, where even the people who voted for Truman expected Thomas E. Dewey to win in a landslide, Harry S Truman won. With a plurality in Minnesota, the DFL had helped keep the incumbent from having to move out of the White House.

Humphrey would have been happy to see the DFL candidate installed in the State Capitol in St. Paul, but the re-election of the popular liberal Republican Governor of Minnesota, Luther W. Youngdahl, did not dismay him. Men with brilliant, dynamic personalities, they shared deep moral convictions about human rights and a common interest in "cleaning up" the state. In Youngdahl, many progressive Republicans in Minnesota believed they had found a prototype for Humphrey, and Harold Stassen was also making himself felt in state and national liberal circles. Out of the Humphrey-Youngdahl nonpartisan friendship would come a sleight-of-hand performance that would later have Minnesota Republicans gasping in confusion.

Governor Rolvaag credits much of the success for Humphrey's 1948 election to Orville Freeman, the young Minneapolis attorney who was his campaign manager. It is apparent that these DFL people quickly learned to get themselves involved and efficiently organized, and then worked together in high-spirited harmony.

Hubert Humphrey cleaned out his desk in the mayor's office and closed the door behind him with gentle respect, remembering its importance in his life.

The brand-new Senator set out for Washington by himself. In the suburb of Chevy Chase, Maryland—up above Connecticut Avenue — he found a home the Humphrey family would grow to love. Far from being a "mansion," it was a mint-green, two-story house that cost twenty-eight thousand dollars. He hoped Muriel and the children would be pleased, and they were. There would be warm remembrances of the children skipping through the echoing, empty rooms, exclaiming over and over again, "Daddy, it's beautiful—just beautiful!"

Soon Muriel would put her homemaking talents to work, and later she would have time to make music on the upright piano in the living room. According to a 1960 story in "Newsweek," "When Muriel Fay Humphrey first came to Washington in 1949 she brought along a copy of Emily Post's 'Etiquette.' An unpretentious girl who used to deliver frozen jack rabbits for her food-dealer father in Huron, S. D., Muriel was frankly awed and scared." Even though her sewing ability was not mentioned at that time, Muriel Humphrey was already considered "good copy."

All the Humphrey clan gathered in the Senate to do honor to their kinsman on the day the oath was administered by the late, great Senator Arthur Vandenburg. The former country boy from Doland could glance up, in the old communion of spirit, at the father who had filled him with a sense of excitement about the traditional greatness and unlimited potential of his native land.

Hubert Humphrey Sr., who had seen his son starting up a new "political glory road" that day, would walk beside him for only a brief span of months. But let it be said, from all the printed and spoken evidence, that Dad Humphrey made his days upon the earth twice as long as anyone else's by staying up late and living all his minutes with gusto.

Chapter Seven

Ahead of His Time

There are many Americans who wonder why any-one would want to go into politics. It is not recognized as a "business," from a profit-making angle. In trying to find the key to Humphrey's almost compulsive dedication to politics as a life's work, the career of Carl Sandburg presents a likely parallel. At one point in his early life, Sandburg tried writing for "big money." He voluntarily went back to being the voice of the workaday people—"The People, Yes"—at one fourth the salary. Being "The Poet of the People" is compulsive with Sandburg. Being the "Statesman of the People" is compulsive with Humphrey. Neither has regretted the choice he made.

Much has been written about Hubert Humphrey's "brashness" as a freshman in the austere Senate Chamber during the 81st Congress. Here he was, in the "most exclusive club in the world," but he always seemed aware that he needed to represent a wide cross section of voters—and that he hadn't gotten his seat through some form of "divine inheritance." He certainly shook

up any stuffiness that had settled in the corners, and
he made the name of "Humphrey" famous for his sometimes disconcerting approach to legislative issues.

Talking was the breath of life to the former star
debater from Doland High School, and he was bursting
with human rights convictions. As a young Senator,
Humphrey was sometimes frankly critical of "big business" interests. He was determined to protect the small
businessman, the laborer and the farmer from exploitation by "tycoons" who had gained economic advantages through preferential legislation. In one of his
speeches, he said, "I learned more from one South Dakota dust storm than I did in all my years in college."
He would never forget the closing of those two banks
in Doland. He knew that the first child labor laws were
not far behind him in history, and that the most effective labor legislation was not enacted until the 1930's.
Looking around him, the former druggist felt that the
country still needed a carload of "social conscience
pills" to realize its democratic destiny.

In the surge of sustained prosperity today, Humphrey sees "bigness" as a sign of a healthy democracy,
and he applauds all the wealth, power and prestige that
the capitalistic system represents in the nation's economy. That does not stop him from wondering why
business, which feels justified in being so "big," should
object so strenuously to "big government" and "big
unions."

Back in 1949, as now, he felt that "poor people make
poor consumers." The young legislator reminded the
Senate that "This country is only as strong as its work-

ing people . . . whose boys and girls need homes, need pork chops, need clothes."

In his debates against the Taft-Hartley Law, he criticized "the big boys" who tried to convince small businessmen that the unions were their enemies, and predicted that "Someday . . . the little businessman will wake up and find out that the only important customers he ever had were those who worked in overalls . . . there are not enough corporation directors to keep every store in America busy."

Laudatory references to the New Deal did not exactly endear Senator Humphrey to a heavily conservative Congress. The Roosevelt program, which was being rated as "past history" in the early 1950's, was described in this manner in the Universal Standard Encyclopedia:

"The New Deal was attacked by conservatives as destructive of private enterprise and individual initiative; it was defended by its partisans as a balancing mechanism which would eliminate the recurrent economic booms and depressions of capitalistic production and insure an equitable distribution of wealth and opportunity. Most scholars now believe that the New Deal helped to introduce into the United States a widespread attitude that government regulation of free economy was justified to whatever extent necessary to satisfy the minimum needs of public welfare and continuous employment."

To Senator Humphrey, President Franklin D. Roosevelt's economic adjustment measures would always be a living, breathing part of the nation's history because they would mean so much to so many people for so long. The passage of the Social Security Act in 1935 would serve to remind almost every working citizen, as he reached retirement age, that old age need not be a time of painful insecurity. The young Senator believed that other New Deal measures should be revived to safeguard Americans against depressions like the one that followed the period of "hollow prosperity" in the late 1920's.

Joining Humphrey in the Senate in 1949 was a tall Texan named Lyndon Baines Johnson. Senator Johnson, who had been in Washington during President Roosevelt's administration and shared Humphrey's understanding of the New Deal program, merited the Minnesotan's respect in the sessions ahead. If H.H.H. gradually "soft-pedaled" his fiery civil rights demands, it was because he realized that there were enlightened Southern leaders who felt much as he did and who would some day be helpful in attacking the situation from "the inside out."

His reunions with his old friend, Russell Long, whom he had known at Louisiana State University, made the conflict between civil and states' rights seem less "versus." Russell Long came to the Senate in 1951 to fill out an unexpired term and later became a Chevy Chase neighbor of the Humphreys. After Senator Long arranged a social meeting between Senator Humphrey and a number of Southern legislators, Humphrey acknowledged that they "got to know each other as humans."

Meanwhile, the ebullient Midwesterner was "lobbying" for all the people—of all races and religions—

who had few powerful voices to speak for them. He
was standing on a solid human rights platform when
he demanded that the nation's citizens be better fed,
better housed, better clothed, better educated. These
were not subjects that could be covered in a few well-
chosen phrases—not by young Senator Humphrey at
any rate. He was frank and garrulous, and undoubtedly
he stepped on some prominent toes.

It was considered both imprudent and impudent to
be a "brash chatterbox" in the Senate in those days.
Humphrey was ahead of his time, as he had been with
the civil rights plank at the 1948 convention. Today's
freshman Congressmen — including young Senator
George McGovern from Humphrey's native state—do
not shrink from challenging some of the "kings of the
hill." They seldom get their "ears pinned back," as
Humphrey did in 1950 when he started a campaign to
abolish a fiscal committee headed by the venerable
Senator Harry F. Byrd of Virginia who had been a
member of "the most exclusive club in the world"
when Hubert was still dishing out chili in the drugstore
and helping his father vaccinate hogs.

The senior Senator Byrd, who has now retired from
office, had long been the recognized guardian against
financial excesses in the federal government. After he
had become sufficiently wearied by the young Senator's persistence, back in 1950, the Virginian stood up
on the Senate floor one day and made it clear that any
fiscal committee of which he was chairman was highly
necessary to keep the nation from plunging any faster
into the pits of bankruptcy.

Humphrey did not know that he was facing the most embarrassing fiasco of his talkative career. When he stood up to answer, most of the honorable members of the Senate faded out of the chamber, one by one, and left him talking to a scant handful of sympathizers. A goodly gathering of reporters, up in the gallery, witnessed the distressing episode. Humphrey would never be so young again.

Later he ruefully confessed, "Maybe it would have been better if I had sat back and waited a little." If he had waited until the 1960's, it would have been less difficult to get funds for the humanitarian purposes he had in mind.

After that "chastisement" by the elder statesmen —who undoubtedly believed they were doing it for his own good—Humphrey simmered down considerably, but there are still some people who are not convinced that he deserved the "obnoxious freshman" treatment.

Whether he was on the public platform or in a private gathering, Humphrey was noted for his zest and exuberance. In social groups, the Minnesotan was sometimes carried away by his spontaneous sense of humor. Walter Ridder, in a Saturday Evening Post article, tells of an occasion when Muriel didn't have time to signal her husband as per that etiquette book. At a staid dinner party at the British Embassy, the Senator ended an hilarious political anecdote with the exclamation, "Oh, boy, and then did the manure hit the fan!"

Even after he began to "tone down," Humphrey's prairie heartiness continued to add sparkle to his activities. When he had trouble being sophisticated or fashionably arrogant, it was most apparent that "the country boy" was thrilled to be a United States Senator.

In grateful appreciation for the votes of his constituents, he seemed to feel as though he had to introduce an avalanche of legislation. He was seething with bright ideas; and everywhere he looked, he saw so much to be done. If a vast majority of his bills were shunted aside, at least he was "trying them for size."

Humphrey supported President Truman's civil rights and anti-Taft-Hartley policies. He kept expanding his knowledge of national and international affairs. He was interested in everything from NATO and the United Nations to protecting the dairy farmers of the Midwest from the infringements of colored margarine. He said, on several occasions, that he did not like the idea of price controls but that inflation would be so much worse.

Dr. Charles Gilbert described Humphrey as "an evangelist for democracy." The atom bomb had ended World War II; and only five years later, United Nations forces were trying to halt Communism in Korea. Senator Humphrey was neither a lover of war nor of totalitarian tyranny. He has pointed out that liberals are in favor of peace—unless freedom is threatened. Some of the earliest and fiercest voices to be raised against Nazi barbarism were those of liberals. Humphrey agreed that the Communists must be halted in Korea, but he shared President Truman's anxiety about another world war.

President Truman, who had been elected so unexpectedly in 1948, was serving another sometimes-tumultuous term. General Douglas MacArthur's admirers were indignant at the President's abrupt removal of the Pacific war hero who favored extending the Korean conflict.

At home in Congress, President Truman saw much of his legislation, including his "Fair Deal" program, go down to defeat at the hands of a strong coalition of Republicans and Southern Democrats. The early 1950's will be remembered as a period of emergency and tension, but President Truman won support for a higher minimum wage, increased social security and aid for housing. The voice of Senator Hubert H. Humphrey was raised in eloquent endorsement of these measures.

In 1951, Humphrey was being described as a "political opportunist" by some Minnesotans and a "neat operator" by others. Always an extrovert whose "wide-open approach" made him seem incapable of guile, there was some suspicion that Senator Humphrey resorted to political intrigue in "The Strange Case of the Disappearing Governor."

The progressive Republican Governor of Minnesota, Luther W. Youngdahl, had been elected to three terms and his admirers expected him to run for a fourth term. After that, they believed he could pull Humphrey's cherished Senate seat out from under him— and perhaps climb even higher on the national political ladder.

Governor Youngdahl would have been a formidable opponent. He was also a crusader for human rights, and he drove his messages home with skill and imagination. Humphrey may have been alarmed at the prospect of running against a man he admired so much.

Suddenly, in the summer of 1951, Youngdahl's fans felt as though he had been spirited right out of their midst. He had been appointed a United States District Judge, after a clandestine conference with President Truman. Governor Youngdahl had been accompanied to the White House by a friend named Hubert Humphrey.

Youngdahl issued a statement saying that "the emotional and physical strain of being governor was so great that he would find it impossible to run for a fourth term." Moreover, the law was the Judge's first love. There were several other reasons, but a host of furious Republicans believed that Humphrey had done his best to help Luther Youngdahl eliminate himself from the Minnesota political picture.

Judge Youngdahl would later render brilliant and fearless decisions in the Owen Lattimore and other crucial cases. Partisan politics aside, Senator Humphrey knew that Judge Youngdahl would serve the federal court with distinction and uncompromising devotion to democratic justice.

It was natural that the former druggist from South Dakota should be one of the sponsors of the Humphrey-Durham Drug Act in 1952. He had known that druggists often were "put on the spot" when insistent customers wanted prescriptions refilled without the consent of their doctors. Humphrey and Durham were the only two Senators who had been druggists, and their bill was designed to bring order out of chaos by a uniform reclassification of habit-forming and nonhabit-forming drugs in prescription departments. The bill was misinterpreted as a form of "federal interference" at first, but at last a favorable consensus was obtained in Congress.

The Humphrey-Durham Act is beneficial to pharmacists and doctors because they have definite "guidelines" to follow. Customers are protected from easy access to habit-forming drugs because prescriptions cannot be refilled without the consent of the doctor. Under the act, drugs of that type are required to be labeled "Caution." Although there are a great many new drug regulations on the books now, it was the first major revision of the Food and Drug Act since 1938.

All the details about the 1952 Humphrey-Durham Drug Act were given to me at a very fast clip by a Humphrey staff member named Julius Cahn — as though it had happened yesterday. Young Mr. Cahn's voice is much like Mr. Humphrey's, and so is his energetic exuberance. When I told him that he has a lot of "Humphrey spirit and bounce," he thanked me for the compliment and said, "If you don't have it, you don't last long around here!"

Of special interest was the fact that it was past five o'clock. I had just visited another Vice Presidential office in the same building. Staff members were still pounding typewriters and answering phones in both offices, at a time when most people are "calling it a day." As I left, I asked an elevator boy how late they kept the New Senate Office Building open, and he said that people sometimes worked there until ten or eleven o'clock.

When the average American hears that Congress is not called into session until noon, he jumps to the conclusion that "it's a soft life." Actually, the office buildings and the Capitol are alive with activity long before noon, especially when Congress is in session. One morning, about eighty-thirty, I found myself riding down the escalator to the subway while Senator "Mike" Mansfield was riding up on the other side. (Later I learned that Senator Mansfield's normal working day starts shortly after 7:00.) When I reached Senator Eugene McCarthy's office, he was just leaving for a committee meeting. Congressmen spend most of their mornings in their offices and in committee meetings.

Back in 1952, when Hubert Humphrey had been a Senator for more than three years, President Truman announced that he would not seek another term. The Republicans started a primary write-in campaign to draft General Dwight D. Eisenhower, a candidate whose name would be magic on the ballot. The Democrats began to seek a successor to Truman, and the eyes of party leaders turned toward Illinois. Adlai Stevenson, who was preparing to run again for Governor, finally consented to let himself be drafted.

Senator Humphrey and the Minnesota DFL leaders involved themselves in a vigorous campaign to send Stevenson to the White House. The Illinoisan's campaign slogan was "Talk sense to the people." His whimsical utterances as a two-time presidential contender have been absorbed into the folklore of the nation.

As a man of remarkable intellectual powers, as well as a definitely receding hairline, Candidate Stevenson became famous as the first of the "eggheads." He did not shrink from the appellation. On one occasion, he quipped, "Eggheads of the world arise. You have nothing to loose but your yolks."

The Stevenson wit always emerged in unexpected forms. At one of the annual DFL beanfeeds at the Minneapolis Armory, Senator Humphrey, Orville Freeman and several other Minnesota officials were seated around Governor Stevenson. One of them gestured toward the capacity crowd and said, "Look at all the Minnesotans who have come here to honor you!"

Governor Stevenson picked up his fork and asked with gentle modesty, "Does it occur to you that they might have come for the beans?"

Looking back on the accomplishments of Adlai Stevenson, who was destined to be tempest-tossed as a spokesman for the conscience of the country, President Johnson would say in 1965, "It seems such a short time ago that, out of Illinois, came that thoughtful eloquence summoning an entire nation back from its drift toward contentment and complacency."

The people were weary of the Korean War and price controls in 1952; they liked the promise of Eisenhower prosperity. In spite of Stevenson's reputation for high integrity and humanism in state government, Dwight D. Eisenhower's heroic war record alone would give him a tremendous advantage over the Governor of Illinois.

As the headlines described it in 1952, "Ike" won by a landslide, but the staunch Democrats had given their hearts to the man who said so graciously in his hour of defeat: "That which unites us as Americans is far greater than that which divides us as political parties. We vote as many but we pray as one. With a united people, with faith in democracy, with common concern for others less fortunate around the globe, we shall move forward with God's guidance toward the time when His children shall grow in freedom and dignity in a world at peace." In the "comparative figures department," Adlai Stevenson, in 1952, received approximately as many popular votes as Senator Goldwater received in 1964—with fewer people voting.

As a Congressman, Senator Humphrey considered himself a public servant. He continued to vote the Democratic "party line" in a high percentage of cases, but he was not partisan about any issues that would aid the welfare of the human race. Although he made headlines with "radical" stands on civil rights, fair-price supports, the Taft-Hartley Law, and other programs for social and economic betterment, his backstage talents for conciliation and adroit diplomacy had already been evident during the DFL merger in 1943.

Humphrey saw that the legislative process took flexibility, resiliency, and infinite persistence. When the votes were being tallied, after weeks of committee meetings, conferences, telephone calls, and reams of research and paper work, Humphrey would just about know whether he and the co-sponsors of the bill had a winner or not. It is difficult to give credit to the person who first said, "Humphrey always does his homework," because it has been repeated so many times.

The successful management of a bill might be likened to the training and running of a steeplechase champion. In addition to making certain the entry is sound enough in wind and limb to compete on a congested course, the landscape must be studied for hedgerows and boggy areas, and for all manner of natural and artificial hazards.

Only a minor percentage of all the bills drafted have run the course successfully, in spite of dedication and long weeks or months of "homework." Every Senator believes in the importance of the legislation he seeks to introduce. Senator Everett Dirksen of Illinois recently spoke of the "tediousness" of all the paper work and research involved in the preparation of a bill, but he also emphasized the feeling of exhilaration that statesmanship produces. A capable Congressman must love his work—because work it is.

There was a sense of power to sitting in a Senate seat, but Humphrey realized that the sense of responsibility was much stronger. His legislative interest in education would fill several volumes, starting with a modest aid to education bill for "federally impacted areas" in 1949 and later rising to history-making heights in his sponsorship of scholarship and loan assistance for college students, with credit allowances for those who intended to teach. He has been an articulate advocate of federal assistance for everything from school lunch programs to the expansion of elementary and college building facilities. A dozen years ago, he was visualizing the deluge of "war babies" that is swamping the nation's educational centers—right on schedule. In one manner or another, he has kept saying, "We must not frustrate these bright young people."

Shortly before the 1954 election, when "McCarthyism" was terrorizing the country even more than the threat of Communism, Senator Humphrey introduced a piece of legislation that astonished his fellow liberals. Senator Joseph McCarthy of Wisconsin had started out as a dedicated foe of subversive Communism within the United States; intoxicated with power and finding his quarry scarce, he began to "witch-hunt" blindly in all directions. Patriotic "moderates"—both Democrats and Republicans — found themselves being labeled "Communist dupes" and "fellow travelers."

It was not a rational period. Some Americans began to resemble the ghouls at the guillotine during the French Revolution, crying out for more heads to fall. Robert Esbjornson called it "the most insidious evil the American people have tolerated. They have allowed themselves to fear making forthright statements of opinion; they have allowed themselves to become suspicious of independent-minded men who are not afraid to voice convictions based upon free inquiry into the facts; they have allowed themselves to smirk at scholarly men as McCarthy did, implying that because they were erudite, they were dangerous."

The members of Americans for Democratic Action, in spite of their anti-Communist origin, were considered "scholarly"—a disgraceful condition in the eyes of McCarthy and his followers.

Edward R. Murrow had already gone on record with his "We shall not walk in fear" speech. Senator Humphrey, speaking at an ADA meeting in the spring of 1954, said, ". . . At a moment when all our nation's wisdom should be employed in the quest for solutions to the awesome terrors of the Hydrogen Age, we find ourselves plunged into venomous and often irrelevant fratricidal conflicts that dishonor and debase our traditions." He referred to the machinations of McCarthy and his super-patriots as "this madness of know-nothingness."

McCarthy appeared increasingly determined to turn his witch-hunting talents on some fellow Senators who would soon be up for re-election. Since the Senate did not get around to censuring McCarthy "for abuse of its members and for insults to the Senate during investigation" until December 1954, it was just as well that Humphrey and his associates came up with an "antidefamation insurance policy" in August. His introduction of a bill to outlaw the Communist Party on the grounds that it was "an illegal, subversive conspiracy" under foreign domination—and not actually an American political party by Constitutional definition—was an unusual action for a liberal who believed in freedom in general. But Humphrey had tangled with both Communists and witch-hunters before, and he had the counsel of some astute legal and legislative strategists. It would be difficult for McCarthy to point a finger of accusation at any Senator who backed Humphrey's bill to outlaw the Communist Party.

In his six years in the Senate, Humphrey had not lost his knack for campaigning as though he had to get through that door before it slammed shut. When he went home to ask for support in 1954, it was a case of "Humphrey saturation" in Minnesota. He was all over the state, speaking furiously in person and on radio and television. He employed his familiar "folksy" approach, reminding the people that Humphrey had been conscientiously aware of their best interests in those hallowed halls of Congress. He had demonstrated his belief in their dignity as individuals who had a right to expect a fair share of profit from their honest toil, whether they were farmers, truckers, working-men, struggling businessmen, or members of minority groups that were suffering from discrimination. He also extended his concern to international "sore spots" where the global march toward freedom in underde-veloped countries was being threatened.

The Joe McCarthy factions were "spooking" the ADA even more feverishly that fall. In lauding "Old Hubert's" twinkling sense of humor in a "Harper's" article for February 1960, William S. White recalled that "the dread accusation of ADA membership had been hurled at him by GOP enemies" when he spoke at a meeting of Minnesota dairy farmers during the 1954 campaign.

With a gleam in his eye, Humphrey told White he had assured his accusers that "things had come to a sad pass when a man could be so abused for belonging to that fine old American institution, the American Dairyman's Association."

That was the year when young Orville Freeman was running for Governor of Minnesota, and Eugene McCarthy was campaigning to retain his seat in the

United States House of Representatives. When the votes were counted, the top DFL candidates had won a sweeping victory.

It was an "education in politics" to watch the young DFL Party move forward all through the 1950's. Around election time, Twin Cities papers featured pictures of Governor Freeman with the beauteous Mrs. Freeman, high moments at the annual bean feed, and various state winners posing with nationally prominent Democrats. There was one prize roto-photo of the "Triumphant Three"—Hubert Humphrey, Eugene McCarthy, and Orville Freeman—striding jauntily up the avenue in their overcoats one crisp fall day.

In 1954, according to the Minneapolis Star, "Humphrey drew his big margins in the areas of Minneapolis, St. Paul, and Duluth. But he drew his real victory margin from the farm areas." He had cut into heavily Republican territory all over the state.

Much has been said about Senator Humphrey's interest in the well-being of people whose opportunities and incomes are restricted by forces usually beyond their control, but he tried to be equally fair to all of his constituents—even the affluent ones. Walter T. Ridder wrote in one Saturday Evening Post article: "Minnesota businessmen as a group don't admire and do not vote for Humphrey, but long ago they learned that if they needed something done in Washington, Hubert will do it."

Humphrey enjoyed a fine relationship with one of those Minnesota businessmen—a talkative, optimistic "barefoot boy" who grew up to be Chairman of the

Board of General Mills. Harry Bullis, who referred to himself as a "liberal" Republican, loved to state his views on human relations, and he often jolted the more conservative members of the United States Chamber of Commerce with his pro-labor and pro-Marshall Plan statements. He kept reminding his business colleagues that, if it weren't for the workers, factories would be nothing but deserted buildings filled with idle machines.

Harry had a huge collection of scrapbooks which this author was privileged to examine. Among the many "glossies" of Harry with President Eisenhower, Harold Stassen and other leading Republicans, was a large one of Humphrey and Bullis sitting together at a Minnesota-Wisconsin football game and grinning with good fellowship as they cheered for their respective alma maters.

Anyone who knows the philosophies of both men will realize why they were compatible. Among Harry's sage observations was, "The humanities of business are more important than the techniques of business." He believed that management and labor could and should be able to get along together for the mutual welfare and prosperity of the nation. Humphrey and Bullis shared a common concern for the destitute and underprivileged. Both were appalled at the accepted patterns of misery and illiteracy in Latin America.

Harry referred to Senator Humphrey as "our" representative in Washington. The Senator did not need to worry that his Republican friend, Harry Bullis, would be after his seat in Congress. There was some talk of that, Harry told me, but he had laughed and said, "No businessman could ever beat Humphrey!"

Both Senator Humphrey and Harry Bullis were ahead of their time in visualizing the new business and political climate that would almost be taken for granted in the 1960's. In the meantime, the Senator from Minnesota would conciliate, but he would not deviate.

Chapter Eight

The Importance of Being a Statesman

Early in his congressional career, Senator Humphrey served in legislative areas that were closest to his heart—the Senate Committee on Labor and Public Welfare, and the Senate Committee on Agriculture. When it appeared that the prestigious Foreign Relations Committee would be dominated by isolationist Republicans after the election of President Eisenhower in 1952, Senator Humphrey was chosen by retiring President Truman and Senator Lyndon B. Johnson— then Senate Minority Leader—to serve as the voice of the liberal Democrats on the committee. It meant that he would need to withdraw from the Labor and Agriculture committees and become thoroughly informed on all the day-to-day intricacies of foreign policy. It did not mean that he would ignore the welfare of the workers and farmers. Civil rights and fair employment legislation would continue to be among his major interests. Theodore H. White refers to him as "one of the greatest champions of Negro rights in American history."

As a member of the Foreign Relations Committee, Humphrey plunged into his "homework" with vigor and vision. Sometimes there were on-the-spot missions abroad, and Mrs. Humphrey occasionally accompanied him to the fabulous lands they had once dreamed of visiting. The lady whose eyes and fingertips were thrilled by the texture of fine fabrics was able to shop for exotic materials in the bazaars of foreign cities.

Senator Humphrey met with diplomats and dignitaries on his arrival in foreign capitals. After the official business was concluded, he took special delight in going out among the people, to learn about their attitudes, customs and hopes for the future. He is a man who wants to know everything possible about everything important—and he considers people most important of all. This philosophy was evident in his reports to Congress, and in speeches all over the country, after his foreign inspection trips.

With his interest in international affairs becoming heightened as the tempo of American participation grew more pronounced, Senator Humphrey began to serve with wisdom and dedication as a United States Delegate to the United Nations in 1956. He was active in UNESCO and international disarmament forums. He continued to favor disarmament and the widespread prosperity and freedom from fear that world peace could bring—but he also knew that the leaders of all nations were not men of good will, and he wanted the United States to remain strong in every area of defense.

When Governor Stevenson was running again for the Democratic nomination for President in 1956, Senator Humphrey was a possible candidate for Vice President. Stimulated by the belief that he had a good chance to become Stevenson's running mate, Humphrey campaigned furiously for Stevenson before the primary in Minnesota.

Another top Democratic presidential contender in the same primary was Senator Estes Kefauver of Tennessee, whose crime syndicate investigations had brought him favorable national attention.

When the returns came in, they were disastrous for Stevenson—and for his dedicated champion, Hubert Humphrey. Kefauver's large plurality hit Humphrey right where he lived—in his own home state. Some of the newspaper scribes suggested that there weren't that many Democratic Farmer-Laborites in Minnesota —that a good many Republicans had switched over, to make Humphrey "eat crow." They may even have been getting belated revenge for the Youngdahl debacle.

Robert Esbjornson noted in 1955 that "... it is possible in Minnesota for a Democrat to vote for Republican candidates in the primary and vice versa. . . . Party strategy may call for a wholesale vote for a weak candidate of the other party, who could then be defeated easily in the general election." That has also been true in other states. Undoubtedly that is the reason why Minnesota Democratic presidential candidates are now nominated at the state convention.

By the time the national convention was held in Chicago in 1956, Humphrey—who could have run as a "favorite son" in his home state—was cut off from everything except his allegiance to Governor Stevenson. Because of the way the primary votes had stacked up, the Minnesota DFL group was committed to Kefauver.

Adlai Stevenson was nominated again as the Democratic candidate for President in 1956. In spite of his fondness for Hubert Humphrey, he decided to let the contest go to the floor.

Estes Kefauver, with a backlog of Presidential delegate strength, pulled ahead swiftly for the Vice Presidential nomination. The face of an attractive young New Englander, flushed and smiling from the excitement of making a surprise impact on the convention and the country, beamed out from the milling throng of delegates. John F. Kennedy was crowding Kefauver for second place on the ticket. Hubert Humphrey was lost in the shuffle.

It was a bitter blow for Humphrey. He had thought the door was open, but perhaps it was tightly shut all the time. He had been deserted, unintentionally, by all the forces he had helped to organize and had fought to support. Even though he was depressed and momentarily crushed, he did not hide himself in a cellar and plot revenge. Now was the time for all good men to come to the aid of the Party. He threw himself into the Stevenson-Kefauver campaign as though to sweep aside his visions of a Stevenson-Humphrey ticket by sheer vocal vigor.

Once more, the voters of the nation gave President Eisenhower an overwhelming vote of confidence. On the whole, the economic situation had been favorable, and everyone remembered that Eisenhower had fulfilled his promise to "bring the boys home from Korea." Again, it would have been almost impossible for anyone to beat President Eisenhower in 1956, although Stevenson did receive slightly more than twenty-six million votes. He had campaigned hard, but he had also devoted much of his time to Nuclear Disarmament and World Peace projects.

Back in Congress, Senator Humphrey continued to introduce legislation that leaned toward balancing the scales of economic, educational and moral justice in favor of humanity. He offered ample arguments to support his contention that American "self-interest" could be served in the process of helping one's neighbor to improve his lot in life. It made sense to him that the widespread cultivation of brain power and business initiative would accelerate production and stimulate greater achievement on every level.

If the Humphrey story had ended in the late 1950's, it would appear that his "pet legislation" had not gotten very far. The civil right program had moved forward by fits and starts, as though on rusty gears. There was the school desegregation ruling by the Supreme Court in 1954, with President Eisenhower taking a firm stand at Little Rock, Arkansas, in 1957. But as far as Congress was concerned, the Douglas-Humphrey bill for federal support of a strong desegregation program was considered too much too soon by "gradualists" who were holding out for another 172 years of white supremacy. In the human rights field in general, Humphrey kept working for the creation of a federal Fair Employment Practices Commission of the type he had introduced in Minneapolis.

Humphrey, in the early part of that decade, was learning to compromise some of his differences with even the most resolute of segregationists among his colleagues. The South, with small businessmen and farmers scattered all over a predominently rural countryside, has much in common with the upper Midwest. Senator Humphrey was in favor of protecting small businessmen and farmers on a nationwide scale, and Southern Senators often found themselves voting on the same side of the fence with the man whose eloquence had been responsible for the "Dixiecrat walkout" in 1948. Because they were glad to hear his persuasive voice raised on issues that were important to them in their home countries, they began to feel more reasonable about the Minnesota Yankee's point of view on other legislation.

The Senate came to know Humphrey as a man who wanted to keep the lines of communication open, seeking advice and knowledge among his colleagues and showing respect for their experience and erudition. He revealed a spirited eagerness to keep learning, although his basic philosophy remained the same—almost as though he were waiting for the country and the world to see the moral logic of it.

He often found intellectual enlightenment and humor to match his own among the Southerners in the Senate. He learned what almost every "damnyankee" learns in the South—that educated Southerners may object to integration in political principle, but that most of them list several "colored people" among the friends they admire most.

Exuberantly prolific in the exercise of his legisla-

tive duties, Humphrey said he had no intention of settling down to becoming "the world's greatest expert on
the boll weevil."

In his sponsorship and co-sponsorship of thousands
of pieces of legislation, Senator Humphrey seems to
have been more of an "influencer" than a "credit-
seeker." Although there are no major bills that bear
his name, his eloquence and strength of purpose have
often furnished the momentum that made passage possible. He has moved behind the scenes, with a conciliatory pat on the shoulder here, with a shrewd bit of
horse-trading there, with appeals to loyalty and good
conscience all over the place.

Humphrey's fellow Senators knew him as a man
who cared more about "fighting the good fight" to get
a worthy piece of legislation passed than about the
glory of having it named in his honor. He has viewed
certain bills with enthusiasm when he was just one of
twenty or thirty co-sponsors.

There has been a deathless quality about Senator
Humphrey's legislative tenacity. President Franklin
D. Roosevelt had tried to include some health legislation in the New Deal program. In 1945, part of President Truman's health care program was passed; the
section that would have provided hospital and medical
care for senior citizens was eliminated. In 1949, young
Senator Humphrey introduced a medical insurance bill
for the elderly, to be financed through Social Security.
It was shrugged aside as more "pie-in-the-sky," but
Humphrey resorted to various types of strategy to keep
it coming up in the Senate regularly. It was a case of

try-try-again, with a teacher's patient understanding that people's consciences need to be educated.

Where major legislation was concerned, Senator Humphrey never considered his efforts an exercise in futility. He kept pounding the anvil for fair minimum wage laws, as a spur to economic stimulation and higher standards of living for more millions of Americans.

Back in 1947, Mayor Humphrey of Minneapolis had cheered the news of President Truman's veto of the Taft-Hartley Law; the predominantly Republican Congress had promptly overridden the veto. For almost two decades, Section 14 (b)—the "right to work" provision—would be the target of reform by Humphrey and other liberals who believed that economically depressed areas would benefit from increased labor union activity. It is a fact that the Deep South, where unions have been unwelcome, has had less economic vitality, more illiteracy, and a lower per capita income than the states in which unions are strong.

Humphrey has always believed that unions and business organizations should learn to get along together, for the increasing prosperity and welfare of all American citizens. He does not believe that all unions should have to suffer for the transgressions of a few dishonest labor leaders—people who would be dishonest or greedy in any field in which they might be operating. Humphrey likes the beneficial accomplishments of labor unions. In their drive to emancipate the laborer from the "old sweatshop" era, they have inspired industrial leaders to be equally magnanimous in offering extra benefits.

The "extracurricular activities" of labor unions are dear to the heart of Hubert Humphrey. They have led the fight for sanitary working conditions, for safety measures to protect workers, for decent housing and education in the areas where they operate. It has been more than just a matter of higher wage scales.

In his survey of the labor situation in "War On Poverty," Humphrey noted the great gap between the wages of white people on one hand, and Negroes, Indians, and other minority groups on the other. As an example, about one fourth of all semiskilled Negroes are truck drivers, but they average at least $1,000 a year less than white drivers of comparable ability. The average income of the American Indian—our original native citizen—is about $1,500 a year.

Harry Golden made a delightful observation about the "vertical equality" of white and Negro customers at the checkout counters in Southern super markets. This equality does not extend to the groceries that are being purchased, unless the Negro is shopping for his or her white employer. The seeds of revolt may be born in the heart of a $150-a-month colored person who sees the white man unloading packages of steak and pork chops from his grocery cart, while he is trying to raise a family of decent American citizens on macaroni and potatoes and having to squeeze every cent to do it. Abraham Lincoln's face must sometimes break out in a cold sweat on those overworked pennies.

There is more freedom today. There is more hope for the underprivileged, the illiterate, the desperately poor. Americans are becoming aware of the "shame, misery and degradation" of poverty. A popular wise-crack, when Hubert Humphrey and the rest of us were young, was "I'm free, white and twenty-one!" What of the millions of less fortunate Americans who were enslaved by poverty and illiteracy, warped by racial inequality, suffering the helpless desolation of old age? It is safe to say that no one in the Humphrey family ever boasted, "I'm free, white and twenty-one!"

This is a time in history when foresight is more important than ever before. Hubert Humphrey started long ago to do his "homework" on the effects of auto-mation on the labor market. He believes that this is a two-way street and that audio-visual aids should be applied more extensively. "We are permitting automa-tion to create a large army of unemployables while refusing to use these same automated techniques to train our labor force," he wrote in "War On Poverty."

Some of the large industries are involved in experi-ments with audio-visual training programs, in coopera-tion with government agencies. That is a point Hum-phrey emphasizes often — that the highest level of achievement can be reached when business, labor and government march side by side in the development of programs that will lead to greater production and more earning and spending power. There is no force in his-tory to compare with that type of "bigness."

The National Commission on Technology, Automa-tion, and Economic Progress, which was created through legislation originally proposed by Humphrey, is seeking to develop more intermediate institutions between the laboratories and universities, where basic research takes place, and the existing and potential industries that can deploy it to make new products, develop new markets, and offer new jobs. The Federal Government invests about fifteen billion dollars a year in research and development — some in government laboratories, but mainly in industry and educational institutions.

Humphrey has studied men and events from every angle, and he is convinced that there are solutions to almost every human problem. In the words of the United States Air Force, "The impossible only takes longer." Sooner or later, he knows mankind must come to grips with its difficulties or perish. He often sounds as though he will fight to the last ditch to keep mankind from becoming a victim of its own bullheaded folly.

In his concern with the current unemployment problem, Humphrey sometimes re-examined the New Deal programs that helped to hoist the country out of the depths of the Great Depression in the Thirties. There was the Civilian Conservation Corps which transported thousands of unemployed youths from sweltering tenement ghettos to the fresh country air of forest and mountain work camps. For many of the young men, it meant the difference between delinquency on the city streets and a future life as capable American citizens. The primary effort, according to former WPA Administrator Humphrey, was to develop sound work habits. He believes "The most fundamental of all so-called job skills is the ability to appreciate the value of work, hard work, for its own sake."

In a 1959 article in "Harper's" entitled "A Plan to Save Trees, Land and Boys," Senator Humphrey rec-

ommended the establishment of a Youth Conservation
Corps. In Washington and other great cities, he has
seen idle teen-age dropouts, loitering around the streets
and prowling the alleys in sinister-looking gangs. Restless, rebellious, bitter young people, existing in a
vacuum of hopelessness — today, tomorrow, forever.
"Good-for-nothings, that's what you are! That's what
you'll always be, nothing but good-for-nothings!" They
heard that same record, played over and over again,
until they believed it. "So what?" was the retort that
covered the seething mass of frustration, boiling up
unchecked.

In 1959, a Labor Department planning group made
a study of Senator Humphrey's proposal for the establishment of a youth conservation corps which would
combine basic study courses and some military discipline with work on a variety of forest and conservation
projects. In its initial stages it would have taken
150,000 young dropouts away from tenement jungles
and taught them "sound work habits." A version of the
bill cleared the Senate in 1961, but it aroused very little
enthusiasm in Congress.

It was not until 1964, when President Johnson—
who was in no mood to fiddle while Rome burned—
ordered an assault on poverty that would include a
full-scale Job Corps program for teen-agers who had
left school before they were prepared for life. Even
though it was pushed forward at an accelerated rate,
the Job Corps was just gathering momentum in 1965.
When any nation refuses to shoulder its responsibilities soon enough, history often catches up with it. If
Congress could have looked ahead to the big city riots

that erupted during the long, hot summers of 1964 and 1965, it might not have considered Humphrey's 1959 youth conservation proposal another slice of pie-in-the-sky.

Humphrey considers unemployment a waste of valuable human resources. "The poor," he repeats, "make poor consumers." They must be trained to work and earn, to achieve all the dignities of citizenship. The more they earn, the more consumer products they will be able to buy—which will multiply the number of workers needed to supply those products.

Sceptics look at the job market and say, "There is nothing new under the sun." Under the Manpower Training and Development Act, the U. S. Employment Service has joined hands with private business to set up three hundred apprenticeship training programs for future chefs and cooks. Instead of scanning the horizon for new industrial categories, the Manpower directors faced the fact that there are never enough professional cooks. In a recent newspaper account, it was noted that Chef Binon, who presides over the kitchen of the Shoreham Hotel in Washington, takes personal pride in the progress of his four trainees.

All the apprentices may not have as glamorous a tutor as the one at the Shoreham who is described as looking like "a famous French chef—a round pink and white man with zesty accents, sweeping French gestures and a jolly Santa Claus chuckle." However, they can all find encouragement in a statement by Dominique D'Ermo, the food and beverage director who set up the training program at the Shoreham, that "due to the chef and cook shortage, none of the boys will have difficulty finding work."

The modern arm of the federal government is growing longer. It is reaching out into areas where stagnation and apathy have blighted the landscape for centuries. It points a forefinger and asks searching questions; it makes comparisons about human values. There is that business about farm surpluses, with the government paying millions of dollars just for rental storage every year. Senator Hubert Humphrey began to outline his "Food for Peace" proposals early in the 1950's, and was instrumental in obtaining grants for the famine-stricken people in India and Pakistan.

It was often stated with finality, by the experts, that we could not share our abundance with our hungry fellow men, because it would upset the economy of the world. The Senator from Minnesota couldn't swallow the sanctimonious argument that children in other lands should starve while American wheat was locked away in elevators. It went beyond moral consciousness. He saw the danger of presenting a picture of a rich, well-fed Uncle Sam to the ragged, diseased, undernourished billions in the "slums of the world."

The United States could not afford to be wealthy and selfish in a world growing turbulent with the political unrest and hunger pangs of billions who were becoming impatient for a better way of life. Even if they could not read, many of them had seen colorful, tempting pictures in American and European magazines. Communism kept trying to label American capitalism as deficient in humanitarianism; that "line" became a major propaganda weapon. It is true that isolationist voices often drowned out those of moderate liberals who understood the nightmarish incongruity of gaunt, desperate faces pressed up against our glittering windows in a world suddenly shrinking in size.

Both President Truman and President Eisenhower saw the moral and practical wisdom of nourishing the hungry of underdeveloped countries, but Humphrey had to keep "selling" Congress on each step forward in the people-saving "Food for Peace" program. The attention of the country was turned inward on McCarthyism, isolationism and the prosperity theme. It was not until the Russians hurled the first Sputnik into space in 1957 that Americans realized a new era was rushing upon them with giddy speed. Large-scale atomic war would be made too easy. No man—and no nation—could be an island. Many of the old ways of thinking would need to be scrapped.

While millions of Americans went into a panic of disbelief at the early space achievements of the U.S.S.R., Senator Humphrey intensified his study of the peaceful as well as the military aspects of the situation. He saw no conflict between working diligently for eventual world disarmament and building the United States missile arsenal up to peak strength. There were no other practical choices.

He believes in "weapons for peace" as well as for war, and the sharing of farm surpluses with the less fortunate seems the most appealing of friendship-makers. He has had little patience with the people who poke fun at our bountiful harvests. These are blessings

—we should take pride in an agricultural system that keeps the American "horn of plenty" overflowing, year after year. Nowhere else on earth can a nation complain of such a "miracle of abundance." We can sell it on world markets to bolster the American economy; we can use it for foreign aid to bolster our "brotherhood credit rating."

The fortunate American, with two cars in his garage, two TV sets in his house, and a new diet every week because his world is loaded with too much rich food, demands to know, "How can we afford all these 'handouts?' If we give too much away, we won't have anything left."

Hubert Humphrey insists that we may not have anything left if we do not share with those whose living standards we have outdistanced by centuries, too often through no fault of their own.

The Senator, who had to pinch pennies during so much of his early life and had often condemned thoughtless extravagance in any area, is aware that the nation's "money barrel" is not bottomless. He has been ruthlessly critical of foreign aid practices that permit expensive American machinery to rust in weed patches on the other side of the world and that do not get food supplies to the people who desperately need them. But he sees the miracles that can be accomplished by men of good will who—though fully aware of our wealth as a nation—are determined to make every dollar work to its utmost for democracy.

For more than ten years, the idea of sending "peace representatives"—rather than military personnel—to assist with economic and educational development in "emerging areas" of Africa, Asia and Latin America has been under consideration by some enlightened members of Congress. Humphrey was especially enthusiastic about the prospect of helping to nourish the minds, as well as the bodies, of illiterate people who had never learned to read under colonialism and were still bogged down by primitive agricultural and industrial practices. It was a challenge to make an ex-teacher's eyes shine; the U.S.S.R. had already launched numerous programs to capture the minds of men.

Senator Humphrey, during the 1950's, made a full-scale, practical study of the situation and often referred to a "Youth Peace Corps" in his speeches.

When the Senator first introduced his Peace Corps bill in the summer of 1960, it was greeted with as much derision as the "medicare" proposals of the 1930's. "Ole Hubert" was really chasing after rainbows this time! But "Ole Hubert" wasn't finished—he was letting Congress "try it for size."

True to his heritage as the son of a small business-man, and himself a druggist for a time, Humphrey was a dedicated co-sponsor of the Small Business Investment Act of 1958. Dad Humphrey had managed to scrape up enough credit to get the family drugstore through the Depression, but his son remembered all the small businessmen who had been ruined for want of a small loan when they needed it most.

The Senator from Minnesota waged a relentless campaign for universal disarmament, never lapsing into apathy in his belief that ". . . nuclear weapons re-

main the greatest single threat to man's survival."
After President Eisenhower appointed him Chairman
of the Senate Disarmament Subcommittee, he explored
the subject of nuclear-weapons testing with scientific
experts and a group of concerned advisors.

In a report issued in 1956, Humphrey supported
Adlai Stevenson's appeal for the banning of nuclear-
weapons tests. During succeeding years, as they in-
vestigated every aspect of test banning, including nuclear fallout, sufficient detection systems, and research
into the technical, scientific and political issues involved, Humphrey and his colleagues often realized
that they were "before their time." It was difficult to
get the message across to people who could not comprehend the dangers of nuclear fallout to themselves
and their descendants. They could view an automobile
accident with horror, but "strontium 90" was both invisible and unfamiliar.

Senator Humphrey staged a relentless campaign
to make "fallout" a household word. As a "teacher"
who realized the need for a test ban, he recalls, "In the
week before Easter, 1958, I spoke on the subject in the
Senate every day, once for four hours. Lyndon Johnson, then majority leader . . . urged all Democratic Senators to be in the chamber for this speech." He recalls
the overwhelming public response: "Americans appeared to be somewhat ahead of their elected officials
in understanding the urgency of the test-ban proposal."

Although he has not complained about receiving
almost no credit, Humphrey did a great deal of "homework" on the proposal to send a fleet of medical ships
to bring modern medicine and health information to

underdeveloped countries. The plan has already been put into practice with the good ship "Hope."

This is only a sampling of the major legislative activity that bore Senator Humphrey's imprint during the 1950's, and much of it would be a "continued story" as the nation moved into the next decade of the Twentieth Century. If the Senator from Minnesota had been able to look into a crystal ball, he would have been astounded at the panorama of pathos, triumph, tragedy and political drama that lay ahead.

Chapter Nine

Not a Dull Life

"HUMPHREY TALKS WITH KHRUSHCHEV FOR EIGHT HOURS" was headline news in early December 1958. It was an amazing feat, for more reasons than one, in the eyes of most Americans. The Iron Curtain had never been rung up that far before. But, if there were ever two men who could set up such a long-distance record for conversation, it was agreed that the President of the U.S.S.R. and the senior Senator from Minnesota could do it.

Undoubtedly there were no dull moments. Television viewers at home can almost see the gears meshing together in Humphrey's mind when he is the object of rapid-fire, point-blank interview. Even while a question is being asked, Hubert apparently is assimilating, digesting, agreeing, disagreeing, approving or rejecting —and he is ready with an emphatic answer, complete with figures and background material, the moment his interrogator finishes the query. Sometimes Humphrey's quick mind even anticipates the next question, before it is asked. There are two things that mark him as an extremely modern man — his computer-type brain and his sensitivity to all world problems.

Both the former President of the U.S.S.R. and the former Senator, Humphrey, were famous for their verbal dexterity, and Khrushchev may have been intrigued at the idea of discussing the state of the world with another "wizard of words."

In "Life" magazine for January 12, 1959—which carried a cover picture of the Senator sporting a handsome Russian fur hat and a lively smile—Humphrey reported at length on the trip and the historic interview. The eventful journey was publicized in newspapers and magazines all over the world, with reporters mobbing the Senator to ask for "journalistic tidbits" on his way home from Europe to report to President Eisenhower and some mighty flabbergasted colleagues in Congress.

Senator Humphrey had not gone to Moscow to visit Premier Khrushchev. He was on a mission to eight European capitals to promote international medical research, a subject that had interested him when he was Mayor of Minneapolis. At Geneva, on the 1958 trip, he had also participated as a Senate observer in United States-Soviet nuclear test-ban negotiations.

During the week in Moscow, Humphrey became the first major American government official to speak on television to the Russian people. In "War On Poverty," he recalled that there is no equivalent Russian word for "opportunity." The interpreter looked puzzled when he tried to translate it.

There are some revealing character clues in the "Life" article, in which Senator Humphrey reported that he "spent much more time with the leaders of research in medicine, health and agriculture than with politicians. Mrs. Humphrey, who traveled with me at our expense, broadened our nonpolitical experience by separate visits to schools, hospitals, and libraries, and on our Sunday in Moscow we did what we would have done at home: we went to church."

When Senator Humphrey indicated that he would like to see Premier Khrushchev before he left Moscow, he realized that some Americans might be critical about his talking to the top Communist leader, but he believed that by keeping the lines of communication open he might perhaps obtain some "valuable information for the free world."

Since he did not know whether his request was even being considered, Humphrey was astonished to be informed, at 2:30 on the afternoon of December 1, that the head of the Russian government would be ready to see him at 3:00 o'clock. He was whirled away almost immediately to the Kremlin, to be escorted down two huge, carpeted corridors in the building where Premier Khrushchev had his office, and into the presence of the plump, balding man whom much of the world regarded with awe and trepidation.

There were the customary news pictures during the handshaking preliminaries, and the two principals exchanged some joking comments. Then the two men took each other's measure and "squared away for the main bout."

Humphrey told Khrushchev that he had been "fighting Communism for twenty years in one way or another."

"Good—now we can talk, for we each know where we stand," the Soviet Premier replied.

The Senator remembered that "the informal meeting was fascinating, covering a huge range of subjects, including the American political scene." In debating Capitalism vs. Communism, Khrushchev willingly discussed nuclear disarmament, Berlin, international medical research, NATO, peaceful co-existence, economic competition, and just about every other subject —including Red China's stubborn determination to make all the errors that had proved impractical in Russia. He referred specifically to the Chinese experiments with communes.

Humphrey almost jumped when he heard Khrushchev refer to communes as "old-fashioned." The Russian leader continued, "You know, Senator, what those communes are based on? They are based on the principle, 'From each according to his abilities, to each according to his needs.' You know that won't work. You can't get production without incentive."

Humphrey was hearing the leader of world Communism rejecting the basic core of Marxist theory! (Khrushchev later described this exchange as a "fairy tale" straight out of Humphrey's imagination. The Russians were on good terms with Communist China at that time, but Khrushchev's 1959 references to Chinese stubbornness may have been "a straw in the wind.")

President Khrushchev had chosen a top-notch interpreter, who translated so smoothly and unobtrusively that it seemed as though it were a two-man conversation. Oleg Troyanosky, son of a former Soviet Ambassador to the United States, seemed to know every shading of American idiom. "He even had the Russian word for 'lousy.' "

Khrushchev often referred to his age—sixty-five in 1958—and Humphrey gathered that the Soviet leader felt he had "no time to waste." The Premier impressed Humphrey as vigorous and dynamic, especially when he told about all the political in-fighting in which he had been involved before he reached the heights of power in the Kremlin. "I gathered that he would rather outtalk or outsmart his opponents than exile or liquidate them. He gives you the idea that his way is more fun." That is one reason why Humphrey later described Khrushchev as a "practical politician, a new type of Russian leader."

In an exchange about missile strength, Khrushchev laughingly complained that their missiles had such great range that they didn't have the space to test them. In a right neighborly manner, Humphrey replied, "Well, if you are having all this trouble, we will be glad to test your rockets for you." There was a fair amount of good-natured banter, often with "deadly serious undertones."

Khrushchev seemed to feel he had scored a major point when he extended his "gratitude" to the United States for its embargoes, trade restrictions and other brands of "negativism." They had made the Russian people feel that the Americans did not care about them. That attitude had been helpful in compelling the citizens of the U.S.S.R. to depend on their own resources, Khrushchev declared.

It is possible that Premier Khrushchev had looked forward to "outtalking and outsmarting" the loquacious Senator from Minnesota, because it was the type of "fun" he enjoyed. He was still going strong as the witching-hour of midnight approached, after more than eight hours of verbal "in-fighting" in which his visitor valiantly upheld all phases of American democracy, including the policies of Secretary of State John Foster Dulles.

When Humphrey had said he wished to see Premier Khrushchev, he was aware that it took an extrovert type of courage to match wits and ideology with the most powerful Communist of his day. Although much of the world referred to Mr. K. as "a smart old fox"— with varying degrees of affection or scorn—perhaps Khrushchev was more astute than anyone knew. Humphrey was not exactly in the upper echelons of the Senate, and he did not represent one of the more influential states in his country. Was Khrushchev psychic enough to guess that this man might someday reach the heights of the American political ladder, or was he merely attracted by Humphrey's reputation as "a great talker"—a trait they had in common?

Premier Khrushchev, who had seemed to feel that he had "no time to waste," was suddenly "retired" from power in 1964—just about the time that Mr. Humphrey was elected to a very illustrious position in his own country. No Communist leader with a personality as dramatic as Khrushchev's has emerged among his successors. Even though they denounced him to kingdom come when he was the blustering symbol of world Communism, there are many Americans who now speak of him with a hint of nostalgia in their voices. On the world stage, he was an actor who never forgot his lines.

When the man in the fur hat came home from the Kremlin, the first low murmurs of "Humphrey for President" began to swell in volume. The Humphrey presidential boom was soon highlighted by Mrs. Eleanor Roosevelt's "spark of greatness" endorsement.

During subsequent speeches, the country began paying closer attention to what Humphrey was saying about the international situation. Linguists even commented that he was the only official in the government who could pronounce "Khrushchev" correctly.

Whereas it had seemed as though Senator Humphrey was overreaching himself for the Vice Presidential nomination in 1956, his loyal supporters saw him as a logical Democratic Presidential candidate in 1960. The 86th Congress, convening in 1959, was illuminated by "the new liberal spark," and Humphrey was recognized as the man who had kept it glowing. Progressive moderates and liberals of both parties were making themselves heard above the complacent voices of the strong old conservative faction.

The fact that blind complacency might threaten the future of the country was to be a major issue. Large segments of the world were already on the march for freedom, for the right to determine their own governments and seek their own salvation—as the Thirteen Colonies had done in 1776. Communism also was on the march, and the United States saw indications of international turmoil ahead.

On the domestic level, the liberals of the Democratic Party began to lift up the handsome "prosperity rug" and bring to light some of the stains and squalor that had been accumulating underneath for decades and even centuries. The two Democratic candidates who campaigned most actively during the early 1960 primaries spoke of millions of Americans who were going to bed hungry every night—who were living below the ragged edge of the poverty line.

John Fitzgerald Kennedy, the attractive young Senator from Massachusetts, who had crowded Estes Kefauver for the 1956 Democratic Vice Presidential nomination, had a well-organized staff of consultants to compile the "poverty figures" that he quoted. Many of his comfortable fellow Americans registered disbelief and varying degrees of scorn. Any Americans who went to bed hungry, they said, must be on a diet.

Senator Hubert Humphrey, who appeared to be Kennedy's neck-and-neck rival at the time of the first primary, had been studying the problems of poverty for so long that he didn't need to be brought up to date on them. He had seen poverty at close quarters during the Depression, and he had started fighting squalor, wage inequality, and discrimination back in Minneapolis in the 1940's.

Both men were dedicated to the improvement of the Family of Man. Wealthy young Mr. Kennedy was known as a Senator who sometimes voted against his own and his father's pocketbooks. A majority of reporters and commentators considered Humphrey more popular with his fellow Senators. In his survey of "Humor in Politics," in "Harper's" for February 1960, William S. White described Humphrey as "a genuine, and genuinely cheerful, extrovert. . . . He can readily halt amidst a violent political scrum . . . to find and proclaim some absurdity that does not necessarily serve his own cause.

"It is this quality that makes many Senators—including the blackest of Republicans and the most deplorably Deep of the Southerners—privately chuckle and call him 'Ole Hubert' even while he is bouncing happily up and down in ideological hobnailed boots on their most sensitive toes. . . .

"He can give up nothing of principle and still stay on the best of terms with antagonists in bitter combat. . . . He has, moreover, the engaging ability to laugh genuinely when the joke is on 'Ole Hubert.' And he knows that a really good story is much too good to keep to one's self."

The doorway to the 1960 Democratic Presidential nomination appeared to be standing wide open, and Humphrey set out for it with one cheerful flying leap after another. In the frantic whirl of speeches, half-nibbled dinners, press conferences, and meetings with campaign workers, he came as near as possible to doing a human imitation of "perpetual motion."

Reporters, skimming the ragged edge of exhaustion and panting to keep up with him, considered Humphrey's astonishing vitality a wonder to behold.

An hour or so of sleep on planes or trains, a quick shower and some vitamin pills, and the effervescent campaigner was "off to the races" again.

Muriel Humphrey, who had taken her duties and

privileges as an American mother so seriously during the early years in Washington, was able to travel with the candidate more often since the four young Humphreys were no longer children. She usually wore lovely suits and dresses "fresh from her own sewing machine." Sometimes Muriel was the guest of honor at ladies' coffee parties, where all the other housewives felt at home with her.

The scene of the first serious Humphrey-Kennedy primary contest was Wisconsin, right next door to Humphrey's home state of Minnesota. He had worked as hard for the dairy farmers of western Wisconsin as for those in Minnesota, and he was considered popular with big city labor leaders and the progressive intellectuals in the University of Wisconsin area. There is a large Catholic population in Wisconsin, but Humphrey had many Catholic friends and he would never allow the question of denominational differences to rear its ugly head. As far as he is concerned, there are no controversial "differences."

Photographers caught Humphrey making indoor and outdoor speeches, dancing a high-spirited polka on the street with a delighted matron, and playfully tossing a handful of snow at a TV cameraman.

There were some episodes that tugged at the hearts of Humphrey admirers. Often he stood at factory gates in the bleakness of early dawn to shake hands with workers coming off the graveyard shift. Bareheaded and shivering slightly in his dark coat, trying to meet indifference with a hopeful greeting, there was an atmosphere of "brother-can-you-spare-a-vote?" to those gray scenes.

Humphrey had some financial help, but he could not afford an extravagant campaign; he had to carry a large share of the activity on his own shoulders. He had a group of passionately devoted supporters who would almost knock themselves out, night and day, for him and his liberal cause, but it was difficult to compete with the better-organized and more sophisticated political style of the Kennedys.

The maestro of the political saga, Theodore H. White, wrote sympathetically about Humphrey's "romantic, almost quaint faith in ordinary people," in "The Making of the President—1960." He told of a middle-of-the-night trip from Milwaukee to Madison, in Humphrey's drafty bus, with three newsmen, two aides, his seventeen-year-old son Douglas, and his future son-in-law, Bruce Solomonson. It was brittle-cold outside, and White said that Humphrey sat with his chilled companions "hunched forward about him, for he is a very lovable fellow." They listened while the Presidential campaigner spoke at length about the virtues and good sense of "the ordinary people."

In the same book, White made the following reference to the speaking abilities of the rival candidates: "Kennedy . . . is, in private, one of the more gifted conversationalists of politics, second only to Hubert Humphrey in the ease, simplicity and color with which he talks."

During the Wisconsin campaign, Humphrey carried the banner of the liberal cause. In one Milwaukee speech, he said, "We believe that liberalism is more than intellectual capacity — intellectual liberalism must be buttressed with an understanding of people and a love of them that goes far beyond texts and documents. For if you can't cry a bit in politics, the only thing you'll have is hate."

In 1949, freshman Senator Humphrey had rated a cover picture on "Time" magazine. It happened again in 1960, when he and John F. Kennedy were in the Wisconsin contest. According to a lengthy story in the issue for February 1, Senator Kennedy had announced that he had to confront Humphrey in Wisconsin. "If I take Humphrey in Wisconsin, they can't take that away from me."

The night when the primary election returns were being counted in Wisconsin was not a happy time for Senator Humphrey and his family and friends. All of them had worked themselves to a state of taut nerves, and suddenly they were numb with shock. The young Senator from Massachusetts had pulled ahead and was holding his lead, especially in the heavily Catholic areas. There was also some evidence of the old "Republican cross-over" that had made mincemeat of Stevenson and Humphrey in Minnesota four years before. Humphrey did get solid support from the rich Wisconsin dairy and farmlands which border Minnesota, and from the Second District in which Madison and the University of Wisconsin are located, but it was not enough.

The door to a presidential future had begun to close slightly, but Humphrey was still optimistic about his chances. He would meet the Kennedy challenge next in West Virginia, a state where the people would certainly feel kindly toward a fellow like Humphrey—a man of the "ordinary people." West Virginia has many virtues, but it is not one of the wealthier states.

In the Appalachia section of the state, there were scars of old coal mines, and Kennedy was as sympathetic about unemployment and poverty as Humphrey was. The ordinary people of West Virginia did not have a charming, wealthy young man with a Harvard accent in their midst every day, asking them not to be bigoted about religion when they went to the polls. Where lives were drab, he and a small army of Kennedy relatives and friends brought color and an unaccustomed aura of glamour. They gave him their votes. So did the citizens who were comfortable and prosperous, resenting Humphrey's references to "disaster areas" in West Virginia. As it turned out, Humphrey was right, and he has continued to work for the correction of economic ills in the Appalachia region right up to the present.

Hubert Humphrey was the first to know that the door had slammed shut, on that damp, dreary night when he squared his shoulders and went over to congratulate Kennedy. Temporarily crushed to the roots of his spirit, Humphrey had also been the first to speak words of comfort to his despondent family and small band of supporters. Would he bounce back from this latest blow with his vigor and faith in human nature undiminished? There is a typical South Dakota expression that he often uses, "Yessirree!"

As he said when Khrushchev sent for him on such short notice, Humphrey did not believe he had been put on this earth to lead a dull life. Mighty miserable, sometimes. But not dull.

Chapter Ten

The Kennedy Door

Humphrey's campaigning in Wisconsin and West Virginia had been more arduous because he refused to neglect his Senate duties. In the first place, he was conscientious about wanting to rush back and cast his vote for important legislation. In the second place, his second term in office would expire that year. In the back of his mind, he knew he would certainly want to retain his Senate seat—if he were not a candidate for a higher office.

By the time the Democratic Convention convened in Los Angeles in July, Humphrey had little more than a block of Minnesota "favorite son" votes—good only for bargaining purposes.

Other distinguished members of the Democratic Farmer-Labor Party from Minnesota were prominent at the convention. Governor Orville Freeman, who was only able to talk again by a miracle of medical science, nominated John F. Kennedy for President.

Eugene McCarthy, who had been elected to the Senate in 1958, nominated Adlai Stevenson with an

oration that reached the heights of Stevenson's own
lofty rhetoric. Listeners were profoundly stirred as the
tall, forceful junior Senator from Minnesota leaned
forward from the convention lectern and entreated
them, "Do not leave this prophet without honor in his
own party."

Even though Stevenson was reluctant until the last
minute, his supporters managed to whip up a frenzied
stampede for him. It was a last gasp. The other leading
contenders had lined up strong support, with the Kennedy contingent operating most efficiently.

Kennedy went "over the top" on the first ballot,
with Senator Lyndon B. Johnson running a strong second, and Senator Stuart Symington a weak third—
which indicates the shifting trend toward Senators for
the highest offices in the land.

The choice of John F. Kennedy as Democratic nominee for the Presidency of the United States would not
arouse Hubert Humphrey to bitterness, even though
he had again leaned toward the nomination of Adlai
Stevenson. Some caustic remarks had been exchanged
in the heat of the primary political battles, but it had
been a fair fight. In the Senate, and even among those
who sometimes have opposed him strenuously, it is
agreed that Hubert Humphrey does not carry grudges.

Humphrey was so far down the line that he didn't
expect to be mentioned for Vice President in 1960, and
he wasn't. From the outside looking in, it appeared
that Senator Symington would be the logical choice,
even though he ranked third in delegate strength.
Every space-age youngster knew that Symington was

an authority on rockets and missiles, but Senator Johnson's talent had been confined mainly to legislative
business in Washington. Very few people in the country even knew that his wife's nickname was "Lady
Bird."

Many Northern liberals considered Johnson's home
territory—Texas—as distinctly Southern, segregation-
ist and conservative.

One sentence from Theodore H. White's "The Making of the President—1960" reveals the bizarre state of
affairs when reporters and cameramen were gathering
outside the Kennedy suite for news about the Vice
Presidential decision: "Gradually, in the course of the
day in the hot, packed corridor, the press of human beings built up a sweat that hung like a meaty animal
odor over the whole matter of choosing a Vice President of the United States."

As all the world learned, John Fitzgerald Kennedy
of Massachusetts chose Lyndon Baines Johnson of
Texas for his running mate; and neither of them, on
that day in the summer of 1960, could appreciate the
profound significance of that "moment of truth."

Certainly the senior Senator from Minnesota, short
on funds for the Congressional battle he must now
wage in his home state, would have thought himself
the last man to inherit any of that upper-stratosphere
power and glory.

Both Kennedy and Johnson surprised the country
during the Presidential campaign. John F. Kennedy,
in spite of his wealth and social prominence, spoke
from a conscience that sounded much like Hubert

Humphrey's. He had taken a long look at the wretched poverty areas of the nation—at bleak regions in which illiteracy and intolerance had been flourishing for centuries—and he promised to lead the nation forward into a New Frontier of progress and dignity. He handled the religious issue with warm sincerity, explaining carefully that he would not be "taking orders from the Pope in Rome."

As for Lyndon B. Johnson, he went barreling merrily through the South, jovially demanding of his home folks, "We aren't against anybody's religion, are we? We want equal rights for everybody, don't we?" And so great was the challenge of his charm and wit, the people of the South roared "No!" to the first question and "Yes!" to the second.

"Herblock" immortalized that phase of the campaign with a cartoon of the Vice Presidential candidate beating out a rollicking tune on the keyboard. The caption read, "They laughed when I sat down at the piano." Lyndon Johnson was putting on a great performance, and the country was yet to learn that he meant every word of it. He was nobody's "stereotype." Hubert Humphrey knew the score; he and Senator Johnson had been friends for a long time.

The Republican candidate, Vice President Richard Nixon, had already received a warm welcome in the Twin Cities. The DFL leaders were proud to have their candidate, Senator John Kennedy, as their honored guest at the festive DFL Beanfeed in Minneapolis. The auditorium was packed that night, with an overflow crowd milling outside for a glimpse of the dynamic young New Englander.

Senator Humphrey was in his glory as he stood on the brightly lighted stage, surveying the people who had gathered in the huge murky room below, looking up expectantly. This was their leader—the man who had welded two reluctant parties together and set them on the road to victory in election after election. He may have left his most indelible impression of the evening when he remarked, "There are some faces here that I haven't seen for quite awhile—I see you are coming back into the fold." Perhaps he was referring to Eisenhower Democrats, or even to ultra-liberals or ultra-conservatives who had been slow to make their peace with the DFL merger. Only they would know. Hubert usually leaves people with something to ponder on.

The Democratic Presidential candidate received a lusty ovation. Where he and Humphrey had been apart during the first two primaries, they were now very much together. Humphrey was the first to set a good example for his loyal followers who had resented the lopsided primary contest.

John F. Kennedy dodged in and out of the auditorium with all the skill of a touch-football champ that night. Just a flashing smile and a quick wave as his bus threaded through the crowd outside, and he was gone.

Sometimes Senator Humphrey was on the national campaign trail for Kennedy and Johnson, and sometimes he was campaigning for Humphrey and the DFL ticket in Minnesota.

There would be a fierce battle inside Minnesota, where the political picture always emerges in vivid shades of "technicolor." The Republicans were grimly determined that the next governor would be named Elmer Andersen—not Orville Freeman.

In 1960, with so many conflicting issues at home and abroad, neither major party had an "edge." It was often riotously exciting, with moods ranging from good cheer to nasty sarcasm. Partisan statements were made that were better left unsaid.

Which way would it go? There were the hard-core loyalties, from generation to generation—but this time a new unknown quantity, religion, had been added. There were the unpredictable "mavericks" whose voting records had vaulted from La Follette, to Hoover, to Roosevelt, to Truman, to Eisenhower—a crossword puzzle that defied solution.

Minnesota, like several other northern states, is a political "stew pot" that seethes and boils, with some of the ingredients refusing to "get done" until it is almost time to get to the polls. But the voting gets done.

In Minnesota, in precinct after precinct, voters have stood in long lines—outdoors and in hallways—for an hour or two before they have reached the voting machines. In the Southern states in the early 1960's, a newcomer could easily get the impression that there were more election officials than voters in the polling places.

The political vitality of a state is often the barometer of its economic and educational health. If the people are content to say, "Let Harry do my voting for me," they are going to be apathetic about other vital considerations. And some day, when Harry needs their support like tarnation, they won't even be registered.

During his campaign for the Senate in 1960, Humphrey stressed all the Christian, democratic principles that had guided his legislative activities—his sincere belief that it is "right to feed the starving; it is right to heal the sick; it is right to lead the blind; and it is right to teach the illiterate."

It was also no less than Christian justice for the small businessman, the industrial worker and the farmer to earn decent returns for their contributions to the nation's economy. Humphrey felt a special sympathy toward the man who still clung to the small "family farm," with the encroachments of "large mechanized spreads" threatening to sweep him aside. Here was the backbone of America since pioneer days— solid, reliable, healthy as a 4-H Club. You didn't need to worry about farmers' sons growing up to be juvenile delinquents. If the family farm should ever pass from the American scene, Hubert Humphrey will be the chief mourner.

A week or so before the elections—while the U. S. Senatorial candidate was barnstorming the Minnesota countryside and trying to get as much television and radio exposure as he could afford, a "Humphrey panic" materialized. It was in the same class with most "scuttle-butt." From some mysterious source, the word had gone out, "There's a shift away from Humphrey! Humphrey's going to lose!" Some national publications sent the news whistling far and wide, because Humphrey had been a serious contender for the Presidency. Had

Kennedy deserted Humphrey? Obviously someone was trying to drive a wedge between the two Democrats. The Democratic Party waited for a message from its chosen leader, who was then in California. When he heard the news, John F. Kennedy reacted with all the necessary indignation: "They say Hubert's in trouble in Minnesota—I can't believe it!" Jack had not deserted Hubert.

The second Tuesday in November 1960—election day—was as far into November as a second Tuesday can get. On November 8, the adults of the United States went forth to exercise their rights as citizens. The country would wait, and wait some more through the long night, and then it would drop its weary head on a pillow while the returns were still inconclusive. Jack Kennedy, like his predecessor, Harry Truman, did not know for certain that he was President of the United States until he awoke the next morning.

The weather had been sleety and rainy in many parts of the country, but election day was fair and fine in Minnesota. The Humphreys were waiting out the day in their small, attractive home at Lake Waverly, near Minneapolis. Far from losing his Senate seat, Humphrey would go back to Washington filled with the self-confidence of a man who has topped the opposition by almost 250,000 votes.

It is interesting to note, in relation to those two primary contests in which Humphrey was pitted against Kennedy, that Wisconsin rejected Kennedy in November, but West Virginia stayed with him.

Minnesota had been a strong Eisenhower state, and

it was touch-and-go for Kennedy. It would be difficult
to analyze all the "stew-pot" ingredients that finally
gave Kennedy a margin of about 25,000 votes—every
one precious, considering that Kennedy won in the
nation by only 118,550 votes out of more than sixty-
eight million. The Catholic Democratic vote in St. Paul
was strong for Kennedy and the Protestant Republican
vote in Minneapolis supported Nixon, but this author
knows of people in both parties who refused to indulge
in religious prejudice.

The DFL Party suffered one shattering casualty;
the new governor would be named Andersen, instead
of Freeman. Running for a fourth term, Freeman had
been defeated by a slim margin. Minnesota Republicans said gleefully, "Well, we got him out of there!"
So what happened to poor Orville Freeman? President
Kennedy appointed him Secretary of Agriculture,
much to the delight of the Minnesota DFL and the con-
sternation of the Minnesota GOP.

Many of President Kennedy's new appointees
would be Harvard men. Cleveland Amory's "Celebrity
Register" describes Orville Freeman's witty reaction
to his Cabinet assignment: "I think I got it because
there's no Aggie School at Harvard."

Among the other early DFL volunteers who received special appointments was Mrs. Eugenie Anderson who had served as Ambassador to Denmark under
President Truman and was named Minister to Bul-
garia by President Kennedy.

Hubert Humphrey had done immeasurable service
to the Kennedy cause by helping to bring the candidate

and the issues to center stage early in the primaries
and by working to shift Minnesota into the Democratic
column in November. The election of John Fitzgerald
Kennedy was, to Humphrey, another thrilling break-
through in the march toward true democracy, and he
was glad he had been a part of it. Here was a milestone
—a monument—to mark the place where a man's religion would never again be a handicap at the national
polls.

As for Kennedy's running mate, Lyndon B. John-
son, another "bugaboo" had been laid to rest. The
Negro, labor union and civil rights factions in the
North had been as alarmed at the idea of a Texan on
the ballot as the South had been about a Catholic for
President.

It was a case of prejudices colliding with cross-
prejudices. Even though soldiers of the North and
South have fought as comrades in two great wars in
this century, election day usually finds much of the
South falling back on its old Civil War battle lines.
That attitude antagonizes the North to the point of
returning the compliment.

It is difficult to know whether the Deep South
states voted their loyalty to a native son, Lyndon Johnson, or whether a majority of parents had come a long
way from the days when a father would rage, "I would
rather see my daughter daid at my feet than married
to a Catholic!" (Or a "damnyankee," as the case
might be.)

But the ballot is secret, and no matter how many
political analysts may rack their brains until dooms-
day, the pattern will probably never come quite clear.

Senator Hubert Humphrey was there—he was very much there—on Inaugural Day, January 20, 1961. Granted that he had run short on financial backing, and sometimes on friends who did not revere Adlai Stevenson as he did. Granted that he had needed to "run scared," for no reason at all, to get through the door to his third Senatorial term.

It had been "just plain rough" sometimes, but it would all seem worth-while as he listened to the words of the new President of the United States as he told the nation in his Inaugural Address:

"Let the word go forth from this time and place, to friend and foe alike, that the torch has been passed to a new generation of Americans . . ." And so it had.

It was going to come out all right, this new era that would be lighted by the glow of "our ancient heritage . . ."

Hubert Humphrey seemed to be eating with gusto at the Inaugural luncheon. For once he was not having to dash from one campaign speech to another, from a distant part of the country back to the Senate, from one telephone conversation to another, from one plane or bus to another. They were letting him alone—the luncheon guests who were pressing around the colorful Kennedy family.

Did Humphrey know that a television camera had swung around to catch a back view of him as he sat at the table, and that the voice of a commentator singled him out for a special salute lest the nation forget that he was probably the best "publicity man" that John

F. Kennedy had: "Here is Senator Hubert Humphrey. If it hadn't been for Senator Humphrey, there might not be a President Kennedy today."

Hubert Horatio Humphrey kept right on eating— with enthusiasm.

Chapter Eleven

The New Frontier

Some Congressmen seldom get attention in Washington papers, but Hubert Humphrey always seemed to be doing something newsworthy. There was the time he charged into the Capitol City's public schools and let out a blast of indignation about the battered, outdated textbooks and the deplorable facilities. He believed that caring about Washington schools was a Congressman's business, and the newspapers agreed with him. Long before the Kennedy victory, Senator Humphrey had ceased to be a "comer"; he had arrived.

The road pointed upward for Humphrey after the election of 1960. As "majority whip," he would not be as much of a "free agent" in the Senate. On the other hand, he would have more power to shepherd the President's legislation through Congress.

After Lyndon B. Johnson's elevation to the Vice Presidency, "Mike" Mansfield of Montana became Senate majority leader. Humphrey's appointment to assistant majority leader was definitely a promotion—a recognition of his ability as a legislative leader in the most select forum in the most powerful democracy in the world.

Humphrey had always enjoyed thinking of the United States as a country with great power; he also wanted to think of it as a country with a great mind, a great heart, and the highest potential for modern progress that the world has ever known.

Whenever the opportunity has presented itself— and even when it hasn't—Humphrey has voiced his admiration for President Kennedy. Different in social background, personality, and financial status, the two men had a common respect for intellectual achievement, good conversation, humorous anecdotes, and the welfare of the human race. Especially the welfare of the human race.

The beginning of the sixth decade of the Twentieth Century marked the swelling of a fresh new tide in American thought and action. This is not to belittle previous Administrations, each of which had its own type of personality and competency in certain areas. History will give its "just deserts" to those who merit them.

A great democracy thrives and prospers through a combination of forces. Occasionally it stands still or goes backward because the central forces become sluggishly content with themselves. They close their windows on the country and the world and tell themselves that everything is fine—because they themselves are fine.

After the election of 1960, it became apparent that the opposite would be true of the new Administration.

If any windows had been closed, they were opened wide—even though the scenery might be sickening.

Hubert Humphrey is a great man for wanting to improve the scenery. Teddy Roe, a member of Senator "Mike" Mansfield's staff, tells of the time Senator Humphrey voiced his indignation—in no uncertain tones—about the bare and desolate condition of some flower beds on the Capitol grounds. He was persistent about it, and the message got through. "Two weeks later," Teddy recalls with lingering amazement, "there were huge flowers in those flower beds — in full bloom!"

The Minnesotan has always been a booster for a more beautiful, more hospitable Washington. Grace Tully, who was FDR's private secretary and has known Humphrey for years, says he keeps talking up the idea of "sidewalk cafes" on the Capitol plaza, to give tourists a place to rest and refresh themselves during their foot-weary treks around the marble corridors.

When the Beautification Program became official, with Mrs. Lady Bird Johnson as its "spade and trowel" leader, Humphrey was quick to note that "association with beauty can enlarge man's imagination and revive his spirit. Ugliness can demean the people who live among it. What a citizen faces every day is his America."

Senator Humphrey loved "beauty for beauty's sake," but he also viewed it with appreciation from practical angles. Beautification projects, especially in slum areas, would create jobs for young people in their own neighborhoods; and sidewalk cafes at the Capitol would add new business life where there had been none before.

The Kennedy Administration in 1960 brought a new "style," an atmosphere of youth, and in some instances a new political approach to the problems of the nation and the world. The new Senate majority whip, who was born in the eleventh year of this century, was young enough to swim vigorously with the tide of youth and mature enough to know where the shoals and whirlpools were located. He certainly had never been timid about getting his feet wet, even when that was not the style.

Looking back, it is apparent that Hubert Humphrey was a Senator who knew which way the country would need to go and he was holding himself in readiness for the "great push forward." This year—or next year—or the year after that, the signal would come. When men of good will would reveal an innate respect for justice and human dignity, they would find that Humphrey had already done his homework.

Men and women would put their lives in jeopardy during the years ahead—not for the sake of money or glory, but for principles that are as old as the story of the Good Samaritan. The Peace Corps and the Civil Rights crusade would fit into that category.

In the summer of 1960, when Humphrey had introduced his Peace Corps bill, many members of Congress had scoffed at it. It was considered farfetched, impractical and too idealistic. Humphrey had never denied that he was an idealist. He was thinking that the Peace Corps volunteers would do as much for themselves and their country as they would do to promote favorable impressions abroad.

The prairies of South Dakota had been far distant from the Bohemian life of Greenwich Village, when Hubert was a young man, but there had been vivid stories about creative frustrations in those cold water flats, in the magazines at Humphrey's Drugstore. Hubert understood the groping idealism of youth. He had not yearned to run away to the Village in New York and write the Great American Novel. When he was able to make his first trip East, he headed for Washington, D. C., and his own quest for self-expression was part of the pattern of youth in any age.

Humphrey knew that each generation produces its restless, searching young crusaders—the contemplative nonconformists who often are more interested in the human problem than in settling down to a socially-acceptable pattern of Babbittry. So much idealism going to waste, because so few of them would be able to write the Great American Novel or major books of poetry—or sit in Congress for that matter.

Humphrey considers the waste of talent and idealism an extravagance we can ill afford in this period of our history. The Peace Corps would give thousands of young Americans—and some older ones, too—a specific outlet for their visionary energies.

If the program proved workable, the benefit to underdeveloped countries would be incalculable. Moreover, our "pioneers in human responsibility" would show that there were Americans who sincerely believed that they were "their brothers' keepers."

The Senator had been persistently gathering additional support for the Peace Corps Bill in Congress, and the climax was reached with the strong endorsement of the man who achieved the highest office in the land in 1960. President Kennedy's imagination was more than equal to the Peace Corps challenge. On March 1, 1961, the Peace Corps program was set up on a temporary basis by Presidential order. It would become a permanent project under the brilliant direction of Sargent Shriver. At the time when Peace Corps legislation was passed by Congress late in the summer of 1961, President Kennedy credited Senator Humphrey with having originated the idea.

The Peace Corps grew from a few hundred volunteers in 1961 to fourteen thousand in 1965. In its early months, the program was subjected to much "nit-picking" from critics who seemed hopeful that it would fall flat on its face. Now it would be difficult to find anyone who scoffs at the Peace Corps.

In addition to other obvious services to mankind, the Peace Corps will be a brimming reservoir of future diplomatic talent—of young people who know the languages, the customs and the political atmosphere in the most remote areas of the world. When there has been unrest in various foreign localities, Peace Corps personnel have been able to act as interpreters between native inhabitants and American "trouble-shooters." The Peace Corps is "at home" in the world, and its success has led to the formation of similar teaching and economic development programs in deprived areas of the United States.

Other issues that were mutually important to both President Kennedy and Senator Humphrey—strong civil rights enforcement, increased aid to education, reduction of unemployment, Food for Peace, a substantial tax cut, and medical care for the aged—were debated with varying degrees of success or failure in Congress.

During those early years of the Kennedy Administration, Hubert Humphrey could feel as though history had begun to move in the orbit of healthy human progress that he had been visualizing for so many years. It was a happy combination of personalities and circumstances, in spite of the continued opposition of a strong bloc of conservative Republicans and Southern Democrats to many aspects of civil rights enforcement, aid-to-education, medical care for the aged, and redevelopment of economically distressed areas. At least they were being recognized as respectable subjects for Congressional debate.

If it seemed to the opposition that Humphrey was intent on promoting legislation that would cost money, Humphrey was equally convinced that money had been taking precedence over people for most of the world's history. That conclusion can be drawn from his undeviating support of minimum wage laws. As a student of economics, he believed that multimillionaires should not quibble about paying their workers at least a dollar-and-a-quarter an hour. As a wise statesman, Humphrey does not want to regulate the bird that is laying the golden egg; he is most happy when the bird regulates himself in the best interests of everyone concerned.

Humphrey tries to keep all "diplomatic channels" open, whenever possible. Early in 1962, when President Kennedy was denouncing a price rise by U. S. Steel, the Wall Street Journal noted that Senator Humphrey was having an amicable discussion with a top steel executive about the Mesabi Range ore reserves in northern Minnesota.

Senator Humphrey was still very much a Minnesota Congressman, taking a keen interest in educational, industrial, agricultural and road-building programs in his thriving state. Its accent on health and education has put Minnesota near the top in selective service examinations, and its fair employment program —pioneered by Humphrey as Mayor of Minneapolis— has been setting an example for the nation. The young state, only a century old in 1958, has a per capita income that is higher than twelve of the older Southern states, and it also ranks highest in its own Plains region.

On his visits home, Humphrey continued to "have fun," even with bipartisan audiences. Several years ago, when he and former Governor Elmer Andersen were appearing on the same dinner program, Humphrey gave the Republican a mischievous grin as he started his speech. He confided to the audience, "Governor Andersen and I have been getting acquainted; we've been eyeing each other and sizing each other up. . . ."

The eyes of the nation were drawn to Minnesota's gubernatorial contest in 1962. It was more fascinating than the average "cliff-hanger" because the DFL candidate, Karl Rolvaag, was kept in the basement of the Capitol until it was determined that he had won the election. He is destined to remain in the office upstairs for twice as long as any of the previous governors; the gubernatorial term is now four years.

In 1961, with the approval of the Kennedy Administration, Senator Humphrey successfully reintroduced a bill to establish the Arms Control and Disarmament Agency. In 1963, he was the first of thirty-three Senators to co-sponsor Senator Thomas Dodd's limited test-ban treaty. Humphrey, who had worked for more than a decade for just such an agreement, was present on June 10, 1963, when representatives of the United States, the Soviet Union and Great Britain signed the historic treaty suspending nuclear testing above ground.

An enlarged college building and scholarship measure received Congressional approval under the Kennedy Administration. Both President Kennedy and Senator Humphrey were personally concerned about the enactment of a Mental Health and Retardation program; a younger sister of the President had been confined to a hospital most of her life, and it appeared that Vicki, the Humphreys' first grandchild, would need more care than the average youngster. The wholesome attitude of the Humphrey family is summed up in a columnist's assertion that ". . . you can count on Muriel to brag about what her little retarded granddaughter can do rather than talking about what she can't do."

The Administration's "medicare" proposal was still under strong fire from the American Medical Association, and a Republican bloc kept introducing counter-proposals.

Civil rights continued to be an inflammatory subject. Attorney General Robert Kennedy, the President's younger brother, was instrumental in bringing suit against Southern forces that had consistently defied court orders relating to desegregation. "Freedom riders" became active participants in the struggle for racial justice, and some were beaten by mobs of "white supremacists." Hubert Humphrey was anxious about the sinister aspects of the situation, but he knew that the South must no longer halt the hands of the clock. It was obvious that some cities of the North and West would also need to do some soul-searching.

It might be said that President Kennedy was more popular with the people of his country—and other nations—than he was with his own Congress. The thirty-fifth President of the United States was the epitome of a modern "Prince Charming"—enlightened, debonair, and idealistic. His chic and enchantingly lovely wife and two "picture-book" children added glamour to every first-family scene.

In Congress, opponents of the Administration gave every indication of "digging in" for an eight-year battle. There was grim suspicion of the New Frontier by reactionary forces and special interest groups. President Kennedy had to make the initial "breakthrough."

The ominous antics of Fidel Castro, in Cuba, helped to gain support for the Alliance for Progress which was set in motion in July 1961, to counter social inequality and economic stagnation in Latin America. "Castro is a political pygmy, and that will be proven when we really get under way with the Alliance for Progress," asserted Senator Humphrey.

Earlier that year, the Bay of Pigs invasion had been launched by Cuban exiles. In "October's bright blue weather" a year later, the young President of the United States was forced into his "toe-to-toe" confrontation with Premier Nikita Khrushchev. The world held its breath until the secretly installed Soviet missiles were removed from Cuba. It was becoming increasingly clear that this age of nuclear hazards demanded cool, deliberate courage and iron nerves—but never blind ruthlessness, or there might not be any tomorrows for deliberation.

The huge Civil Rights march, with more than two hundred thousand Negro and white comrades singing and praying their way through the streets of Washington on August 28, 1963, had the blessing of the Administration. As that gigantic mass of faces gazed upward at the Lincoln Memorial at the climax of the demonstration, the Civil Rights movement presented a dramatic picture of unyielding solidarity—of total mobilization for human justice and dignity. Men of good will, of all parties and religious affiliations, had shown their determination to "walk forthrightly into the bright sunshine of human rights," as Humphrey had put it in 1948.

The John F. Kennedy era of "High Hopes" ended with shattering finality at noon on November 22, 1963. On the eve of the tragedy, speaking before a National Mental Health group, Humphrey had declared, "We live in a world in which the penalty for rash judgment is monstrously out of proportion, in which the misjudgment or miscalculation of a powerful leader can bring down civilization in death and destruction or where the act of an emotionally unstable person or irresponsible citizen can strike down a great leader." Twelve hours later, an undoubtedly "unstable person" did strike down "a great leader." In the years ahead, Humphrey would consider the construction and staffing of hundreds of well-equipped mental health centers "a living memorial to President Kennedy."

The news of the catastrophe reached Senator Humphrey at an embassy luncheon. Heartsick with grief beyond comprehension, he was one of the dignitaries who stood with bowed head and reddened eyes as Air Force One touched down at Andrews Air Force Base that evening. Now the Minnesotan heard the voice of his new leader—his close colleague and friend in the Senate for so many years—calling upon the country to stand with him in that hour of incredible tragedy.

After the assassination came the days of shocked disbelief. President Kennedy had been so young, so vibrantly alive. How could so uncivilized a tragedy have come to pass in a country that considered itself civilized? But hatred is not one of the cultural refinements, and there was an atmosphere of hatred, from the extreme left as well as the extreme right, that was no more civilized than the air from a dank cellar. It was an atmosphere in which the indulgent snuffing out of a human life could be made to seem rational in the warped mind of an irrational individual.

It threw a sharp spotlight on the frightening legacy that had been handed down—to several school children who applauded the news of the President's death, and to the youth who called an Atlanta "open mike" show to say, "Any white man who did what he did for niggers should be shot." Irrational hatred, yes—and in the same class as the vulgar humor of the Red Chinese.

But there were millions of Southerners whose sorrow was as profound as that of their fellow Americans. They were all caught up in the inexorable throbbing of muffled drums and the majestic drama of the mourning period — shadowy unreality beginning to blend with stark reality for Americans who had felt as though they would awaken soon and find that it was only a bad dream.

The mighty of the world—kings, presidents, rulers, statesmen—came to pay their respects to the slain young leader as he lay in the East Room of the White House. It was said that Senator Humphrey "wept unashamedly." It would be impossible for him to blot out memories of the past—to stop remembering the conferences about pending legislation, the times they had laughed appreciatively at each other's wit, and the novel informality of discussing the state of the union and the world as the two of them swam back and forth in the White House pool.

John F. Kennedy's neighbors and countrymen came to pay their respects at the flag-draped casket, as it rested in the Capitol Rotunda on the catafalque that had been used for the lying-in-state of Abraham Lincoln almost one hundred years before. They marched past the bier, in a weeping, grieving procession, hour after hour, all through the chill of the long night, until the casket was borne slowly through the streets to St. Matthew's Cathedral on the following morning.

His Eminence Richard Cardinal Cushing, archbishop of Boston, received the body on its arrival. Then all who had come to pay homage moved into the hushed aisles of the cathedral—the young widow with her face set in lines of nobility, the two winsome children still trying to comprehend, the distinguished mourners from all over the world, the new President of the United States and two former Presidents, and a host of Congressmen and statesmen.

At the heart of the moving pontifical Funeral Mass was Cardinal Cushing, beloved friend and spiritual mentor to the Kennedy family for many years, who had presided over the marriage of John F. Kennedy and his bride and had baptized their children. Even the final ritual sprinkling of holy water, at the graveside in Arlington Cemetery, was performed with almost ferocious tenderness by the dynamic Prince of the Catholic Church as he commended "this wonderful man, Jack Kennedy," to God and to the ages.

Chapter Twelve

"Let Us Continue"

Congress had adjourned in a state of numb bewilderment on Friday, November 22, when the news of President Kennedy's death had halted a discussion about federal library services. It was Chaplain Frederick Brown Harris who spoke the most appropriate words in the Senate—repeating a message delivered on a similar occasion ninety-eight years before. On the morning of Lincoln's death, Representative James Garfield of Ohio had said, "God reigns and the government lives in Washington."

There had been no panic on that November day in 1963—only a bleak sense of loss for awhile. "The government lives . . ."

The new President, Lyndon Baines Johnson, was a Texas man, tall in the saddle and possessed of his own special brand of Pedernales glamour. He would take up the reins before they could grow slack. He was no "loner," no amateur. He had been in the government long enough to know where to look for instant support and strength, and it was offered to him on every hand.

On the evening of the assassination, the man who had been President for only a few hours was already conferring with Congressional leaders.

All over the country, Lincoln scholars were suffering from "history-itis." This was too much of a coincidence! "Andy" Johnson, a Southerner from North Carolina and Tennessee, had been Vice President at the time of Abraham Lincoln's assassination. Caught in a bitter struggle between his sympathy for the South and his loyalty to the Union, the first President Johnson was almost impeached by Congress.

Now, a century later, which way would this new President Johnson go? When it came right down to brass tacks, the average American didn't know much about Lyndon B. Johnson. As a Texan, how would he feel about integration, and a strong federal government, and foreign aid—and all those things that Southern politicians usually vote against? He had done quite a bit of diplomatic traveling, and the country had chuckled with delight when he brought back a camel driver from Pakistan for a grand tour of the United States. But how did he feel about the Kennedy program? Americans were surprised to learn that the former Vice President had been exceedingly busy on Equal Employment, space, the Peace Corps and security advisory committees. The news just hadn't gotten out.

Looking back, it appears that the vigorous Texan must have been mighty restless sometimes. There was nothing puny about the man who suddenly had to hoist himself into the saddle and ride out to the world's greatest roundup on a day late in November 1963. He had to pull the nation together, strays and all, and keep going across the New Frontier into something that he would call the Great Society.

Hubert Humphrey respected the fact that his old Senate friend had suddenly become the most powerful political figure in the world, but he still liked him anyway. He liked him even better, because he could appreciate seeing all that reserve energy unleashed; it would be more dramatic than "Captain Applejack." This was his new "Leader," and he was familiar with the great bundle of political vitality that was Lyndon B. Johnson in action. The tall Texan had come striding out of the wings, ready to dominate the scene—as he was supposed to do—without vacillation, coyness, or partisan expediency.

The Kennedy Administration had been lining up legislation for a war on poverty, medical care for the aged, a stronger civil rights bill, a foreign aid bill that would channel more economic and educational advantages down to the "little people" in underdeveloped countries, and all the other New Frontier programs that would eventually have helped to make a better country and a better world—by the Grace of God, and Congress.

Even while the pageant of mourning moved forward with stately rhythm, President Johnson kept conferring with Congressmen and American businessmen — checking the "political temperature" of the country. He wanted to go before the American people at the earliest possible moment, to let them know that this Republic is founded on rock, not quicksand.

Before the liquid notes of taps were fading in Arlington Cemetery on the afternoon of Monday, November 25, Hubert Humphrey was realizing that the new President of the United States would expect to know the score—the exact score—on Senate bills. That was the way LBJ felt about a pending Mundt bill which would have made it practically impossible for the United States to sell wheat or any other products to Russia, under any circumstances. The Senate was to vote on the measure on the day after the assassination, and Humphrey had to get a preliminary report, as well as the final favorable tally against the bill, to the President.

Hubert Humphrey was also lending his creative talents to the composition of the President's first report to Congress and the people. While the country waited and wondered, Humphrey knew. Among other enlightened suggestions for use in the address, he is credited with contributing three key words: "Let us continue."

On Wednesday, November 27, President Lyndon B. Johnson delivered his first speech to the joint session of Congress and to his fellow citizens of the country and the world. Of President Kennedy's program, he declared, "No words are strong enough to express our determination to continue the forward thrust of America that he began. . . . Now the ideas and ideals which he so nobly represented must and will be translated into action. . . ." The torch had been passed into strong, steady hands.

The country always worries about its "prosperity status" when a new President takes office. There had been an atmosphere of economic stimulation, except for Black Monday—May 28, 1962—when the stock market took a wicked plunge. A few days before his death in 1963, President Kennedy had pointed out in a speech to the Florida Chamber of Commerce that "corporate profits were at an all-time high, production and personal incomes had risen, the rate of United States business expansion led most of Europe for the first time in many years, and profits had not been eaten up by an inflationary spiral."

But what about the new President's attitude toward integration, a subject that was anathema to Southern politicians? It might be said, "Only a person who is mentally and spiritually 'walled-in' will conform to the same pattern, day after day and year after year."

Out of the nation of Israel have come many mighty prophets. Although Harry Golden does not usually specialize in that line of business, the editor of "The Carolina Israelite"—a good friend of Lyndon Johnson, Hubert Humphrey and many other great and small people —predicted in 1959:

"Only a Southerner will eventually smash the caste system of the South, a Southerner who will have gained political power in the only way a Southerner can gain political power—filibuster against any and all civil rights proposals. But at the right moment this Southerner will gather all the white supremacists into one room and knock their heads together. I have a strong suspicion that the Majority Leader, Senator Lyndon B. Johnson, might possibly be that man."

During conferences and "Presidential Leadership

Breakfasts," Senator Humphrey learned that he would be responsible in Congress for the passage of the President's appropriations bills. This was no small order, because the President was moving forward with unprecedented momentum; all the pending legislation might well be marked "expedite," and most of it required money. It was a time to recall that President Kennedy had run into some Congressional opposition that had resembled the Berlin Wall. Was President Johnson going to be any more successful, with the same type of legislation? "Let us continue," said Mike Mansfield, John McCormack, Hubert Humphrey, Everett Dirksen, and scores of distinguished Congressmen of both parties.

Even before that time, Humphrey had said, "If I work less than fourteen hours a day, I feel that I have denied both my work and my official duty." His working days were not destined to get any shorter.

Within two weeks, a remarkable amount of legislation was being readied for the President's signature. The House and Senate were voting appropriations for the manpower retraining program, river and harbor projects, the Atomic Energy Commission, public works and other aid for depressed areas, the Peace Corps, various college and vocational programs, and foreign aid.

Some commentators, watching with awe, suggested that Congress wanted to make things as easy as possible for the new President—until he got used to the job. That was partly true, but a good many Congressmen had been watching Johnson operate as a "professional" for years. Depending on his area of influence, he had always been a captain who knew how to get the best out of a team. After he became President, he started calling many of his "team plays" over the telephone.

The Senate majority whip, Hubert Humphrey, said he used to get so many calls from the Chief Executive that he had trouble finding time, in between, to take care of the requests that were discussed. The eminent Republican leader, Senator Everett Dirksen, said that President Johnson had a "hot line" to his office too. With almost "artless" finesse, both President Johnson and Senator Humphrey have refused to let partisanship interfere with their personal friendships.

In "Humphrey: A Candid Biography," published by Morrow, Winthrop Griffith wrote, "A dozen Senators admitted in interviews in 1964 that they were irritated occasionally by Humphrey's frantic pace and long speeches, but most agreed that he was probably the only member of the Senate who did not have a personal enemy in the place. His humor and decency also appealed to most reporters."

The new Administration did not tolerate a whole lot of dilly-dallying on old bills. The Civil Rights Bill was still stuck in committee at the time of President Kennedy's death. Representative Howard W. Smith of Virginia, chairman of the House Rules Committee, had delayed the 1960 Civil Rights Bill in the same manner. The careful strategy of President Johnson and his "team" could be detected in preparations to force hearings by circulating a "majority-vote" petition to discharge the committee. When he heard about the plan,

Representative Smith graciously agreed to hold hearings "reasonably soon in January."

When Senator Harry F. Byrd of Virginia, chairman of the Senate Finance Committee, said that it would be impossible to act on the proposed Tax bill until the committee had seen the President's budget in January, President Johnson assured Senator Byrd that the committee would receive a preliminary report on the budget in December.

Perhaps President Johnson's greatest political talent has been the ability to delegate heavy responsibility in delicate legislative areas. He knew that the 1964 Civil Rights Bill, for all its merits and historic consequences, could not simply be jammed down the throats of segregation-calloused Southerners. One hundred years ago, a bloody war had been fought on the same lines that were being laid down in Congress in the middle of the Twentieth Century. Who was the man who would best understand the tensions of both sides, who could operate tactfully but firmly—without making the South feel as though it were being driven to its knees?

He knew a man who was famous for saying, "I am prepared to walk the extra mile . . ." and who even threatens to go down on his own knees in dramatic appeals for cooperation. The fact that the President chose Senator Humphrey as floor manager for the Civil Rights Bill in 1964 revealed that he knew the right man for the right job. Humphrey was identified with the lengthy crusade; he was co-leader, with Thomas H. Kuchel of California, of the Civil Rights bipartisan coalition in the Senate.

The subject of equal rights and opportunities for
Negroes had been a "hot potato" for a hundred years.
The 1964 bill was designed to outlaw discrimination in
public accommodations, schools, employment and voting.

On Monday, March 30, when Senator Humphrey
introduced the 1964 Civil Rights Bill to the Senate,
after its passage in the House, his eloquence was rem-
iniscent of the young mayor of Minneapolis who had
spoken on behalf of the same cause of freedom at the
Democratic Convention in 1948. This time he spoke as
a veteran statesman, with patience but with the same
sense of urgency. He told the Senate, "As I have already said, we believe this historic bill must receive a
full and fair debate."

For those who sought revelation in the words of the
Founding Fathers, he quoted the Preamble to the Constitution: "We, the people of the United States, in order
to form a more perfect Union, establish justice, insure
domestic tranquility, provide for the common defense,
promote the general welfare, and secure the blessings
of liberty to ourselves and our posterity, do ordain and
establish this Constitution of the United States of
America."

And he continued, "I cannot help but marvel at the
impact, the directness and the sense of destiny of those
fifty-two words. I cannot help but marvel at their rele-
vance to the responsibility which now confronts the
Senate of the United States.

"The preamble to the Constitution might very well
have been written as a preamble to the Civil Rights
Act of 1964.

"We, the people of the United States . . .

"Not white people, colored people, short people, or tall people, but simply:

"We, the people

"In order to form a more perfect union . . .

"We know that until racial justice and freedom are a reality in this land, our Union will remain profoundly imperfect. That is why we are debating this law . . ."

He told of the inequality of the highway, where Negro tourists and business people are locked out of rest rooms, and rejected at hotels and restaurants, so they often have to drive hundreds of miles as outcasts in their own country—these "alien taxpayers" whose ancestors were among the first families in the New World. He invited the Senators to ask themselves how they would like to be rejected because of the color of their skin, and only because of that. When traveling with their families on a highway and seeking a place to rest, how would they like to be told that " 'there is no room in the inn,' as it was said 2,000 years ago."

Senator Humphrey, in that speech, spoke of travel guidebooks that are printed for owners of dogs, and also for Negro tourists. A comparison of the two directories had proved enlightening. In Augusta, Georgia, there were five hotels and motels that welcomed dogs, and only one where a Negro could go "with confidence." In Columbus, Georgia, there were six places for dogs, and none for Negroes. Prominent in all the restaurants in that area were those intimidating signs, "We reserve the right to refuse service . . ."

This debate, he said, had world-wide implications. "... In a sense, America is now in the midst of a struggle of anticolonialism. Those of us who seek to impose the yoke of superiority—which is nothing more or less than a refined definition of the ugly practice of colonialism—will find that the yoke of superiority will be ripped from our hands . . ." Senator Humphrey believed in the free exercise of "a full and fair debate," but he knew the day of reckoning must come when he said, ". . . If the American Negro can wait a hundred years for the promises in the Emancipation Proclamation to become a reality, I can wait a hundred days, if necessary, in this debate."

It was an exceedingly long, hot summer on the Senate side of the Capitol, in spite of the air conditioning. The lines of tourists lengthened as the weeks of "debate" continued. The occasion was historic, and everyone wanted to see what was going on.

Almost nothing was going on, most of the time— unless you were lucky enough to be there for a quorum call. All the productive discussion on that bill, and dozens of others, was going on in committee rooms behind the scenes.

A first visit to the Senate Gallery will banish some misconceptions. The Senate Chamber is not as huge and lofty as its reputation makes it seem. The visitor feels a sense of identification with the distinguished gentlemen, and one or two ladies, who might be present at the desks below. Some of them are immediately recognizable from TV programs and newspaper pictures. Who could possibly fail to identify Senator "Mike"

Mansfield or Senator Everett Dirksen at first sight? If Senator Wayne Morse is talking, he can be recognized by what he is saying.

On one memorable day during the debate, the inimitable Senator Dirksen declaimed in his best oratorical voice, "I do not want my grandchildren to grow up in a country in which there is racial discrimination." As he picked up his glass of water, he added a bit of typical Dirkseniana, "I do have grandchildren, you know."

That was a day when there were more Senators on the floor and more reporters in the press gallery than is usually the case. A witty Russian visitor is supposed to have said, "Congress is so strange. A man gets up to speak and says nothing. Nobody listens—and then everybody disagrees." That quite often seems to be the case, but during the 1964 Civil Rights filibuster, nobody listened and nobody bothered to disagree because the practice is recognized as a "stalling operation." Years ago, when those "long-distance" talkathons were still a novelty, one Senator read the phone book—with emotion.

It is difficult to trace the origins of the thick volumes of loose-leaf material that were used during the 1964 filibuster. Among the sentences that registered with the listeners in the gallery was a spectacular one that went something like this: "The South is economically backward because the North freed the slaves and there was no one left to work the plantations."

Most of the time, there would be a bare sprinkling of Senators sitting at their desks. The "filibusterer of the moment" would be standing at his desk, his voice droning on and on, while one of his states' rights colleagues sat near him, nodding occasionally, either to give him moral support or from drowsiness.

On an impressive rostrum facing the semicircle of Senatorial desks are seated what appears to be the "high tribunal." In the center sits the "President pro tempore" who is addressed as "Mr. President." Legally this is the Vice President's chair, but there was no Vice President in 1964. Younger Senators often preside as "President pro tempore." The secretary of the Senate and other staff members are grouped at desks in front of the higher podium, and the young pages sit on steps around the edges.

Pulses quickened in the Senate gallery whenever the signal sounded for a quorum call. Everyone leaned forward to see the Senators pouring into the chamber, some briskly, some slowly, usually continuing a conversation that had started somewhere else or beginning a new one. They would answer when their names were called, and some would drift right out again and others would remain for awhile.

During one afternoon quorum call, Senator Hubert Humphrey arrived shortly after the bell sounded and gave every indication of staying until midnight. In the minutes before they got down to business, the Senator from Minnesota was surrounded by groups of colleagues. There was an air of good-natured authority about him, and he answered questions and joked informally. He abruptly turned his attention to the next speaker on the filibuster schedule. Going over and flicking the thick sheaf of pages in the notebook of the junior Senator from Georgia, Humphrey gave fair warning that there would be a number of quorum interruptions before midnight.

The Majority Whip had a bit of conversation with Senator Dirksen, greeted Senator Margaret Chase Smith with a comment that made her laugh, and then sat down behind his desk in the front row—a position he had earned by devotion to democratic statesmanship.

Quite often the "filibuster teams" yielded to other legislative business, but the 1964 states' rights marathon was destined to last for seventy-five long days— often until long past midnight.

Hubert Humphrey brought his own whimsical touch to many of the civil rights sessions. According to Teddy Roe, who spent most of his time in the Senate during those seventy-five days, Senator Humphrey's patience and sympathy were a joy to behold. During one all-night session, when West Virginia's Senator Robert C. Byrd was the marathon speaker, the two men began quoting poetry at each other. About 2:30 in the morning, the verses started getting too sentimental for words, and someone suggested that Humphrey "say it with flowers." The Senator from Minnesota, after only a few hours of sleep, was back again at 7:00 on the same morning. Sure enough—he marched into the Senate, strode all the way across the chamber, and deposited a bouquet on the desk of the Senator from West Virginia who was just concluding his night-long flow of words.

On another occasion, when Senator A. Willis Robertson of Virginia was roundly criticizing the fair housing section of the civil rights bill, Hubert Humphrey somehow cajoled him into agreeing that he had been seriously misinformed on some facts basic to his argument. By the time the debate ended, the two distinguished Senators had their arms around each other's shoulders—and Robertson had decorated Humphrey's lapel with a Confederate pin. Undoubtedly Humphrey was applying the Biblical admonition, "A soft answer turneth away wrath."

History reaches its crossroads by diverse routes. Day after day, Senator Humphrey appeared to be testing the "political temperature" in the Senate. He was respectfully granting the opposition a chance to let off steam and simmer down. In the meantime he was lining up votes to invoke cloture for the second time since 1917. If the rule to close debate received a two-thirds majority, each Senator would be allowed to speak on the pending bill for just one hour before the final vote was taken.

Humphrey's "resiliency" in the Senate did not alter his determination to line up the votes to pass the 1964 Civil Rights Bill before the summer was over. It was necessary to invoke the cloture rule to do it, and some compromises had to be made because Humphrey considered the South—with its many fine people and its high potential for educational and industrial development—a very important part of the nation.

Humphrey recognizes, just as Abraham Lincoln did, that there are wounds that must be bound up. "If I believe in something," he says, "I will fight for it with all I have. But I do not demand all or nothing. . . . Professional liberals want the fiery debate. They glory in defeat. The hardest job for a politician today is to have the courage to be a moderate. It's easy to take an extreme position."

In a subsequent statement about the Civil Rights Bill, Humphrey wrote in "War On Poverty," "There will be no miracle wrought overnight. Rather, then will come the real test of the maturity of our people."

Senator Humphrey's "management" of the bill added up to a bipartisan triumph—a victory which could not have been achieved without the dedicated leadership of Republican Senators Everett Dirksen and Thomas Kuchel, and Democratic Senators Mike Mansfield and Jacob Javitts and dozens of other human rights statesmen of both parties. Even a dying man, Senator Clair Engle of California, insisted on being there in his wheel chair. It was only by a scarcely discernible movement of his eye or his hand that he could cast his vote both for cloture and for the Civil Rights Bill.

Senator Humphrey was becoming accustomed to being invited to the White House, and his appearance there on July 2, 1964, is described as "the highlight of his legislative career." That was the day when President Johnson presented him with one of the pens he had used to sign the historic Civil Rights Bill.

The President also gave Senator Humphrey a copy of the speech he delivered to the Nation upon signing the bill. Inscribed on the speech were these words:

"To Hubert Humphrey—without whom, it couldn't have happened."

Chapter Thirteen

"A Man Who..."

The people on Capitol Hill remember how Senator Humphrey reacted to the news that much of the overflow crowd could not get into the Senate gallery for the final vote on the Civil Rights Bill. All through that last week, when the one-hour speeches were tapering off, visitors stood in endless lines for hours—hoping that, if and when they got into the gallery for their few allotted minutes, they might hear the final history-making tally.

Those who were still waiting, after the moment of triumph, looked up and saw Senator Humphrey coming down the steps of the Capitol to greet them. They shouted approval and applauded, and some of them blinked back tears as he walked among them shaking hands and sharing the jubilance of Negro and white Americans alike.

That moment was a reminder of Dr. Martin Luther King's inspiring words during the great Civil Rights March of 1963: "I have a dream that one day on the red hills of Georgia the sons of former slaves and the sons of former slaveowners will be able to sit down together at the table of brotherhood. I have a dream that even the State of Mississippi, a state sweltering with people's injustices, will be transformed into an oasis of freedom and justice. . . ."

The more he learned about the world, the more Humphrey hoped that every oppressed, stagnant area of the world could become "an oasis of freedom and justice." When the names of Vice Presidential prospects were being discussed, Humphrey's vigorous promotion of the Alliance for Progress in Latin America and his practical recommendations for educational and economic aid in all underdeveloped countries were mentioned as some of the high points in his favor. There were many other considerations, including his ability to get things done in Congress.

In his doctoral thesis, Charles Gilbert made a significant point about a "conflict" within Humphrey's political philosophy. Humphrey believes in government by the majority, but he has always been the champion of minorities. How could he know that the minorities—and the people who would come to care deeply about their welfare—would add up to a great majority in the latter half of the century?

In addition to all his other achievements, Hubert Humphrey was the author of three books during 1964. "Integration and Segregation," published by Crowell, is a well-balanced appraisal of the racial issue. A "New York Times" reviewer pointed out that "The text of the Supreme Court's school decision is followed by the Southern manifesto denouncing it. There are legal and sociological analyses." The Library Journal said of "Integration and Segregation," "In many respects this is the best of many books written about the problems of legally enforced integration since the 1954 Supreme Court decision. . . . Recommended generally."

"War On Poverty," published by McGraw-Hill, is rich with quotations that are part of our contemporary life and that will prove substantial for many years to come. According to E. T. Buehrer of the "Christian Century," "There is solid stuff here, and we may want to refer to it again from time to time—perhaps in the campaign of 1968."

The third book, "The Cause Is Mankind"—subtitled "A Liberal Program for America"—was published by Praeger. In less than two hundred pages, it covers a huge variety of subjects, viewing domestic and foreign policy through the eyes of a statesman who believes that large-minded, progressive liberalism must move in and tackle the responsibilities that narrower minds have neglected and ignored. Our blighted cities, our escalating unemployment problem, our educational deficiencies, and our agricultural surpluses are only a few of the subjects he explores with constructive vigor and imagination. "The Cause Is Mankind'" throws new light on subjects that have lain dormant during most of the century. As it says on the jacket: "His theme here is victory—the victory of mankind over the traditional enemies of poverty, hunger, disease and ignorance. Americans of all persuasions — Republican or Democrat, conservative or liberal — should heed his stirring voice."

The Civil Rights Bill had been signed on July 2,

1964, but it was also the year of the "greatest political circus on earth." No one was forgetting that the Presidential elections would be held in November.

The primaries were notable mainly for the struggle between moderates and conservatives in the Republican Party. Because it appeared that an alarming percentage of Americans seemed capable of voting their racial prejudices, the early candidacy of Governor Wallace of Alabama threatened for a time to demoralize the entire political picture.

Senator Barry Goldwater, a devout conservative who had voted against the Civil Rights and Anti-Poverty Bills, proved to have the most vociferous support behind him at the Republican Convention in San Francisco in mid-July. Senator Goldwater's name was placed before the convention by Senator Everett Dirksen, the one Republican "colossus" who could nominate so controversial a candidate without losing a whit of his own stature. William Edward Miller of New York became the Republican Vice Presidential candidate.

Because President Johnson had proved himself to be a combination of "Mr. America" and "Mr. Democrat," it was universally understood that there would be no contest for the Democratic Presidential nomination.

The Vice Presidential race was the center of suspense, and it would be a cliff-hanger right up to the grand climax. In speeches and interviews, a number of distinguished Democrats had been admitting with varying degrees of reluctance, solemnity and bravado that they would be glad to offer their services for the second spot.

All the people who had considered Humphrey their champion over the long haul—including labor and civil rights organizations, various farm and urban groups, and educators far and wide—started campaigning vigorously and vocally for Humphrey's nomination.

There are conflicting reports on the degrees of eagerness with which Hubert Humphrey publicly "announced" his candidacy. It was obvious that he wanted it and he hoped he would get it, but he demonstrated admirable restraint about not throwing himself at the President; if President Johnson wanted him, that would be a doorway that any man would be honored to enter sedately — but no astute statesman would plunge toward it with brash eagerness. All the potential candidates seemed aware that the tall Texan could easily eject any of those who gave themselves premature "head starts." It was apparent that the President had a contemplative eye cocked on that door—and all the windows too. He made it known that he would welcome suggestions, but he was not about to be "crowded."

Hubert Humphrey made one comical reference to the competition, which was becoming numerous enough to fill a good-sized room. "The President sent Bobby Kennedy to the Far East," he lamented with a twinkle in his eye. "He sent Sargent Shriver to deliver a message to the Pope. Adlai Stevenson got to escort Mrs. Johnson when she went to the theatre in New York, so I asked the President, 'Who is going to enroll Lynda Bird in George Washington University? I'll volunteer.' "

But most of the time, Senator Humphrey concentrated on the business of being a Senator. He did listen attentively, on July 30, when President Johnson eliminated a dozen of the top contenders with one sweeping announcement: "With reference to the selection of the candidate for Vice President on the Democratic ticket," he stated, "I have reached the conclusion that it would be inadvisable for me to recommend to the convention any member of my Cabinet or any of those who meet regularly with the Cabinet."

This ruled out Attorney General Robert Kennedy, who had been considered next in line in the "Kennedy dynasty," and also the United States Ambassador to the United Nations, Adlai Stevenson, and the Peace Corps Director, Sargent Shriver.

Later in the summer, the President indicated that he wanted to work with a man who had learned to live with defeat and disappointment without losing his sense of proportion. Heaven knows Hubert Humphrey had suffered all the "slings and arrows of outrageous fortune" and had not carried grudges or compromised his loyalty.

Only once did Hubert "impishly" hint that he considered himself a candidate for Vice President. He slipped a magazine picture of a Johnson-Humphrey campaign button under LBJ's glass at the White House breakfast for congressional leaders. The President took one look and burst into hearty laughter—which could have meant almost anything. But Senator Humphrey laughed right with him.

Going into the home stretch, Humphrey was a survivor, and still very much in the running, except for several dozen Congressmen, governors, and assorted businessmen and military officers — many of whom probably had suffered defeat at some time or another.

When the Democratic Convention delegates gathered in Atlantic City on August 26, their platform reflected many of the positive aims of the "New Frontier-Great Society" programs. Both the Democratic and Republican platforms agreed on maintaining military strength and keeping Red China out of the United Nations. Republicans continued to maintain that education was the responsibility of state and local governments, while the Democratic platform strongly supported federal aid to education with this statement: "Our task is to make the national purpose serve the human purpose: that every person shall have the opportunity to become all that he or she is capable of becoming. We believe that knowledge is essential to human freedom and to the conduct of a free society. We believe that education is the surest and most profitable investment a nation can make."

The ardor of the Democratic convention delegates was momentarily dampened by the sight of a huge billboard bearing a picture of Republican Candidate Barry Goldwater and the GOP campaign slogan, "In your hearts, you know he's right." One night, the words "extreme right" were inserted beneath the slogan—presumably by a Democrat.

Outside the convention, there were clambakes and formal parties, with a three-ring circus atmosphere along the famous old boardwalk. It was slightly difficult for the Vice Presidential contenders to get away from the thoughts that were in the backs of their minds. Members of the Humphrey family had come from South Dakota and Minnesota to rally 'round their famous kinsman and share the tense hours of waiting for the final verdict.

The convention's keynote speech was delivered with such fiery zeal by Senator John Pastore of Rhode Island that some of the visitors started "talking him up" for the Vice Presidency.

Curiosity about the second-place choice grew so intense that it sometimes overshadowed the seating dispute between "white supremacy delegates" from Mississippi and the predominantly Negro Freedom Democratic delegates from the same state. The Freedom delegates based their right to be seated on the fact that the "regular'" delegates had not been chosen by a majority of both white and Negro Mississippians. Alabama also was challenged on the right of its delegates to represent the Democratic Party in a state that had just passed a law that would keep President Johnson's name from appearing on the Alabama ballot. The delegates watched closely, and so did the cameras, as Senator Humphrey waded into the fray as a mediator.

All the delegations were requested to sign a loyalty oath. The Alabama delegates walked out, as they had done in 1948. After refusing to sign the pledge, all except three Mississippi delegates walked out.

Two of the Freedom delegates were seated, and the rest made their point by staging sit-downs, inside and outside the hall. It appeared to be the only solution to an awkward situation, and a disastrous floor fight was barely avoided. On paper, it was resolved that "at the Convention of 1968, and thereafter, no delegations would be seated from states where the Party process deprived citizens of the right to vote by reason of their race or color." This was one of the major achievements of the convention, but it went unsung in the midst of the clamorous hullabaloo.

The Vice Presidential sweepstakes kept being the big item of news. Majority Leader "Mike" Mansfield eliminated himself by declaring emphatically that he would not be a candidate. The excitement mounted as the unofficial choice began to narrow down to two Senators—Hubert H. Humphrey and Eugene J. Mc-Carthy—both from Minnesota. The television camera-men followed them both around Convention Hall, re-peating the same question over and over, "Have you heard anything from the White House?"

It was a time to listen to thoughtful remarks from Minnesotans who were familiar with the fine records of both men. One Catholic was heard to say, "I like McCarthy very much, but William Miller is a Catholic —and it would seem like a deliberate case of 'me-tooism' if the Democrats choose a Catholic too."

Most people were pointing out that Humphrey was better known, had more political experience and would balance the North-South ticket best. About that time, on the afternoon of August 26, it was learned that the President had sent for Senator Humphrey. The plot thickened as the public learned that Senator Thomas J. Dodd had also been called to the White House. All the masters of mystery drama—from Poe to Hitchcock —needed to look to their laurels that day.

It was the most solemn moment in the life of "a country boy" there at the White House on August 26. At last Hubert Humphrey stood outside the door that was unlike any ordinary door, and he saw that it was wide open, and the President of the United States said, "Come in, Hubert." And he went in.

That evening all the statesmen and officials at the White House got into the President's plane and went flying gaily off to Atlantic City. The President had already been nominated by acclamation, and now the pent-up emotion could be unleashed in frenzied applause as the candidate appeared on the rostrum. There was party unity. Gone were the delegates who refused to support the ticket in November. Those who remained to set the rafters ringing with resounding hallelujahs were ardent New Frontier-Great Society moderates.

Whether or not Hubert Humphrey had anything to do with it, the temper of the national Democratic Party in 1964 bore some similarity to the Minnesota DFL Party in the late 1940's, after it had either rejected the uncooperative extremists or insisted that they mend their ways and start moving forward.

In his acceptance speech, President Johnson answered the Goldwater charge that only the GOP could offer the people "a choice, not an echo." The President assured the convention, and the nation listening on radio and TV, "We do offer the people a choice, a choice of continuing on the courageous and the compassionate course that has made this nation the strongest and the freest and the most prosperous and the most peaceful nation in the history of mankind."

And there sat Hubert Humphrey, with his wife Muriel, while Mr. LBJ played out the scene to the last drop of suspense. The President of the United States was nominating a Vice Presidential candidate in the accepted style, except that this would be final. He wanted a man who was "experienced in foreign relations and domestic affairs . . . a man of the people who felt a compassionate concern for their welfare." He wanted a man who was "attractive, prudent and progressive." He had consulted carefully with people all over the country, right up until the last minute, and he had reached the firm conclusion that Hubert Humphrey "would be the best-equipped man in this nation to be President if something happened to the President."

President Johnson had nominated "the man who," and the cheers swelled again to a deafening crescendo as Hubert and Muriel Humphrey joined the Chief Executive at the convention lectern.

Humphrey, who has sometimes been described as "the most articulate American," was ready to unleash all his eloquence for that almost unbelievable moment of his life. The clock had struck midnight, and he had not been turned back into a pumpkin. He could speak all his hopes for the future with evangelistic fervor, knowing that the campaign had started as soon as President Lyndon Johnson had spoken his first words before the convention.

Now the word went forth "to friend and foe alike" —to people who were sitting in their homes smiling affectionately and nodding, and to people who were sitting in their homes cussing and scoffing. The Vice

Presidential candidate knew the situation, and he sounded a clarion call for positivism in his acceptance speech when he said, "While others may appeal to passions and prejudices, we of the Democratic Party call upon all Americans to join us in making our country a land of opportunity for our young, a home of security and dignity for our elderly, and a place of compassion and care for our afflicted."

He appealed to all of them—Democrats, Republicans and Independents—extending a warm hand of fellowship. "We ask you to join us tonight, for this President, my fellow Americans, is the President of all the American people. . . . I am proud to be the friend of this great President, and I am very proud that he has asked the convention to select me as his running mate. . . . And I ask you, my fellow Americans, I ask you to walk with us, to march forward with us, to help President Johnson build a great society for the America of the future." During his twenty-four minute acceptance speech, the rolling tide of applause interrupted the Senator more than thirty times.

There was a heady whiff of victory in the air even in Atlantic City, but the face of the Republican candidate, high on that billboard above the boardwalk, had loomed like a ghost at the wedding feast. And there had been all those Wallace votes—thirty per cent in Indiana, and forty-three per cent in Maryland—in the primaries. A party with a strong civil rights plank would have some cause for anxiety. But you had to have faith in the people—otherwise there was nothing. The President and his Vice Presidential candidate took it from there.

All during the demanding days and nights of rigorous campaigning ahead, Senator Humphrey would be sustained by the words President Johnson had spoken about him at the convention, "I feel strengthened knowing that he is at my side at all times in the great work of your country and your government." It was symbolic of the spirit of unity that would characterize the Democratic campaign of 1964.

The nation's columnists began reviewing the past achievements of Mr. Humphrey, the boy from a small South Dakota town who considered politics "a distinguished and honorable profession." They studied his record and found their imaginations stirred by his prolonged dedication to the welfare of the family farmer, the small businessman, the worker in the factory, the neglected elder citizen, the wayward young person, and the victim of discrimination. They were fascinated, in 1964, with his old reputation as a long-winded speaker. They recalled that trip to Russia in 1959; it was possible that no one in the world—except perhaps Mrs. Khrushchev — had ever held President Nikita Khrushchev's attention for a solid eight hours.

As a Vice Presidential candidate, Senator Humphrey was asked during the campaign to describe the type of President he would like to be if that possibility should arise. "A great nation needs a strong President," he answered. "The Presidency is the only office in our constitutional system that holds together the many divided parts of the executive branch; that connects the executive with the legislative and judicial branches of the government; that binds the government to the people, and that represents the nation as a whole in the political arena. A man called to the Presidency must cast from his heart and mind all narrowness of spirit. The very word 'President' is a summons to greatness."

Back and forth across the country went the four major candidates. Wherever his plane landed, Hubert Humphrey was likely to find some old friends or neighbors among the thousands of potential voters gathered at the airport.

A scheduled stop at Peoria, Illinois on October 21, was typical. As he walked along the fence shaking hands and greeting as many people as he could reach, he suddenly recognized a familiar face from the days of his and Muriel's youth in Huron, South Dakota. "Why, Edith!" he exclaimed. It was Mrs. R. C. Lee, the former Edith Smith, who still remembers when "Pinky" and his father used to come into the bank where she worked. When Edith looked around for Muriel, the candidate explained that she was on her way to Alaska.

According to some lengthy stories in "The Peoria Journal Star," Senator Humphrey paid attention to all the age groups, frequently leaning down to say "Hello, kids" to the youngsters, and saluting his "student friends" when he saw a delegation from Southern Illinois University waving signs proclaiming "ISU Thinks Humphrey's Great."

In his address from a temporary platform at the airport in Peoria, Humphrey charged that Goldwater was being supported by a "radical right faction" which included the Ku Klux Klan, the John Birch Society and the Minutemen. This was in answer to attacks on Humphrey's membership in the so-called "radical ADA." Humphrey asked Illinoisans "to redeem the pledge of civil rights made by that great Republican, Abraham Lincoln, by defeating the people who have now captured the Republican Party." He reviewed Goldwater's record of "no" votes against a variety of aid-to-education and scholarship bills. He pointed to the GOP candidate's votes in the Senate against minimum wages, tax cuts, civil rights and agriculture. "He has voted against everything except Mother's Day," Humphrey declared.

In that speech and others, Humphrey referred to Goldwater's brand of radicalism as "selfish irresponsibility which appeals so directly to various extremist groups in America."

Although he confined himself mainly to partisan remarks, Humphrey said with feeling that the news of President Herbert Hoover's death had "saddened every one of us," and he paid special tribute to the former President's monumental food and relief projects after the two Great Wars.

Theo Jean Kenyon, staff writer for the "Peoria Star Journal," said that Humphrey warmed up the audience on that chilly day with his "cheerful manner and his buoyant dissection of the opposition candidate whom he called 'the temporary chairman of a fraction of a faction of reaction.' "

The Senator from Minnesota received a special "pharmaceutical souvenir" that day. David Hubert McMaster, a Junction City pharmacist, presented him with a small gold mortar and pestle "in honor of their mutual profession." The erstwhile druggist from South Dakota assured Mr. McMaster, "We're two of the greatest pharmacists in the world!"

It was a good thing Humphrey was "a veteran campaigner." The day before, flying in the four-engine Electra named "The Happy Warrior," he had carried the Great Society crusade to Oklahoma, Illinois and Kentucky. In addition to the Peoria speech, he appeared at Decatur, Carbondale and Chicago—and then set out for the "backlash area" of Gary, Indiana, where Governor Wallace had made an impression in the primaries.

Wherever he spoke, Senator Humphrey appealed to the voters to support the state and local Democratic candidates, as well as the national ticket.

All of the Humphrey family took an active part in the campaigning. When Muriel was guest-of-honor at a luncheon attended by more than seventeen hundred women in Los Angeles, Mrs. Edmund G. Brown introduced her as "the Democratic Party's secret weapon."

According to columnist Kim Blair of the "Los Angeles Times," Mrs. Humphrey established instant rapport with her audience by talking about young people who, she said, impress her because "they are zooming with excitement."

She said that the three Humphrey sons, two of whom were past twenty, were keenly interested in the campaign. The Humphrey daughter, who was born while Hubert Humphrey was still a struggling young student at the University of Minnesota, had trained to

become a nurse before her marriage to C. Bruce Solomonson. At that time Nancy and Bruce were the parents of two small daughters, and Mrs. Humphrey spoke
with grandmotherly pride about Vicky and Jill, for
whom she loved to sew when she had time.

She talked with her usual matter-of-fact tenderness
about Vicky, the older grandchild: "As the mother of
a nurse, and the grandmother of a lovely little girl who
happens to be retarded, I know what the programs for
which my husband has done so much can mean—like
pioneering the Nurse Training Act and the new community mental health programs. They are programs
that spell life and exciting progress to people."

Muriel also "stumped" Alaska and Hawaii, and she
didn't lose either one.

The political mood was in a state of fluctuation,
with more and more moderate Republicans publicly
beginning to endorse the Johnson-Humphrey ticket.
It looked favorable for the Democrats, and the polls
indicated a sizeable victory. But Thomas E. Dewey had
looked just as good on the eve of the 1948 election.

Much of the Solid South probably would need to be
"written off." In the pre-election issue of "The Carolina Israelite," Harry Golden pointed out that peren-
nial Dixiecrats were still beating the political drum
with a wet noodle:

"Throughout the South, millions of men and women
troop to the mailbox to get the federal checks, one after
the other; pension, disability, veterans, social security,
Soil Bank money; and says the fellow, 'The federal government is getting too big.' He says this even as he

holds that brown envelope in his hand. Fantastic, isn't it? Henny Penny, run home and tell the king the sky is falling."

The campaign, gathering momentum as the bite of autumn chilled the air, was more than domestic news. It was a revelation to be in England toward the end of October 1964. During the preceding fortnight, Laborite Harold Wilson had been elected Prime Minister by a slim margin, the Chinese Reds had exploded their first atom bomb, and Soviet Premier Nikita Khrushchev had suddenly been sent into retirement. The sudden power shifts were top news.

No American was a "stranger" in London. On buses, in restaurants, and on the streets, Britons wanted to know if President Johnson had a good chance of winning that election in the States. The great surge of interest had spanned the ocean, and British papers editorialized about the personalities of the Presidential and Vice Presidential candidates and printed apprehensive stories about the last-minute scandal charges that were launched.

All the planes were filled, on November 2, with homebound Americans who wanted to vote on their native soil.

Chapter Fourteen

Landslide 1964

Several hundred hardy souls, with two brass bands to play a "welcome home" serenade, waited at the Twin Cities Airport. A raw fall rain had slowed to a sloggy drizzle and stopped as midnight neared. The well-wishers had begun to assemble at 11:30, while it was still November 2, 1964.

At 1:30 in the morning, "The Happy Warrior" touched ground in a happy landing and taxied toward the terminal. It was already election day—November 3—as Muriel and Hubert descended from the chartered plane to the sudden hilarity of greetings and laughter and the jubilant strains of the "Minnesota Rouser." The Minnesota Senator and his wife had come "back to where we want to be" on that day of all days.

Accompanied by DFL officials, the Humphrey party went from the airport to the Sheraton-Ritz where a tenth-floor suite would be the Minneapolis headquarters for the Humphrey family during that long, historic day.

When he had come to the end of the campaign trail in Utah, after two hectic months of one speech after another, the Senator had been close to exhaustion. He "deplored the kind of a campaign it had been," but he was satisfied with his part in it. One colleague reported, "He thinks he played it clean and above the belt and honorably."

Here again was the man whom Minneapolitans had known as their skinny, energetic mayor. Back in those early days, one reporter had described him as "a strange combination of good sense, political erudition, imagination and enthusiasm." Except that he wasn't as skinny, he was still the same man—only more so—twenty years later.

What does a Vice Presidential candidate do, while he is waiting for the tidings-of-a-lifetime on election day? Hubert Humphrey spent the day at Waverly— casting his vote at Marysville Township Hall, puttering around the house, and visiting with old friends. The next time he saw his fellow townspeople, things might be considerably different. Security officers were already standing by.

The Humphrey family, after being scattered all over the country during the campaign, had begun gathering at the Sheraton-Ritz suite for what they hoped would be a grand victory reunion. After his day in the country air at Waverly, the Senator joined them there.

Before the night was over, it would be evident that many Minnesota Republicans—including businessmen who remembered that Senator Humphrey had gone to bat for them in Washington even when he knew they wouldn't vote for him—had crossed the ballot to endorse the top Democratic candidates. They felt chilly toward the GOP nominee who had condemned big business, big labor and big government.

During the campaign, men of power and influence had formed the Business and Professional Committee for Johnson and Humphrey, some of them expressing convictions that this great nation could afford "to take care of its own" and be prosperous too. Which was exactly what Humphrey had been saying all along.

The atmosphere in the Humphrey suite became more jubilant as the evening advanced. The family smiled for photographers and reporters and accepted the good wishes of DFL supporters who had "believed in Hubert" all along. This was a world away from several doors that had banged shut in Hubert Horatio's face—a world away from that "let-down" feeling at the 1956 Convention, and those dark-of-the-night rejections in Wisconsin and West Virginia.

As the tide of Democratic votes rolled in, the victory rally at the Hotel Radisson ebbed and flowed. They sang "Waiting for Humphrey" over and over again— but no Humphrey. There was a smaller victory rally at the Sheraton-Ritz too, where Humphrey also waited. Protocol required that President Johnson, down in Texas, should make the first statement. Perhaps the President was waiting too—for the Republican candidate to concede—but Senator Goldwater went to bed.

At last the President spoke, inviting all his countrymen to help build the Great Society and partake of its blessings. When tragedy had called him to office a year before, President Johnson had said he wanted to be the President of all the people. This was the night he learned that his feelings were handsomely reciprocated. He had his "consensus."

It was 1:45 when a hoarse cheer set off a jubilant chain reaction at the Radisson. The Vice President-elect of the United States had arrived at Democratic headquarters, and his name was Hubert Humphrey. Humphrey of Minnesota, as they said in the newspapers. Although Humphrey kept repeating, "This is President Johnson's night and his victory," the cheering Minnesotans could not be blamed for feeling that this was also "Humphrey's triumph."

Now they could go home and collapse, all those exhausted Humphrey fans who had stayed for a first glimpse of the first Minnesotan to become Vice President of the United States.

The Administration had hoped to move the nation forward with an overwhelming vote of confidence from citizens of all political persuasions, races, creeds, and financial backgrounds. The election results revealed that the United States shared President Johnson's vision of a Great Society in which our wealth and resources would be used "to enrich and elevate our national life and to advance the quality of American civilization."

A landslide victory for the Johnson-Humphrey ticket broke just about every voting record, including Franklin D. Roosevelt's previous high plurality total in 1936. Only his home state of Arizona, and the five southern states of Alabama, Georgia, Louisiana, Mississippi, and South Carolina, ended up in Senator Gold-water's column. President Johnson's name did not appear on the Alabama ballot, and former Deep South conservative Democrats had switched their allegiance to the Republican Party. "Republicrats," you might say. A new national political pattern was emerging, with the "white backlash" vote receding into the Deep South. That is one reason why it is unfair to accuse the North and West of strong civil rights opposition.

Analysts would call it a great year for "ticket-splitting." Millions of Republicans, in a dozen states, voted for President Johnson and Vice President Humphrey, and then switched over to the Republican column. In the over-all picture, however, the Johnson victory swept a flood of energetic young Democrats and even some liberal Republicans into Congress, to give the President the legislative support he would need.

Maine and Vermont startled the nation by going Democratic. So did Virginia, which had not supported a Democratic President since 1948. South Dakota, traditionally Republican, voted for her native son and his friend on the top of the ballot and then elected a Republican governor by a slim margin. Analysts credit Humphrey with "bringing in the harvest" all through the Republican Middle West.

Minnesota was fabulous, bestowing a solid plurality of more than 400,000 votes on Johnson and Humphrey. They saluted gallant Senator Eugene McCarthy, who did not become the Vice Presidential candidate, with a similar whopping majority. Heavy Republican support was quite "visible" in the Minnesota totals.

Even before the polls were closed on the West Coast and in Alaska and Hawaii, it was apparent that President Lyndon Baines Johnson and Senator Hubert Horatio Humphrey had no cause for anxiety. As though it seemed almost beyond belief, considering all the circumstances, Hubert Humphrey was heard to say aloud on election eve, "I'm the Vice President!" He must have been "trying it for size."

As the President had said during his election night address to the nation, he was looking forward to a post-victory meeting with his new partner—the sooner the better. The Vice President-elect and Mrs. Humphrey arrived at the LBJ Ranch in Texas on November 4, after only a few hours of sleep. President Johnson "duded" his pardner all up in a cowboy suit and he got another upward boost—into the saddle of a frisky quarter horse. Riding his own Tennessee walker, the President took Mr. Humphrey out to help round up the cattle. From some of the cartoons afterward, Humphrey was game for the unaccustomed exercise but found it slightly bruising. He might have preferred to go out on another campaign tour and round up votes from a standing-up position.

After the barbecued ribs and the scenery along the Pedernales River, the Vice President-elect got back to the normal routine again. As thrilled as he was with the high office he would soon assume, Humphrey's sense of humor and his sense of history produced some whimsical anecdotes. During one speech, he read a list of names, looking up every few seconds to ask, "Do you remember him?" or "Does that name ring a bell?" Grinning triumphantly at his mystified audience, he at last let go with the punch line. "They were all Vice Presidents!"

When the Humphreys returned to Chevy Chase, their neighbors had gathered to welcome them home. The country learned, then, that the new Vice President had not stopped playing basketball when he finished high school in South Dakota. Some of the Chevy Chase youngsters were carrying a sign announcing, "We have lost a basketball player, but we have gained a Vice President."

"Nonsense," said Mr. Humphrey, "we're going to keep right on playing basketball!" But there hasn't been much time for "shooting baskets" in the Humphrey yard since the election, and the security guard might get in the way.

A full-time security officer was soon installed in the basement playroom at the Humphrey house, and there are also two secretaries in the house to attend to Mrs. Humphrey's mail and keep track of her busy schedule.

At Holiday time, in 1964, the Vice President-elect paid a special "sentimental visit" to Huron, South Dakota to bring flowers and a Christmas present to his attractive eighty-four-year-old mother who lives in a nursing home there. The Huron "Daily Plainsman" for December 21, 1964, featured a large front-page picture of Humphrey and his mother and a story about the illustrious American statesman "who made his usual first stop at the family drugstore, managed by brother Ralph, to scan the store's Christmas stock and straighten shelves, and talk business with Ralph." He

attended services at the First Methodist Church, and
that was one of the few times when he was not flanked
by the group of Secret Service men who were now part
of his daily life.

In reading Ed Trandahl's story in "The Daily
Plainsman," it is clear that Humphrey does not agree
with Thomas Wolfe that "You Can't Go Home Again."
The Humphrey exuberance always responds to any
mention of Doland or Huron or the cities and towns he
knew so well in Minnesota.

The former Huron druggist did not have a long
"holiday" in South Dakota. It was wedged between
public appearances in Sioux Falls and Chicago. In addition to their mutual sympathy for every facet of the
Great Society program, President Johnson had gotten
himself the most reliable speechmaker in the country.
Where other "traveling orators" might appear breathless and weary, Hubert strides to the lectern looking
cheerful and unruffled, eager to speak vigorously for
this dynamic era of the Great Society. As one Humphrey admirer put it, "He's had a lot of practice talking, and now it's paying off. He never needs to fumble
for words."

Technically, Hubert Humphrey was still a Senator
for several months after the election. He lived up to
his reputation for "political erudition" when Minnesota
Attorney General Walter F. Mondale was chosen to
fill out his unexpired term. As soon as Governor Rolvaag announced the appointment, Humphrey made
plans to "abdicate" early and yield seventeen days of
salary—to give Mondale that much seniority over other
new Senators. For a couple of weeks before the Inaugu-

ration, Humphrey often quipped that he knew how it felt to be numbered among the "unemployed."

But he would soon have a "job" again. The Vice President-elect was in a healthy frame of mind about his future relationship to the Chief Executive. He had stated firmly, "The President of the United States is not a committee but one man—and this one man is the captain on the bridge. The second-in-command must support the captain, lighten his burdens, counsel him, but he must never forget who is captain."

The first weeks of 1965 were a prelude to the Inaugural ceremonies, the grand finale to every Presidential election. After showing newsmen the LBJ branding iron — with which he might have wanted to "autograph" the forthcoming 1965 budget—President Johnson returned to Washington from his ranch in Texas. That was Sunday afternoon, January 17, the beginning of seven days of hectic activity with an unexpected climax.

Often that week, the President and Vice President-elect and their ladies were in the midst of the multitudes of formally attired couples that packed the gala ballrooms in the Capitol City. Chatting, laughing, they switched partners without missing a step. President Johnson and the Vice President are at the top of the list of favorite dancing partners in Washington, and undoubtedly Muriel still thinks "Pinky is the best dancer in town."

There were dinners, receptions, speeches, meetings, and reunions with relatives, political dignitaries and friends who had come from all over the country to salute the victorious Administration. An astronaut's training schedule would have been appropriate for the principals involved in that frantic round of merry-making.

The work of directing the government went on, early in each day, with the ceremonial functions and parties often keeping LBJ and HHH dashing around in a whirl of activity until long after midnight. They appeared fit and jovial, at one event after another.

The Tuesday schedule had included the Governors' Reception at the Sheraton-Park, the Inaugural Concert at Constitution Hall and a party afterward at the State Department. As usual, the hands of the clock pointed to a new day before Hubert Horatio Humphrey went to bed in the same suite at the Mayflower that President Franklin D. Roosevelt had occupied before his first Inauguration in 1933. It was both a sentimental gesture and a good omen for a very modern man who still cherished his New Deal legacy.

Ahead was a day of breathless significance. In a nation of almost two hundred million people, the former druggist from South Dakota and Senator from Minnesota would stand where few people are destined to stand and repeat words that few mortals are privileged to speak.

Chapter Fifteen

"True Faith and Allegiance"

"I, Hubert Horatio Humphrey, do solemnly swear that I will support and defend the Constitution of the United States against all enemies, foreign and domestic; that I will bear true faith and allegiance to the same; that I take this obligation freely, without any mental reservation or purpose of evasion; that I will well and faithfully discharge the duties of the office on which I am about to enter: So help me God."

The oath of the Vice President of the United States was administered by Speaker John W. McCormack. Hubert Humphrey stood with his right hand raised and his left hand on a Bible that belonged to Muriel's family. He had to speak more slowly than was natural for him, and it was obvious that he was concentrating almost too intensely on each impressive phrase because his usually nimble tongue slipped a bit.

It was a moment to think back in time to 1948, when he had stood up in the Senate to take his first oath as a national statesman—to remember that Dad Humphrey had been looking down from the gallery with tears of pride in his eyes, and to wish that his father could be among the thousands gathered here at the Capitol at noon on Wednesday, January 20, 1965, to witness this awesome ceremony.

It was also a time for the new Vice President of the United States to turn and kiss the lady whose Bible he had borrowed, and to remember how far they had come and how bumpy the road had sometimes been for both of them in the three decades since he had written to her about his dream of Washington and "bigger things."

The usually smiling face of the Vice President was solemn as he listened to his Chief Executive say again to the people of the country, "Let us reason together." More specific than anyone realized at the time was the clarion call for justice that must go ringing down the corridors of America's future, as the President declared that ". . . the hour and the day and the time are here to achieve change without hatred; not without difference of opinion, but without the deep and dividing divisions which scar the Union for generations.

"In a land of great wealth, families must not live in hopeless poverty. In a land rich in harvest, children must not go hungry. In a land of healing miracles, neighbors must not suffer and die untended. In a great land of learning and scholars, young people must be taught to read and write. . . ."

And out on a snow-whitened slope of Arlington Cemetery, where a few people kept a silent vigil, the eternal flame flickered with life and light. The faith would be kept.

This time, at the Inaugural Day luncheon, the ex-Senator from Minnesota did not sit quietly in the background. He was one of the two "leading men" in that day's festive extravaganza. In addition to the political elite, there were Johnson and Humphrey "kinfolk" by the dozen to greet—plus a large slice of the population of Doland.

Waving and smiling, the President and Vice President rode at the head of the Inaugural Parade, from the Capitol to the White House.

In view of later developments, reporters would recall that the President was not wearing a coat when he jumped from his limousine to greet some Texas girls along the parade route. With the thermometer registering between thirty and forty degrees, he had dashed around coatless and hatless most of the week, in contrast to the warmly clad people around him.

Even Vice President Humphrey, accustomed to the "arctic winters" of Minnesota, put on his coat for awhile in the glass-enclosed viewing stand that had been built at the White House. President Johnson went circulating around, coatless as usual.

The parade was as lively and exuberant as the spirits of the Presidential party. Maybe this was even better than the Clyde Beatty Circus—to see the big University of Minnesota Band swinging up Pennsylvania Avenue toward the White House, playing the "Minnesota Rouser" as though it had become Humphrey's "theme song." Vice President Humphrey applauded with all his might when the 61-piece Doland High School Band went past playing the "King Size" march.

He likes to remember that he played the baritone horn in the Doland Band—back in the days when both he and the band were smaller.

Despite the challenges of the preceding days, the President and Vice President and their wives made a grand tour of all five Inaugural Balls on Wednesday night, remaining long enough to greet the guests and dance several dances at each one. People who tried to keep track of them were tottering with exhaustion.

When Americans had time for a few meditative moments that week, their thoughts turned to Sir Winston Churchill. As his condition continued to decline, news of his passing was expected momentarily. But it was almost as though the invincible old English statesman refused to cast a shadow over the Inaugural festivities by dying at so improper a time. He was still clinging to a spark of life in his Hyde Park home in London as the last strains of 1965 Inaugural music in Washington faded away into history.

The Executive branch of the United States government had a full schedule of business lined up for the next two days, Thursday and Friday. Humphrey, who often mentions that he has gotten along fine on six hours' sleep at night since he was ten years old, was planning to fly to Minnesota on Saturday morning to officiate as grand marshal of the gigantic Winter Carnival Parade in St. Paul.

The newly inaugurated Vice President was working in his office on Friday night and didn't get home to Chevy Chase until almost one in the morning. At 3:30 a.m., he was awakened abruptly by a telephone

message from White House Press Secretary George
Reedy. President Johnson had been taken to Bethesda
Naval Hospital.

Stricken at the news and in no mood to go back to
sleep, the Vice President went downstairs without disturbing his wife and "just walked around the house."
When he went back upstairs, Mrs. Humphrey was
awake. As though her intuition told her that this was
a night for the history books, she asked if Winston
Churchill had passed away.

"No," her husband answered. "The President is
sick."

As the grand marshal of the Winter Carnival Parade told a luncheon party in St. Paul at noon that day,
he and Mrs. Humphrey had gone downstairs and sat
and talked until a second call came from the White
House. He said, "I then realized my fears and apprehensions were unfounded and I can now smile again,"
and he did.

By that time, everyone knew that the President had
begun to suffer from a cold late on Friday afternoon,
and that he was taken to Bethesda when his temperature had risen during the night.

Upon being notified that his Chief wanted him "to
carry on and fulfill your duties," the Vice President
and Mrs. Humphrey went ahead with their plans to
fly to St. Paul.

It was a relieved and beaming Hubert Humphrey
who donned a fur Winter Carnival hat to ride at the
front of his second big parade of the week. The afternoon was "warm" for Winter Carnival time—eighteen

degrees, with a sprinkling of snowflakes—and the Vice President called it "balmy weather."

The Twin Cities—Minneapolis and St. Paul—had been "home country" to the former Senator for almost three decades, but this was probably the first time he had ridden down those familiar streets from the State Capitol in a bubble-top car. The one hundred thousand cheering spectators along the Winter Carnival Parade route seemed to feel a personal, emotional interest in Humphrey — a Minnesota "figure of destiny" whom they had sent to Congress with their votes.

Humphrey had said, "The President wants us to get on with our work. I intend to do just that." He stayed overnight in the Twin Cities and then flew on to Tucson, Arizona for an antipoverty conference on Monday. Behind the scenes, there was constant communication with the White House, and no more crises were expected. In fact, the indomitable Chief Executive would soon be presiding over a press conference in his hospital suite.

In the meantime, the report of President Johnson's sudden illness had been hurled in banner headlines across the front pages of the world. The American stock market slipped rather badly, and there was international anxiety. Mike Mansfield, Senate majority leader, relieved the tension by observing that "it was probably a good thing for him and for the country that the President is being forced to get a little rest."

On Sunday, January 24, news from London again took over the headlines. The magnificent voice of Sir Winston Churchill, that had dominated the interna-

tional amphitheater for many decades, was stilled forever. He would lie in state for three days in Westmin-
ster Hall, in the heart of the steeples and towers of his
beloved Houses of Parliament. On Saturday, January
30, he would be borne with due ceremony through the
streets of London to St. Paul's Cathedral where he
would be carried down one of the longest and most
majestic aisles in the world, and the "singing bells" of
St. Paul's would toll his passing with voices as sublime
as a heavenly choir.

The world's leaders began to pack their luggage
and set out for London to attend the funeral. Former
President Dwight D. Eisenhower and Chief Justice of
the Supreme Court Earl Warren were heading the
United States delegation. Because nobody told Vice
President Humphrey to pack his bag, the professional
kibitzers would be agog with speculation for months
to come. Some sensational conclusions were drawn:
the President was gravely ill—the President didn't
want the Vice President in the spotlight—the President had suffered a relapse—the President wasn't "getting along" with Humphrey.

It would have been undramatic for anyone to suggest that the Vice President was so busy with Administration business, on a policy-making level, that he
would not have had time for the London trip. Although
President Johnson was making a normal recovery, he
was suffering the same period of lassitude that ordinary mortals do, and it was good to have a hale and
hearty Vice President handy when he needed him.
Even while he was in the hospital, President Johnson
was seeking passage of legislation that would provide

for an "Acting President" in the event of "disability" in the highest office.

The President did not need to explain how he felt about Winston Churchill or Vice President Humphrey. His laudatory remarks about both of them are a matter of record.

The skeptics were not easily appeased about the Churchill funeral. Humphrey has noted that "there are more fight promoters in Washington than peace-makers." As an art that is filled with ambiguities and hollow conjectures, "second-guessing" can be an enter-taining part of the American political scene, if it is not spiteful. Back in late January 1965, with the inau-guration scarcely over, the pundits were asking why LBJ was "punishing" HHH by keeping him home from the Churchill funeral. Six months later, some of the same "fight promoters" sounded frustrated because LBJ and HHH were getting along so well together.

The critics kept forgetting that there was supposed to be a sparkle of newness to everything in the Great Society—that no possible area of rejuvenation would be neglected. A war on poverty was being launched in underdeveloped areas. It is not strange that the Vice Presidency should be viewed as an "underdeveloped area."

To his eternal credit—and the world might well benefit from his example—President Johnson was in-troducing a full-scale concept of dual political harmony in the upper echelons of national government. It is a form of insurance for the perpetuation of stable gov-ernment, a grim necessity in this era of complicated international politics. At the head of many nations of the world, there is one supreme leader "playing king of the hill"—jealously and suspiciously guarding his exalted position against any possible successors. The rest of the world does not know the names of the people upon whose shoulders their mantles might fall, or their qualifications, or whether they must claw their way to power through revolution.

Whether it was completely deliberate or not, President Kennedy was fortunate in having a successor with a progressive spirit so similar to his own. President Johnson, from all his public statements about his choice of a Vice President, was not leaving anything to chance. As he said, he had set out "to find the man best qualified to assume the office of President if that should ever be necessary."

Anyone who examined President Johnson's programs for the Great Society should have known—long before he chose his 1964 running mate—that Hubert Humphrey would regard President Johnson with unadulterated admiration. They might disagree on a small point now and then, but where would he find another "leader" whose practical idealism so closely paralleled his own—who honestly cared about first-class citizenship for every American, for amicable business-labor relations, for wider educational opportunities, for health care for the aged, for replacing slums with decent housing and making cities livable? Where would he find another President with such a high regard for space exploration, for American world leadership, and for the general welfare of little people as well as big people? Most of all, where would he find a President who would be so ready to take giant steps forward, right from the word go?

In other words, it would be difficult for political skeptics to drive a wedge between two men who are viewing the country and the world from the same plateau. Too often in the past, the President has appeared to be standing on one high peak, and the Vice President has been relegated to a lower peak on the other side of a deep chasm—to listen meekly for an occasional yodel.

Although the Vice President makes none of the final decisions, he and the President are equally well-informed. The President has arranged to keep his Vice President in up-to-the-minute touch with affairs of state. Every morning, on his way into the city, Humphrey studies cables and classified reports that fill him in on what has developed in "daytime areas" of the world while most Americans were sleeping. He is "briefed" frequently during the day. In the evening, the Vice President usually reports to the President on the activities of each committee in Congress during the day. Both of the men know where they stand and how to get things said and done together.

A complete recital of the varied activities of the Vice President during a period of only a few months would fill a shelf of books. Almost immediately, he was actively supervising a multitude of vital government programs with which he had already become familiar in Congress: outer space, public welfare, aid to education, health, science, the war on poverty, farm problems, natural resources, the Alliance for Progress, the

Food-for-Peace program, disarmament and arms control. It was a far cry from being "the world's greatest expert on the boll weevil."

When the "Pacem in Terris" convocation assembled in New York, wise men from all over the earth gathered to discuss the requirements for world peace as Pope John had described them in his historic encyclical. As the opening speaker, Vice President Humphrey said that "the next major step" in controlling nuclear arms would probably be "finding ways of preventing the further proliferation of nuclear weapons in Asia, Latin America, Africa and the Middle East." His statement was regarded as a "policy" signal that the United States will give priority attention to creating nuclear free zones.

When the Vice President and Mrs. Humphrey flew to Florida one week-end late in February, it was more of a change of pace than a "holiday." Humphrey attended a President's Club reception, spoke at an Israel bonds dinner, and met with AFL-CIO leaders while he was there.

For many years, Senator Humphrey dramatized the need for a youth conservation program. On February 29, the first of many work-and-education projects — the Catoctin Job Corps Center near Thurmont, Maryland—was dedicated. On March 13, Vice President Humphrey told the first group of Federal Job Corps trainees at Camp Kilmer, New Jersey, that they have a war to win "against the faceless enemy of poverty." "The government," he explained carefully, "does not owe you a living or a salary, but owes you an opportunity to make a living and earn a salary. That is what we are trying to do." As an example of government-industry partnership, the Camp Kilmer center is being operated by a subsidiary of a large private corporation under government contract.

In mid-March, Humphrey talked about Farm Aid plans at the National Farmers Union Convention in Chicago. He assured his audience that President Johnson "will not let you down on legislative programs designed to put more money into farmers' pockets." He referred to the export market as "the big area of potential expansion for U. S. agriculture; if we compete —if we sell—and if we don't price ourselves out of the market."

In a discussion about possible cuts in the farm budget during the meeting, Budget Director Kermit Gordon upset the group with a suggestion that not all of the three and one-half million farmers in the country can expect a good living off the land. Proving that he had not changed his mind about that topic, the Vice President said, "I reject any solution that would in effect force the small farmer off the land." He does encourage farmers to convert some of their acreage to resort and recreation centers, whenever possible.

With a former mayor of Minneapolis handy, it was natural for President Johnson to appoint Humphrey as chief liaison man between the Administration and city and county officials. At a meeting on March 31, the Vice President warned that forces of growth and decay are converging on cities and require not only new building programs but better education, higher incomes and a lifting of "oppression" which is used "to deny some of our citizens their rights." He said that "American cities today are at a time of great decision. We can be crushed by their unchanneled vitality if we do not impose civilizing controls." On May 5, during his third conference with mayors and city managers, Humphrey stressed the need to formulate plans to "defuse the explosive potentiality" of having some two million unemployed youths on their streets during the approaching summer.

Humphrey has also written extensively on the subject of urban problems. In a guest editorial in "Saturday Review" for July 3, he began by emphasizing that it is later than we think: "Robert Herrick said in the seventeenth century that great cities seldom rest: if there be none to invade from afar, they will find worse foes at home. We know those foes today. They are slums, crime, a lack of playgrounds and parks, overburdened schools, inadequate transportation, crowding, lack of clean air and inequality of opportunity."

When the Vice President made a last-minute appearance at a party being given by U. S. Chief of Protocol and Mrs. Lloyd Hand, at Blair House one evening last spring, he almost slipped up on his protocol. In answer to their questions, he was busy telling guests and reporters about the lively life of a Vice President in the Great Society—five or six hours a day on civil rights, plus much intensive concentration on numerous other programs, and speaking dates and miscellaneous administrative business. He was still talking half an hour after he was due for a dinner conference with Undersecretary of State Thomas C. Mann. Someone asked him if he were about to leave.

"Oh my, am I holding up the party?" he asked, hurrying to say good-by to his host and hostess as the last handful of guests lingered. "I just can't get used to the protocol of these things. Can't you leave until I go?" he asked reporters.

"Heavens, no, Mr. Vice President," one of them said. "You are news, and we might miss something!"

Mr. Humphrey went flying buoyantly from the 1965 Opening Day ceremonies at the World's Fair in New York to co-starring with Luci Baines Johnson at the Azalea Festival in Norfolk, Virginia. When he spoke to eight hundred civic club members in Norfolk on April 23, he said of the Azalea Queen, "There is no lovelier flower than Luci."

He also made it clear that the Administration would not pursue an isolationist policy. He declared that ". . . the United States should not drop the torch of internationalist leadership. . . . We hear many voices these days saying that America is overextended in the world—that other people's problems needn't be our problems—that we ought to close up shop overseas and enjoy our blessings here in the good old U.S.A. My friends," he told the Norfolk audience, "when that time comes, this nation is doomed. Who in the world will work for democracy if we do not? Who in the world can set the example, can offer the needed hand, if we do not?"

On the afternoon of April 28, the Vice President dedicated the new Washington Veterans Administra-

tion Hospital. He pointed out that "We don't help anybody by maintaining an institution that is obsolete.
. . . We hear about the closings, but we are engaged in
the largest building program in VA history." He
stressed the necessity for providing top medical care
for veterans. "We are determined to put medical care
within the reach of all," he said, "but the veteran has
the first claim, based on his service to the country."

The next day, Mr. Humphrey spoke to an audience
of more than one thousand, at the annual banquet of
the White House News Photographers' Association. Referring to fine photography as "the art of the times,"
he suggested the possible establishment of a national
gallery of American photography. Still vivid in the
minds of the association officials were the pictures of
Humphrey's horseback ride at the LBJ Ranch. They
presented him with a rocking chair, which they said
would probably be a safer seat for him than a Western
saddle.

Humphrey's faith in the power of "pictorial history" was affirmed in the starkly shocking "Profile
of Poverty" exhibit—a photographic display of the
bleak faces of poverty in squalid city slums and rural
hovels. The Vice President had suggested "the grim
photographic exhibit," which was assembled for display at the Museum of History and Technology in
Washington from mid-May to mid-June, 1965. It was
indeed "the art of the times"—a reproach to complacent Americans who say that "everyone has an equal
chance to better himself."

The Vice President was probing every area of Administration policy during those first few months in

office. When it came to caring about the welfare of less-privileged Americans, he was still the same young Senator from Minnesota who had told his distinguished elders, "I learned more about economics from one South Dakota dust storm than I did in all my years in college," and "I believe that if we put more emphasis upon the human element we will take care of the financial element."

All through his legislative career, Humphrey had revealed both practical and intellectual versatility. He had already discussed the Mesabi Iron Range with Roger Blough, and he had been on handshaking terms with business people all over the country; but when Washington newsmen got together for their annual Gridiron "spoof" in the spring of 1965, they came up with a whimsical exaggeration of the "new Humphrey image:"

I'm a maverick stray from the ADA
And I used to play Walter Reuther's way,
But I'm steppin' out in different company now—
Henry Ford, Fred Kappel and Roger Blough—
We're saddled up with businessmen somehow,
Yippee-yi, LBJ!

Chapter Sixteen

The Ides of March —1965

The final weeks of March 1965, may well be considered both magnificent and tragic in the history of mankind. Brave men were fighting against totalitarian aggression in Vietnam. Brave men were assaulting the law of gravitation in space. Brave men and women were marching from Selma to Montgomery in the struggle to end political white supremacy in Alabama. Morally, physically, and scientifically, humanity sought to throw off the shackles that had kept it "earthbound" for centuries.

Although it sounds farfetched to suggest that the Russians keep their rockets waiting on the pad for just such a moment, the glory of the first two-man American space flight was slightly marred when the Soviets sent two cosmonauts into orbit early on Thursday, March 18. By the time Voskhod 2 landed on the next afternoon, Soviet Cosmonaut Lieut. Col. Alexei Leonov had become the first human being to "take a walk in space."

While the world was still gasping at Leonov's spectacular feat, American scientists on March 21 launched another photographic moon probe that reached a grand climax with the relaying of live close-up pictures as Ranger 9 reached its bull's-eye point of impact near Moon Crater Alphonsus, on the following Wednesday morning.

Another historical "launching" occurred on the Sunday that Ranger 9 departed for the moon. In Selma, Alabama, thousands of Civil Rights marchers set out on the fifty-mile trek from Selma to the capital city of Montgomery, Alabama. With them went the blessing of President Johnson who, in his "We Shall Overcome" message to Congress on March 15, reminded his countrymen of the tragedy of Selma on the previous Sunday. "There, long-suffering men and women peacefully protested the denial of their rights as Americans. Many were brutally assaulted." He spoke of the Boston minister, the Rev. James Reeb, who had been fatally clubbed in Selma. "One good man—a man of God—was killed."

Seated behind the President, during that special joint meeting of Congress, the faces of Vice President Humphrey and House Speaker John W. McCormack reflected the strain of an hour in history when democracy must answer yes or no. Everyone knew that they were adding the strength of their own resolution to the noble phrases that the President was speaking:

"Rarely are we met with a challenge, not to our growth or abundance, our welfare or security—but to the values and purpose and meaning of our Nation.

"The issue of equal rights for American Negroes is such an issue and should we defeat every enemy,

double our wealth, conquer the stars and still be un-
equal to this issue, then we will have failed as a people
and a nation. . . ."

With the applause of a vast majority of members
of Congress ringing in his ears, the President prepared
to send a stronger human rights bill to the lawmakers
—one in which "the heart" had better not be eliminated this time, when it came back for his signature.

Both of the top statesmen in the nation were highlighted on special TV programs that evening. Shortly
after the President had finished speaking, "CBS Reports" featured an interview with Vice President Humphrey.

He appeared agile-minded and physically at ease
as he told about the status of the Vice President in the
present Administration. It was noted that many Vice
Presidents of the past have been "forgotten men" but
that Humphrey would have difficulty finding anyone
in Washington who hadn't heard of him.

Obviously a man of Humphrey's vigor and vitality
would burst if he had to sit around and twiddle his
thumbs. He assured his interviewers that he has always
been included in the Administrative circle—that President Johnson wants him to be entirely familiar with
all areas of governmental control. He and the President
work in "reciprocal harmony." The President conscientiously keeps the Vice President informed about messages he will be delivering and other governmental details, even though they might not be of current concern
to him.

On the other hand, Hubert Humphrey clears his

statements with the White House before they are released. When he was asked if the President sometimes
suggests a more temperate line, Humphrey laughingly
recalled the comment attached to one of his speeches,
"Quit being so soft. Get a little tougher."

All of the Vice President's answers indicated a good
spirit of camaraderie between himself and his "Chief."
They might not always agree on every detail, but he
has no desire to challenge the authority of the President—and he added with a grin, "He who giveth can
taketh away." He is motivated by an inspired sense
of loyalty toward the President—by a desire "to march
beside him, instead of getting in his way."

What about that memorable night at the White
House, when President Johnson said he had chosen him
for his running mate? As he tried to recapture the high
point of those months of suspense, the former Senator
said he had been so moved by the news that he had
difficulty recalling exactly what was said. He did remember that the President put his arm around his
shoulders and said, "We're going to be a team." The
President seemed to think Humphrey had already
guessed that he was the top choice, but the man from
South Dakota and Minnesota had been haunted by
memories of earlier disappointments.

No one could be more sympathetic with the President's program than "teammate" Humphrey. Committed heart and soul to an "Emancipation Proclamation" for the Twentieth Century, he also understands
the President's reluctance to make any mistakes that
might prolong the shocking bitterness and violence
indefinitely.

When his interviewers switched to the inevitable question, Humphrey told them he thought there had been "an excellent American delegation" at the funeral for Sir Winston Churchill. He didn't feel that the President had chosen him to be an "official attender of funerals." Even though President Johnson had not been critically ill, it seemed that he had felt more comfortable with the Vice President in the country.

What about the Presidency? Humphrey sounded as though he still felt awed at the thrill of becoming Vice President of the United States. If no other great honors should come to him, how much more glory can a man expect in one lifetime?

All of his remarks, during the CBS interview, added up to a firm resolution to fill the office of Vice President with good manners, dignity, and honor. He strongly favored a bill to insure that there would always be a Vice President. In the event that the President might become incapacitated, the Vice President should be ready to carry the burden—on a temporary basis, and always mindful that "as long as the breath of life is in him, the President is the elected choice of the people."

By word and by tone of voice, on that night of March 15, President Johnson had informed the nation that he would not compromise his moral convictions, and he asked for the support of all his fellow Americans in the war against racial discrimination.

Ahead lay the week of stress and strain that would rise to a crescendo in the gigantic Freedom March, the largest protest demonstration ever to be held by civil rights forces in the Confederate heartland of Alabama.

In the face of the violence that had jolted the consciences of good people everywhere, Hubert Humphrey revealed that he is the opposite of a "wild-eyed radical." To a delegation of outraged citizens who demanded that the civil rights people in Alabama be given immediate protection of Federal troops, he urged caution and patience. He told the group that the President and he were up all night worrying about threats of further violence, "but if we call out the troops now, the hoodlums around Selma may really run wild. And if the troops put down the trouble, the situation will get worse when they leave. Negroes may be in worse danger than ever."

As a good Vice President should, he turned aside bitter wrath with soft answers and assured the group that he would carry their message to the President. By the time the freedom march swung out of Selma on Sunday, the Alabama National Guard had been Federalized and mobilized for guard duty by order of the President of the United States. An undetermined number of FBI and Justice Department men were also on hand.

American flags waving, voices lifted in song—black and white, young and old — they were free to go "tramping through the vineyard where the grapes of wrath are stored," after long weeks of frustration in Selma where some had been beaten and some had been jailed.

Conflicting accounts were emerging during those weeks of the freedom crusade in Selma. One newspaper quoted an "on-the-spot-letter" from an Alabama state trooper, "a true Christian," describing the marchers as "Bearded beatniks, filthy, dirty young white girls dressed like men, so-called preachers in overalls and some priests in their suits with the collar turned backwards . . . all are here, living, eating, sleeping with these Negroes, cursing Alabama and us. . . ."

A report on one of the unsuccessful marches was published in the Catholic Virginian of March 19, 1965. Father Geno Baroni—one of those priests "with the collar turned backwards"—wrote of "Courage, Frustration, and Hope": "As some of the clergymen put it, we were going to Golgotha without the cross. Still, as we marched we couldn't help asking each other what tear gas felt like and hoping that, if there was going to be violence, at least the older clergymen wouldn't be badly beaten. . . ."

Confronted by a solid wall of state troopers, the Rev. Dr. Martin Luther King called upon the people to pray and the frustrated multitude knelt in the road. Father Baroni described the prayers that followed. "Bishop John Wesley Lord, the Methodist bishop of Washington, urged us to love America and love one another. Msgr. Thomas Reese of Wilmington reminded us that Christ had made all men brothers. Rabbi Richard Hirsch of Washington recalled that no men—whites included—are free unless all men are free. . .

"The march . . . demonstrated as never before that the clergy are prepared not merely to speak about the principles of equality and brotherhood but to act upon them. Priests, ministers and rabbis showed that they could walk as well as talk. . . . Catholics, Presbyterians,

Unitarians, Lutherans, Jews, Episcopalians—we got a
new and healthy respect for each other on that highway out of Selma. . . . I think one monsignor spoke for
all of us when he said that the sense of unity and sharing . . . was as close as he expects to come in this life
to the feeling of unity and brotherhood in the next."

Never had the nation been called upon to carry so
great a weight of emotion in so short a span of days.
It was a time when less-determined men than President Johnson, Vice President Humphrey, and other top
officials might have thrown up their hands in despair.
It had been a time for hope to falter, for faith to wear
thin, for justice to weep.

But it was also a time for achievement in the realm
of space exploration. On Tuesday, March 23, Vice
President Hubert Humphrey, in his capacity as chairman of the Space Advisory Council, was an enthusiastic visitor at Cape Kennedy.

He and other official dignitaries watched from the
Mission Control Center at Cape Kennedy as Gemini-
Titan 3 separated itself from the earth with a crackling
roar and hurled astronauts Virgil Grissom and John
Young aloft in a perfect launching. The thrill of initial
success was tempered by a general knowledge of all
the critical periods ahead, before the three-orbit flight
would be completed and the capsule and its precious
cargo recovered from the Atlantic waters north of the
Bahamas.

Although neither American planned to "take a
stroll" outside the capsule as the Soviet astronaut had
done, Air Force Major Grissom was the first earth man

to take a space ride twice. Another momentous "first" was scored when Grissom tested the maneuverability of the craft, successfully shifting from one orbital path to another by firing thruster jets.

About noon, Vice President Humphrey came beaming out of Mission Control and went around shaking hands with maintenance men and other space project workers. "Yessirree—it looks good!" he declared with enthusiasm. "I'm as excited as anybody can be." It was obvious that he was interested in every phase of the gigantic space program.

Later in the afternoon, when it was learned that the men and the capsule were safe after another history-making expedition into space, Humphrey shook all the hands in the Control Center and offered his warmest congratulations.

At the brief press conference afterward, the Vice President saluted the astronauts and the awesome display of teamwork—between military, scientific, industrial and government forces—that had made the Gemini 3 flight a triumphant reality. In a typical Humphrey good will gesture, he also thanked the foreign countries on whose soil the tracking stations are located.

"We will continue with the Gemini program, and then move forward into the Apollo series," the Vice President assured the reporters and TV audience. "We will put a man on the moon—and then go on to explore the universe!"

In answer to the inevitable query about Soviet space superiority, he said in effect that each American has a job to do in terms of his own individual standards of excellence, without wasting energy worrying about the other fellow's rate of progress.

It was a time to remember that President Kennedy had said, at the dedication of a new aero-space medical center at Brooks Air Force Base, on the day before his assassination, "There will be pressures for our country to do less, and temptations to do something else. But this research must and will go on. The conquest of space must and will go ahead."

Is the space race worth all the money that is being invested in it? Humphrey noted that even the "spin-off" from space experiments is paying dividends in earth science areas such as medical research. He believes that this dynamic country can afford both a strong human welfare program and a strong space program. "America's economy is better because of the space program," he noted emphatically at Cape Kennedy. "America's education is better because of the space program. America's industry is better because of the space program. Americans are better off because of the space program."

The Vice President is a man of lively facial expressions—the hearty laugh, the thoughtful stare, the quick smile, the lightning glance. He has a "busy" face that reflects the velocity of his easily stimulated mind.

In the meantime, the Civil Rights march was pressing on toward the capital of Alabama. It was a week of unprecedented "launchings"—two in the name of scientific progress, and one in the name of human freedom and dignity. Perhaps it is the prime paradox of the Twentieth Century that the human rights cru-

saders needed to plod slowly afoot along fifty miles of
Alabama highway, while science was able to send two
men hurtling into space at 17,000 miles an hour.

In spite of pelting rain, some glowering spectators,
and blistered feet, the Freedom Marchers sang the
songs that kept their spirits high and inspired the support of Americans of good conscience all over the country. There were the bright new "freedom songs" and
religious hymns, and reverberating down a century of
years came the grand old melody of the "Battle Hymn
of the Republic."

When the marchers pitched camp for the night,
sometimes on rainy ground covered with a thin layer
of straw, newsmen went among them to ask some of
the distinguished demonstrators why they were there.
One movie actor, pounding a tent stake into the ground
with vigorous blows, paused only long enough to say,
"Because I was born too late for Lexington and Concord."

In Washington, the subject of Civil Rights was con-
tinuously "on the table." During a Cabinet meeting on
March 25, the final day of the Alabama demonstration,
LeRoy Collins, chairman of the Community Relations
Service and former Governor of Florida, reported em-
ployment discrimination in federal agencies in Ala-
bama—in the Federal Courthouse in Selma, the Social
Security Administration, the Agriculture Department,
Craig Air Force Base, the FBI, the Department of Jus-
tice, and the Post Office.

President Johnson responded with a statement emphasizing that the Federal service "must never be

either the active or passive ally of any who flout the Constitution."

Vice President Humphrey, speaking as co-ordinator of Administration Civil Rights activities, said he had named three task forces—on education, employment, and summer activities. He had already been considering programs to help "ease off the tension that might be evident in the summer months."

That was the day when the eyes of the nation—and much of the world—turned toward Montgomery, Alabama. The line of march had been swelled by thousands of new arrivals. With American flags flying, with placards and signs from distant states and from sympathetic national organizations, they began to pour up broad Dexter Avenue—an estimated twenty-five thousand Negro and white Americans—toward the State Capitol. More than an hour later, the end of the long stream of humanity was not yet in sight.

Those who reached the Capitol first did not need to entertain themselves by studying the solid line of state troopers standing guard on the steps above them or by eyeing the Confederate flag flying from the highest point on the Capitol. Assembled around a battery of microphones on a temporary stage was a fabulous galaxy of stars which included Peter, Paul, and Mary, Joan Baez, Harry Belafonte, and Pete Seeger, pouring out their rich voices in one exultant freedom song after another. They sang the hymn of the Civil Rights movement, "We Shall Overcome," and they serenaded Governor Wallace with a heart-stirring rendition of "Let My People Go"—to the polls, to decent jobs, to equal housing and equal rights. They were internationally celebrated artists, accustomed to Jaguars and Cadillacs, but one TV newscaster had been startled to see Harry Belafonte marching along in a cluster of laborers and housewives—just like all the rest. Everyone had marched those last miles—bishops, educators, students, workers, sharecroppers, and several million dollars' worth of volunteer entertainment talent.

The occasion was of such magnitude that it boasted two Nobel Prize winners. Dr. Ralph Bunche told the vast assemblage, "Governor Wallace should understand that no American can be an outsider anywhere he goes in America."

The other Nobel laureate was the "Moses" of the nonviolent civil rights movement, the Rev. Dr. Martin Luther King, who had led the column of marchers during most of the long walk from Selma to Montgomery. That day he was standing up as a prophet in his "home country" to tell the people that "Segregation is on its deathbed. My only concern is how costly the segregationists and Wallace will make the funeral. . . .

"We're on the move now and no wave of racism can deter us. . . .

"We're on the move now and no burning of churches can deter us. . . ."

The Governor had said he would accept a petition from an Alabama Civil Rights delegation after the crowd dispersed, but he had left the Capitol after watching much of the three-hour rally through his windows and on television.

The petition said, in part, "We have come to represent the Negro citizens of Alabama and freedom-loving people from all over the United States and the world. We have come not only five days and fifty miles, but we have come from three centuries of suffering and hardship. We have come to you, the Governor of Alabama, to declare that we must have our freedom now. We must have the right to vote; we must have equal protection of the law and an end to police brutality."

After the Alabama rally, Americans went to bed on the night of March 25 in varied states of emotion. They awoke to hear the bells tolling for another martyr to the freedom cause. Mrs. Viola Gregg Liuzzo of Detroit, Michigan, had been shot to death on a lonely stretch of highway as she was shuttling marchers between Selma and Montgomery. Riding with her was a young Negro who escaped injury.

During that morning, President Lyndon Johnson and Vice President Humphrey and other dignitaries temporarily put aside their anxieties and extended a gala welcome to astronauts Virgil Grissom and John Young. The festive ceremony in Washington included speeches and the presentation of medals to the heroes who had made another "break-through" in the journey toward the moon.

Shortly after the astronauts left the White House, Americans were surprised to see the President, his face taut with strain, looking out at them from their television sets. On one side of him stood a grim-faced J. Edgar Hoover, director of the Federal Bureau of Investigation. It was an unprecedented appearance, during a fortnight of unprecedented events. The President announced the arrest by the FBI of four Alabama members of the Ku Klux Klan who were charged with conspiracy in the slaying of Mrs. Liuzzo. He praised the FBI for their brilliant police work during the long night, and he declared "war" on the Klan. He recalled that both he and his father had fought the Klan in Texas. "I shall continue to fight them because I know their loyalty is not to the United States but to the hooded society of bigots," he declared.

Bond was set at $50,000 apiece for the Klansmen, and three of them were free on bond within a few hours of their arrest.

On the last Sunday in March, Vice President Humphrey visited the home of Anthony Liuzzo in Detroit, to express sympathy on behalf of himself and the President of the United States. He hugged a weeping six-year-old named Sally, one of the five children left motherless by the shooting on Thursday night.

The Governor of Alabama said Mrs. Liuzzo should have been home taking care of her children.

Anthony Liuzzo, the grief-stricken husband, said his wife always wanted to help people.

Governor George Romney, who proclaimed a two-day period of mourning in the state of Michigan, likened Mrs. Liuzzo to another martyr, Joan of Arc.

Shortly after the announcement of the tragedy in Alabama, House Speaker John W. McCormack declared that the Klan belongs "like communism, on the list of subversive organizations compiled by the Attorney General of the United States."

On Monday, March 29, the House Committee on un-American Activities announced it would launch a full-scale probe of the "terrorist activities" of the Ku Klux Klan.

It was the climax to almost two weeks of fantastic heroism on earth and in space.

Chapter Seventeen

"Historyland"

A trip to Jamestown, Virginia, where the Vice President was scheduled to speak on Law Day, was also a good excuse for a tour of Colonial Williamsburg. There, the entire area of the Old Dominion town has been restored or reconstructed as accurately as possible, so now the visitor may take a stroll back in history through the handsome Palace of the Royal Governor, or dine at a "publick house," or imagine how Thomas Jefferson looked when he danced with his fair Belinda at Raleigh Tavern. He may sit in a pew marked "General George Washington" in fine old Bruton Parish Church and recall the time when the Williamsburg patriots staged a prayer demonstration to extend their sympathies to the Boston rebels who had tossed the King's tea into the harbor. He may visit the wigmaker or bootmaker, and tour the gracious homes of some gentlemen who patronized them.

The weather was warm for May, and Williamsburg was ablaze with wisteria, azalea, and forsythia blooms. Dames in colonial gowns and gentlemen in colonial livery were already welcoming tourists to the section of Williamsburg where history pauses to catch the echo of Patrick Henry's voice "rattling the timbers" in the House of Burgesses chamber of the reconstructed Capitol.

About ten miles southwest along the Colonial Parkway from Williamsburg is Jamestown, the site of the first permanent English settlement and center of colonial government in the New World. Here came the three sailing ships—Susan Constant, Godspeed, and Discovery—bearing one hundred and five colonists who had defied the wintry Atlantic in 1607 to seek a new homeland on an alien shore. The foundation stones of old buildings, a thick-walled church tower, and a few mossy graves in the churchyard are among the reminders of those hardy first families of Virginia.

Towering skyward on Jamestown Island is a 103-foot shaft of New Hampshire granite that would have caused the colonial citizens to blink with astonishment. On the terrace of the Tercentenary Monument, erected in 1907 to commemorate the 300th anniversary of the founding of Jamestown, Vice President Humphrey was the featured speaker during the Law Day ceremonies on May 1, 1965.

It was appropriate that more than one hundred petitioners for United States citizenship should be honored at that time and place—at Jamestown, where the spring breezes might still carry the muted voices of other aliens who had volunteered to become Americans there on another May day in 1607.

The "melting pot" quality of the United States was apparent as Mr. Byron C. McAdoo, the Naturalization

Examiner, called the name of each citizenship peti-
tioner. There were solid-sounding names, exotic
names, dramatic names. From all over the world they
had come, seeking to pledge allegiance to the United
States but still retaining the names that were a heritage from their ancestors.

The Vice President, who was scheduled to deliver
the "Charge to Petitioners," was introduced by the
Honorable John C. Butaner, Jr., United States District
Judge.

In 1954, Senator Humphrey had delivered a major
speech favoring immigration reforms. Standing at the
podium in the warm outdoor sun at Jamestown in 1965,
Vice President Humphrey told the assemblage of new
citizens and their relatives and friends that "we welcome new human resources." The United States, he
said in effect, is enriched by new citizens with vitality
and a spirit of dedication and responsibility. As to our
sense of values, we are not opposed to honest, constructive criticism, but we disapprove of anarchy.

His voice was buoyant as he referred to Jamestown
as "History-land." He told the audience that the spirit
of the early settlers is still very much alive—that he
"keeps discovering America every day," as they surely
will. He emphasized that the nation is strengthened by
new people with a variety of backgrounds, skills and
ideals. "What you do with your discovery is important," he said.

Without pointing out that he was one of her American achievements, the Vice President was proud to
recall that his own mother was an immigrant to this
new land.

He had viewed the replicas of the three small ships that had been "tossed about on the turbulent sea" in 1607, and he marveled at the courage and enterprise of the people who had set sail in them. He spoke glowingly of all the settlers and frontiersmen who had built the mightiest nation in the world with their hopes and their hands, and he urged the new citizens to "dedicate their lives to making American history." Voicing new challenges in a land already throbbing with unbelievable manifestations of progress, the Vice President declared that there is still so much building left to be done. "Why, we haven't even barely got started!" he exclaimed with an engaging grin.

We do have freedom here, as in no other country in the world, but with freedom comes responsibility. "We must be prepared to defend democracy . . . and seek to expand the areas of freedom in the world."

In conclusion, the Vice President gestured toward a paragraph engraved at the base of the monument behind him on the terrace. This admonition to the early settlers of Jamestown, he said, is just as relevant in our modern America:

"Lastly and chiefly the way to prosper and achieve good success is to make yourselves all of one mind for the good of your country and your own, and to serve and fear God the giver of all goodness, for every plantation which our Heavenly Father hath not planted shall be rooted out."

Humphrey, who received an enthusiastic standing ovation at the conclusion of his address, had already looked backward in history toward Plymouth Rock and Jamestown in "The Cause Is Humanity," and commented, "Our country became stronger and more creative as each new wave of immigration reached our shores and contributed its own particular energies and traditions." He does not favor "totally unrestricted immigration," but he was a staunch supporter and one of more than thirty co-sponsors of Senator Philip Hart's bill which set forth "a formula based on equality and fair play for all nations," rather than the former discriminatory measures that are an affront to anyone who is not a "white northern European." He wrote, "The enactment of a sound bill now will help restore the image of the United States as a progressive, humane member of the international community. And it will enrich our national life through the infusion of new vitality, new cultures, and new ideas." The immigration reform bill was signed into law by President Johnson at the Statue of Liberty on October 4.

Feeling as he does about welcoming new citizens, it was typical of the Vice President to suggest that he extend a personal greeting to the guests of honor at Jamestown that day. After the Administration of the Oath of Allegiance, the Salute to the Flag, and a spirited rendition of "The Star Spangled Banner" by the United States Continental Army Band, the Vice President and Mrs. Humphrey took their places in a receiving line to shake hands with each new citizen.

As the people filed past, Mr. Humphrey expressed personal interest in each newcomer. He inquired about their countries of origin. At one point, he quipped, "When people hear I'm from Minnesota, they think I should get a visa."

He greeted a number of young men from the armed forces, already walking proudly in the uniforms of their adopted country.

There were some pauses while Mr. Humphrey posed for pictures with the new citizens. He loves children, and it was a time for fond parents to be proud of the attention their youngsters were receiving.

In spite of the wilting noonday sun, Mrs. Humphrey looked refreshingly attractive in a frosty-pink suit with a matching hat. The lovely "pastel lady" shared her husband's pleasure in the proceedings, offering her own congratulations with a gracious smile and an outstretched hand.

As the Vice President and Mrs. Humphrey began to move away from the monument area, the band swung into that familiar salute — "The Minnesota Rouser." Soon the new citizens began to depart too, to go their separate ways and "make their own history" in their new land.

At Jamestown, Humphrey sounded almost poetic about the beauty of the day and the historical grandeur of the Old Dominion. The United States has often been wasteful of her historical resources, but scholars, statesmen, and dedicated citizens have fought the good fight to preserve, restore and renovate large areas where patriots offered their honor and their lives for the cause of freedom. In Boston, in Philadelphia, in Colonial Virginia, and scattered all across the breadth of the land, are shrines that mark the birth and growth of a unique democracy.

Long before his Jamestown appearance, Humphrey

was boosting "America the Beautiful." When the President appointed him director of the "See America First Campaign," the Vice President was eager and more than willing. During an interview with Jack Kerr on television, he rhapsodized about everything from the majestic vistas to the economic prospects of "our wonderful America" in terms of underdeveloped tourist trade.

Much has already been said about trying to keep American dollars at home, to slow down the gold-reserve drain; but no one has been quite as persuasive as Humphrey.

His eyes sparkled, his voice vibrated, and the superlatives cascaded forth as he described the vast panorama of the United States in all its spectacular glory where there is enough variety for anyone—rivers, lakes, mountains, seasides, deserts, great grassy plains —"more beauty than you can find anywhere on earth." Set to music, that burst of eloquence might send Americans dashing to the nearest travel bureau for tickets to Cape Cod, the Rockies, the Black Hills, or the nearest dude ranch where the buffalo roam.

Not only did he ask Americans to start appreciating their own country, but he also stressed the importance of inviting foreign visitors to tour the United States. He noted that there are more than just scenic splendors here; we also have the finest hotels, motels and lodges with splendid conveniences for travelers.

"We need to 'beef up' the tourist business in this country," Humphrey continued. "Americans should know the Grand Canyon as well as the Pyramids. . . . They should try some of our hotels, instead of De Gaulle's." And, "Let's make foreign visitors want to leave some of their francs and shillings here for a change."

He made some observations about "stay-at-home Americans" too, quoting statistics revealing that a large percentage of people in this country have never been much farther from home than "the county court-house."

American tourism, to Humphrey, is a huge, un-tapped resource, and the country needs to get to work on it. We should strive harder to "sell" America as a great recreation land—a major industry that has been sadly neglected. Why have we done so little to promote tourism? Because human nature is like that—"Some-times you can't see the acres of diamonds under your own feet!" Humphrey exclaimed.

To show that the situation is improving, he noted that his home state of Minnesota used to be considered an "ice box" in the winter time. Now, winter sports are transforming it into a winter wonderland. Farm-ers are raising their incomes by converting their acre-age from surplus crops to skiing and skating resorts.

During that TV interview, and on other occasions, the Vice President has referred to the need for inter-national travel centers, with staffs trained to roll out the welcome mat for foreign visitors. In this area, Europe is ahead of us. In airline terminals, in large rail-road depots, in almost every bank in large cities abroad, it is a simple matter to have dollars converted into the local "coin of the realm"—for a small fee. The foreign visitor to Washington usually must find his way to the Riggs Bank downtown, when he wants to leave some shillings and francs here.

The Air France Terminal in the Invalides, in Paris, is an example of a sophisticated European tourism center. In addition to a view of the Eiffel Tower through the windows and the usual American conveniences, there is a multilingual information staff and a currency exchange department. Every hour there are double-decker Cityrama buses to take tourists on a three-hour ride through the streets of Paris. All the bus seats are equipped with individual "speaker systems," and the visitor may listen to a special commentary in his choice of nine different languages. (We always expect foreign visitors to speak "American.") Granting that Europe is a multilingual continent, it is interesting to note that one of the commentaries is in Japanese. In addition to the driver, there is a hostess who goes up and down the aisles inquiring about the comfort of the passengers and answering any additional questions.

These are the homey little attentions that have made tourism a big business in France. The three-hour bus ride, with brief pauses at many points of interest and a fifteen-minute stop at Sacre Coeur atop Montmartre hill, costs sixteen francs—slightly more than three dollars. Night life tours of Paris are considerably more expensive. The important point is this: all arrangements can be made at one efficiently organized international travel center, even on the spur of the moment between planes.

There are some attractive visitors' centers in the United States—the one at Colonial Williamsburg is superb. The addition of currency exchange facilities, foreign language experts, and imaginative tour promotion and advertising would attract more overseas visitors. Other new areas of employment are already being opened up in the field of outdoor recreation. According to the latest survey by the Interior Department's Bureau of Outdoor Recreation, there is already an increased demand for architects, biologists, economists, geologists, historians, and even therapists.

Sleepy little villages and depressed ghost towns are being transformed into picturesque historical shrines. True to the words that were sung more than one hundred years ago, "John Brown's . . . soul goes marching on" in the breathtaking beauty of Harper's Ferry, West Virginia, where scores of scholars, carpenters, architects, and National Park employees have been busy recapturing the historical atmosphere that will lead the tourist down the precipitous little street to the foundation stones of the arsenal where the famed abolitionist made his last stand. Between exploring the quaint old streets and climbing to the heights of Jefferson's Rock to see the Potomac and Shenandoah rivers mingling their waters far below, a lively family of tourists will find their day gone much too soon.

This is what Hubert Humphrey means when he speaks of "Our Beautiful U.S.A." When the nation's Number One Tour Promoter said, "Travel and Tourism is our Gold Rush in 1965!" it was just the start. He knows that every other country in the world would enjoy capitalizing on the variety of historical and scenic charms that Americans have been taking too much for granted.

Chapter Eighteen

The Great Society Moves Ahead

My favorite luncheon companion at the Capitol "Refectory"—where they serve Famous Senate Bean Soup and Famous Senate Apple Pie—is Grace Tully. I do not like Grace merely because she was Franklin D. Roosevelt's private secretary through all the amazing years from 1933 right through that day of international bereavement in April 1945. I like her because she carries her spectacular memories so gracefully and seems so unaware of all the attributes that make her a great lady. Of her fascinating book, "F.D.R., My Boss," she says, "Nobody read it anyway." I love her warm, natural sense of humor—she who has been around some of the world's wittiest and wisest leaders, including F.D.R. and Sir Winston Churchill and still gets her picture in the paper being "smooched" by L.B.J. If anyone thinks that history is not repeating itself, it says on page 4 of Grace's book that billboards were one of F.D.R.'s "pet peeves" when he went riding on the highways.

Shortly after my return from Jamestown, I told

Grace that I had enjoyed going through the Vice Presidential "receiving line" with the new citizens that day —as an "ambiguous alien" from South Dakota—but that it had been disconcerting to have all those security officers breathing down my neck. (Naturally we are all glad that they are so vigilant.)

Grace said that even the Vice President had difficulty getting used to the idea that those Secret Service men were legally and irrevocably "fastened" to him— and that he couldn't politely request them to leave him and do something else. On a chilly February day in 1965, when she was leaving the Capitol, the new Vice President of the United States came rushing out—he doesn't walk when he can run—and gallantly offered her a ride. She suddenly found herself in his limousine, being introduced to a number of gentlemen who had crowded inside with them. Evidently the hatless, coatless Vice President was not planning on a long trip. The limousine halted quite soon, and Mr. Humphrey jumped out. He called over his shoulder, "You gentlemen take care of Miss Tully and see that she gets where she wants to go," and he went dashing toward a near-by government building.

Grace laughed. "Did they take care of me? They did not! They piled out of that car so fast—and went streaking after Hubert Humphrey." Fortunately the chauffeur was still at the wheel.

President Johnson did not choose a man who would get bogged down, fainthearted, or panicky under a heavy load of responsibility. Humphrey has his weary moments, but he recovers fast. In only a few short months, he had involved himself with sheer exuberance in every aspect of the Administration program. Fletcher Knebel, writing with rhetorical zest about the vivacious Humphrey personality in "Look" magazine for April 6, 1965, described him as the "Advance Man for the Great Society" and vouched for the spirit-tingling impact of his speeches:

"As he nears his 54th birthday, vibrating like an electric band saw, the man all Washington calls 'Hubert' has become the all-American antidote for tired blood. You feel run-down, drippy, lethargic? Catch Hubert on the late news show. You are worried, fretting over Red China, Vietnam, the Congo, with nameless chest pains and achy bones? Listen to Hubert's next luncheon speech. He tones the muscles, quickens the blood, buoys the spirit. In adman's lingo, with apologies for syntax, he makes you feel good like a Vice President should." No wonder everyone wants to know Hubert's brand of vitamin tablets!

When the effervescent Mr. Humphrey glories in his role as an American statesman at this time in history, it is not superficial bombast. In spite of some "negativism" to the right and the left, the Great Society is marching through the heartland of America the Beautiful with all its "positive" banners flying. Humphrey keeps saying, "What an age to live in!" How can he help feeling those surges of exaltation when he sees so many people of good conscience—Republicans as well as Democrats—falling into step with Great Society goals? The Great Society is not for political partisans—it is for people, for the Family of Man. Never before in history has a nation talked of banishing hunger and illiteracy and disease on a world-wide scale, and Humphrey glows at the thought of being Vice President of a country that has reached such heights of moral responsibility. He is radiant about the domestic economy and the programs that will make American democracy work, if Americans will work for democracy.

He likes to think of American humaneness as an integral part of the progressive picture, to point out that "we have released human creative talent to a greater degree than ever before in history" and that "we need to prove that human brotherhood, under freedom, has more power to fire the imagination of people of the world than any purely materialistic system. Viewed in these terms, brotherhood has never before been so strong a requirement for our national security."

Terms like "human brotherhood" were not considered worth a nickel on Wall Street, five or six years ago. It has been said that Humphrey uses many cliches and trite phrases of that type. It depends on the way you look at it. We are finally reaching a peak in our personal consideration of "The Family of Man." Scientists have forged ahead, with single-minded purpose, in just a few recent decades; but mankind has been creeping along for two or three thousand years in the field of human relations. Humphrey's cliches about brotherhood and democracy and individual freedom are finally beginning to take hold, to be felt worthy of realistic consideration. The time is ripe for the country and the world to hear those eternal verities again, that they may bear fruit in our generations.

There is much affection in the Humphrey family,

and the month of May 1965, was a time for family happiness. The proud grandfather again, Vice President Humphrey held his one-month-old granddaughter in his arms to show her off to photographers in Minneapolis on May 9. Amy Fay is the third daughter of Mr. and Mrs. Bruce Solomonson. During that same trip back to their "home country," Vice President and Mrs. Humphrey flew on to Huron, South Dakota for a Mother's Day visit with Mrs. Hubert Humphrey Sr.

The Vice President sported his widest grin on May 27, when he and his wife Muriel posed for his 54th birthday picture at the White House. Even though he was born in 1911, Hubert laughingly kept insisting that he is 37. With typical Humphrey humor, he volunteered all the other numbers in his personal life: shirt size, neck 16½, sleeve 34; height, 5 feet 11½ inches; waist, 38 inches; shoes, 9½.

When reporters asked how he planned to celebrate his birthday, he said he would be working as usual. But he added with a twinkle, "I'm going to call up my mother and congratulate her."

Among the bits of whimsey in a biographer's notebook is an item from the "Washington Star" for June 13. Mrs. Humphrey was one of several distinguished ladies who were asked to recall their "most vivid fashion memory." Hers was a nostalgic "dislike" that many an "older girl" can share. The navy blue cotton bloomers and white middy blouses she wore to gym class were "simply horrible." Yessirree!

Shortly after the Inaugural, according to news stories, the new Vice President was "finding some doors closed to him" in the Senate. His routine was described as "full of ceremonial duties, hard work on executive matters, unaccustomed silence and political frustrations." It was reported that he had been "quietly excluded from meetings of the Senate Democratic Conference," which might come under the heading of "frustrations." Although Vice Presidents Alben Barkley and Lyndon Johnson had established precedents by presiding over conference meetings, there had been some strong protests by Senators who contended that as members of the executive branch, vice presidents should not officiate at legislative meetings.

At that stage, it was said that Humphrey was "relegated to the corridors," or had to visit his former distinguished colleagues in their offices. No one in America seemed to be in such a sorry plight as poor Vice President Humphrey. His quarters were not considered spacious or lavish enough, either. Evidently the Vice President could only hope for a "brighter tomorrow" —somewhere in the distant future.

Actually, Humphrey was soon bouncing along his merry way, calling the Senate to order with a sprightly rap of the gavel, prodding legislation in committees, keeping an alert eye on the civil rights and war-on-poverty programs, and acting as buoyant as a booster rocket about his chairmanship of the Space Advisory Council.

A few months later, Robert C. Albright of the Washington Post noted that Humphrey "mingles freely in the cloakroom with his new 'constituents'—all former colleagues—advising, counseling, cajoling, often just plain gabbing," and that he is "determined to live up to the President's own specification for the Vice Presidency."

After the Appalachia bill was successfully passed, the "President of the Senate" scribbled this note to Senator Jennings Randolph who had been the bill's manager: "Jennings: My congratulations. You have done a magnificent job. Proud of you. Appalachia owes you a vote of gratitude. Hubert H." This type of "morale building" is part of the Johnson-Humphrey team play, according to reporter Albright.

On one occasion, Mr. Humphrey told reporters, "As Vice President I have no power, only my powers of persuasion. So I do my best to make myself useful to all members of Congress."

Humphrey is even teaching new Democratic Congressmen, who were swept into office on the Johnson landslide, how to hold their "windfall seats." Faced with the traditional fact that off-year setbacks to the party in power have occurred in practically every election in the Nation's history, Humphrey is telling them how to make more of a "Great Society impact" on their constituents.

Until August 17, the Senate had not realized that its presiding officer was actually suffering from a secret frustration. During that evening session he shouted a resounding "No!" to record his first vote since he had become Vice President. The issue was a minor one that could be defeated by the 45-45 tie, but Humphrey was against it—and, besides, he hadn't had a chance to vote for months.

Mr. Humphrey's relations with Congress have continued to be many and varied. In July, he named six Senators to serve on a newly formed Senate Select Committee on Standards and Conduct. The bipartisan committee "is empowered to receive complaints and to investigate alleged unethical, improper and illegal conduct by Senators, Senate officers, and employees." In August, the Vice President appointed groups of Senators to attend international conferences in New Zealand, Switzerland, and Canada.

On July 18, Administration leaders had started organizing an urban-rural bloc to support a new farm program and the repeal of Section 14 (b) of the Taft-Hartley Act. Both were part of President Johnson's "high priority" legislation—which also included immigration reforms, aid to higher education, economic development, water pollution control and a saline water program. Would the Congress act on them before the end of the session, with tentative plans for a Labor Day adjournment?

Labor Day, 1965, came and went, but the Administration remained patiently persistent.

Vice President Humphrey was deeply involved in lining up support for the two pieces of legislation. On September 14, a huge new farm bill—which would continue major price support and production control for feed grains, wheat, cotton, wool and dairy products —passed the Senate 72-22. To show how complicated these things can get, the AFL-CIO announced it would oppose the measure unless the Senate struck out two provisions dealing with farm labor and wheat shipments to Russia. The farm labor section was knocked out on a hairline vote, with Vice President Humphrey breaking the tie. But the farm bill issue was still not "wrapped up"; the House had passed a slightly different version, and the conflicts would have to be smoothed out. This is just one example of the complexities of the legislative process—and the reason why national politics demands high-quality brain power.

The Vice President summed up his convictions about Congress in a recent speech at Syracuse University, when he said, "I have seen in the halls of Congress more idealism, more humaneness and compassion, more empathy, more understanding, more profiles of courage than in any other institution I have ever known."

As "a man of experience" in Congress, the Vice President eloquently defended the system of compromises by which legislation is enacted. "Through reasonable discussion, through taking into account the views of many, Congress amends and refines legislative proposals so that once a law is passed it reflects the collective judgment of a diverse people," he declared.

After two decades of agitated discussion and weeks of committee meetings and four days of debate, the "Medicare" bill had been passed by the Senate on the evening of July 9, 1965.

Friday, July 30, was the historic day when President Johnson, Vice President Humphrey and a number of Congressmen, journeyed to Independence, Missouri for the formal signing of the bill that would assure health care for the aged and also increase Social Security payments. The "Medicare" ceremony was held in the Truman Memorial Library, because President Johnson said he wanted to share "this time of triumph" with the former President who had sought unsuccessfully to promote a similar plan twenty years before.

Harry Truman said he was glad he had lived to see the enactment of the law which would provide dignity, not charity, "for those of us who have moved to the sidelines."

Observing his custom of signing major legislation with a multitude of pens, the President presented the first one to former President Truman. Mrs. Truman received the second one. The third one was handed to Vice President Humphrey who had "caught the ball" in 1949 and had been making various plays toward the goal line ever since.

Hubert Humphrey had cheered the Gemini 3 space twins at Cape Kennedy, and he was included in subsequent celebrations. One reporter noted that it was raining "Gemini crickets" as Grissom and Young, with the Vice President riding between them, received a rousing ovation in New York.

On March 18, Soviet Cosmonaut Leonov had been the first earth man "to take a walk in space." On June 3, 1965, the world held its breath and then chuckled at the antics of Gemini Astronaut Edward H. White as he cavorted around in space for twenty incredible minutes at the end of a twenty-five foot gold-plated tether cord. He enjoyed it so much that his fellow astronaut, James A. McDivitt, almost needed to coax him back into the capsule.

After having gone "into orbit," with tons of ticker tape and the cheers of millions of spectators in several major cities in the United States, astronauts White and McDivitt and Vice President Humphrey, and the wives of all three of them, flew off to Paris for the international air show. From the time of their arrival at Le Bourget Airport, where a Minnesotan named Charles Lindbergh had landed his "Spirit of St. Louis" in 1927, the Vice President took pride in the personality-plus performance of the Gemini 4 Space Twins. "They were the hit of the show," he reported.

Not long before, columnist Betty Beale had written that the Vice President was chuckling about Mrs. Humphrey's reaction to a newspaper picture of himself dancing (once) with Mme. Alphand at the Swedish Embassy party for Princess Christina. "His wife Muriel, who missed the party and was still out of town, telephoned him when she saw the picture and asked: 'Are relations with France so bad you have to give all that time to Mrs. Alphand?'"

The pursuit of "better relations" was continuing during the trip with the astronauts. Even though it wasn't another "Khrushchev talkathon," Humphrey described his visit with French President Charles de Gaulle, on the afternoon of June 20, as a "friendly, fruitful meeting." For the first time in many months, upper echelon lines of communication were open as the men discussed "a wide range of subjects."

Perhaps too many miracles were expected by people who forget that De Gaulle likes to perform his own miracles. There continue to be some sharp differences of opinion between the United States and France, especially on the handling of the Vietnam situation. In more than one nation, the United States finds itself in the peculiar position of being criticized by the very nations whose perpetuation of "the ugly practice of colonialism" has given rise to many of the problems that we are now expected to solve with efficiency and dispatch.

It is difficult to find a time when the Vice President has traveled merely for recreation. On a trip west, early in May, he toured the Twin Cities area and looked with dismay on the tornado damage inflicted at Fridley, a suburb of Minneapolis. Tornadoes had cut a path of destruction through the countryside, leaving thirteen dead and millions of dollars in property losses.

Going on to Cincinnati for a meeting with three hundred members of the President's Club, Humphrey paused to give his views about the military steps that had been taken to safeguard the Dominican Republic. He termed the West Indian island "essential to our security," noting that "Once before, we miscalculated on Castro."

Speeches at the White House, speeches at the Capitol, speeches at universities, speeches at conventions—as Vice President, the highly articulate Mr. Humphrey continued to be famous for his appearances on a great variety of platforms. It would be difficult to guess how many thousands of speeches he has made, both formally and as the spirit moved him. He has long been rated high with audiences who pay one thousand dollars or more for a prestigious celebrity on their programs, but he has often spoken for nothing to groups with which he has close ties or sympathies. Much of the Humphrey "fortune" was earned on the lecture platform. It was in the conservative neighborhood of $170,000, when Humphrey joined the other candidates in "opening his books" to public view before the last election. The main items included the two comfortable homes in Chevy Chase and Waverly, United States Savings bonds, stocks and bank savings accounts. When his philosophy of life is examined, it is obvious that Humphrey considers himself a "very rich" citizen of the United States.

Both Vice President and Mrs. Humphrey were featured in separate stories in "The Catholic Virginian" for July 30, 1965. Mary Tinley Daly's column, which is syndicated by the National Catholic Welfare Conference Feature Service, dealt wittily with the "Summer Sights" in Washington — especially the spectacle of tourists in "stretch pants stretched to the utmost, shorts and T shirts, bare midriffs, bare legs and bare or slightly sandaled feet, hair in rollers, sometimes not even covered with a kerchief," as the visitors go "trailing around in hordes to the most hallowed historical shrines of our nation, even to churches and cathedrals."

Mrs. Daly noted that, "Beautification of Washington, recently undertaken as a project of the present administration, is being propelled one step further by the wife of Vice President Humphrey when she urges that tourists to our nation's capital dress properly out of respect for the shrines they visit. Mrs. Humphrey does not advocate censoring of garb nor forbidding entrance to buildings and memorials to those inappropriately dressed. Rather, she hopes that the tourists themselves will sense this as out of tune with the purpose of their visit."

In the other story, the Vice President was quoted on his speech at the fifth White House Conference on Education, in which he said that schools can "help demolish the slums and ghettos." He urged that all levels of the American educational system—federal, state and local; public and private—join hands to make slum schools centers of educational excellence in our country."

Among the joys and achievements of July 1965, there was a somber interlude. Adlai Stevenson, United States ambassador to the United Nations, collapsed and died outside the United States Embassy in London on July 14. This time the Vice President flew across the Atlantic, with the United States delegation, to stand with bowed head at the casket and to escort his old friend home.

After the initial shock, Americans affectionately recalled the way Stevenson had "stood up to" the Soviet Ambassador in the United Nations during the Cuban missile crisis, asking, "Do you, Ambassador Zorin, deny that the U.S.S.R. has placed and is placing medium- and intermediate-range missiles and sites in Cuba? Yes or no?" There had been considerable hedging and sidestepping by Zorin, and then the disdainful reply, ". . . I do not wish to answer a question that is put to me in the fashion that a prosecutor does. In due course, sir, you will have your reply." That was the moment when Ambassador Stevenson shot back his famous remark, "I am prepared to wait for my answer until hell freezes over, if that's your decision."

"CBS Reports," with Eric Sevareid as transoceanic host from London, payed tribute to Ambassador Stevenson on the evening of July 19. Lively recollections of the man of "humility and conscience" sparkled from TV screens as four distinguished guests and their equally distinguished commentator spoke with affectionate nostalgia, but not with grief, about the wit and wisdom that had made the late Ambassador to the United Nations a beloved international figure.

The Prime Minister of England, Harold Wilson, recalled that Stevenson was a great human being as well as a great intellectual—that he was delightful with young people, and that he loved a rose named "Peace." The Prime Minister felt that Stevenson should have been born in England, where he was especially admired and might have been more properly appreciated in Parliament.

Secretary of Labor W. Willard Wirtz spoke eloquently of Stevenson as a fellow Illinoisan whose welfare programs and integrity in politics had brought him worldwide acclaim as Governor of Illinois.

Among the many sage observations of poet and playwright Archibald MacLeish, who gently referred to himself as "another egghead," were some of the most penetrating words of the evening. "He had the courage of his doubts." Stevenson, the master of elegant rhetoric, would have been fascinated with that "capsule biography."

Each participant paid tribute to Stevenson's noble quest for world peace—as though it were indeed a Holy Grail—in the councils of the United Nations since he assisted in its founding in 1945.

The CBS salute to Ambassador Stevenson was a sublime demonstration of Vice President Humphrey's transition from "a talkative politician" to an "articulate statesman." After years of practice, his mature eloquence was more than equal to the Telstar company he was keeping that night. His face glowed with delight as he recalled many convivial hours spent with the recent Ambassador to the United Nations.

Humphrey emphasized that there was nothing ponderously erudite about Stevenson's intellectualism. "It was joyful. There was dash and gallantry to his 'eggheadism!'" He had made intellectual statesmanship more than respectable; he had inspired warm human affection as a "pioneer in ideas"—as a statesman "who gave character to the American voice." The late ambassador had possessed the rare ability to play a happy dual role with grace and finesse—to be a "private intellectual" who also radiated a "sense of public happiness."

It was apparent that the Vice President was not wondering what Ambassador Stevenson had thought of him. During the program, he was "caught unawares" by Eric Sevareid who had talked late with Stevenson in London on the night before his death. It was almost as though Stevenson were with him again, when Sevareid quoted him as having said, "Hubert's my buddy!"

Humphrey, deeply moved, responded with a smile that blended boyish pleasure with humility. Perhaps that spontaneous reaction was the finest tribute Ambassador Adlai E. Stevenson could ever receive.

Chapter Nineteen

The Positive Liberal

It is difficult to explain modern American politics to our foreign friends, mainly because there are strong blocs of conservatives and liberals in both of our major parties. In "The Cause Is Mankind," Humphrey traces the development of liberalism through its period of enlightenment and stagnation from the dawn of recorded history. Liberalism, he notes, did not fulfill its social obligations in Europe, and its influence gradually declined. In the 1964 election in England, the Labor and Conservative parties were strongest, with the Liberal Party gaining only a handful of seats in Parliament.

In the United States, in 1960, neither Presidential candidate was a "reactionary conservative," and the election was a close one.

"Authentic liberalism inspired President Kennedy; it inspires President Johnson; it inspires me," the future Vice President said, just before the 1964 election.

In 1964, except for the man who was chosen to represent the Republican Party, almost every major Republican candidate was a "Lincoln liberal." However, the major portion of the Democratic Party has been going through an evolutionary process; it has come around a corner in history and found itself marching right alongside of Abraham Lincoln. During the 1950's, World War II was a prime preoccupation with Americans. In the 1960's, with the spirit of the Civil War Centennial sweeping over the country, Americans of good conscience were asking themselves, "Have we accomplished enough in the field of human rights during the past one hundred years?" Barry Goldwater, the 1964 Republican Presidential candidate, said, "Yes." Democrat Lyndon Johnson said, "No," and the American people agreed with him by a landslide.

Today, many liberal Republicans might appreciate this story more than the Democrats do. In "The Cause Is Mankind," Humphrey wrote, "Because they concern themselves thoughtfully with unique problems, liberals often disagree. Once, when he was asked why the conservatives always seemed united and the liberals divided, F.D.R. remarked that the answer was simple: 'There are many ways of going forward, but only one way of standing still.' "

The new Liberalism often wears a pin-striped or gray flannel suit, or the neat black of the clergy. The "moderate liberalism" of the Great Society, according to Vice President Humphrey, recognizes that a second car and power mowers and dry martinis are not enough. "We stand for the dignity and fulfillment of individual man and woman We stand for the chance for each man to make something better of himself. We stand for free speech and government of the people. We stand for peace without conquest."

In victory and defeat, especially in defeat, Humphrey has often looked at his loyal friends and said, "You are good people." He likes good people, and he does not mind being called a "do-gooder" himself.

In "The Cause Is Humanity," Humphrey explored the extreme-negative forces that confront the human rights reformer. "We now have active in our country a small minority of the extreme, or radical, right. Its members are against civil rights, against the fluoridation of water, against disarmament, against, against, against—really against people, I suppose. They see evidence of sinister conspiracy behind all such causes. The civil rights movement is an effort to 'mongrelize' the race. The United Nations is out to take away the sovereignty of the United States. Fluoridation of water is a part of a plot to weaken us for the communist 'takeover.' The last four Presidents of the United States are supposed to have been in some way part of the Communist conspiracy—either duped by it or willing or unwilling accomplices of it. Those who have this view of life suffer, I fear, from acute detachment from reality. Their fanaticism is as disturbing as the fanaticism of the extreme left was in the 1930's."

Humphrey cautions us not to waste our valuable energy by indulging with fanatic witch-hunters in orgies of desperation and hatred. "The best way to handle the fanatic or extremist is to avoid his tactics and to keep the faith in democracy that he lacks."

A few of Humphrey's ultraliberal colleagues are

disgruntled to see that he is sincerely dedicated to President Johnson's pro-business and international military policies. The Vice President is happy that American big business is forging ahead to set dynamic records for widespread, long-term prosperity. This is a sign of a healthy economic and political atmosphere. The logic of the old debater is present in Humphrey's concept of Great Society goals. Without prosperity, it would be impossible to wage a "war on poverty." This is liberalism in the Great Society tradition.

Mr. Humphrey continues to be interested in business, both big and small. Early in the summer, when he spoke to the American Society of Corporate Secretaries at White Sulphur Springs, West Virginia, he predicted that the U. S. economy can continue healthy and prosperous under "the evolving private-public partnership." He declared, "This Administration is committed to the principle of maintaining sound economic expansion in balance with our economic needs," and he warned both business and labor against actions which might bring about a wage-price spiral. The export picture looked good, he said, and a favorable trade balance of eight and one-half billion dollars might be achieved by the end of the year.

He keeps sounding notes of caution. When he commended employees of the Agriculture Department on their economy drive, he said, "We have great wealth, but it isn't unlimited. We must be ready to fight waste and inefficiency. . . . Every dollar must be put to good use."

On August 19, Vice President Humphrey presented a forty-thousand-dollar check from the Greater Pitts-

burgh Capital Corporation to David B. Shaaf, president
of Gateway Building Products Company of Pittsburgh.
The ceremony marked the 800 millionth dollar invested in small firms under the Small Business Investment Act of 1958, which was co-sponsored by Senator
Humphrey of Minnesota.

The Vice President believes that some of the more
critical members of ADA, which was founded to preserve democratic freedom, should understand why the
United States is remaining in South Vietnam. He has
become an authority on the Vietnam situation. The
only man in the country who could pronounce Khrushchev's name correctly is now pronouncing "Vietnamese
tongue-twisters" just as fluently, as though he has
memorized the map and the positions of all the American units there. By nature both President Johnson and
Vice President Humphrey are very reluctant "men of
the sword." They are "plowshare men" who would
rather be "waging the peace" and getting on with re-
lieving the misery of the world.

In "The Case for the Democratic Party," in "Saturday Review" for October 31, 1964, Hubert Humphrey
pointed out that "it was the United States that took
the lead in proposing the treaty prohibiting nuclear
tests. . . "

Exploring the situation farther, he wrote, "Unilateral disarmament would fatally impair the security
we must maintain to insure the peace. Unilateral initiative is something else. One example of this is our
creation of the Arms Control and Disarmament
Agency, the first such agency established by any nation in history. Its highly specialized staff has done

monumental work in coordinating the complex and interrelated efforts to protect national security and maintain a viable foreign policy at the same time as we look to a reduction in arms. Such work is imperative, but it will take time."

In "The Cause Is Humanity," Humphrey deplored the fact that the world is not yet ready for peace. "Force is present in the world. The only tenable position of a liberal is that despite reluctance to use it unless all other courses are exhausted, one must still be prepared and willing to use force. Only force itself —and the willingness to use it swiftly, powerfully and courageously — can maintain a free government in power when subversion and terrorism are used against it."

But he notes that military force alone is not enough. Military advisers, in a country like Vietnam, are asked about the needs and aspirations of the people "so that we can devise programs and policies that will aid those people and give them the will to fight."

Early in June, Humphrey spoke for most of the "moderate liberals" when he said that he had been deeply concerned over U. S. involvement in Vietnam. Now he strongly supports the kind of action that President Johnson has found it necessary to take there. "I'm still concerned, but I know what we're doing is what we have to do," he said. He is amazed at the bravery of the South Vietnamese whenever he thinks of "the losses they've suffered, the incredible losses, and the terror that has been inflicted upon them." Anti-Vietnam demonstrators do not realize what would happen to those people if United States forces were withdrawn.

Shortly after the Dominican crisis, Mr. Humphrey predicted more Communist revolutionary probes of that type. We must be braced for some time to come, according to Humphrey, "to have the Communist forces in the world test us every place where there is any weakness or possibility of success."

The Vice President cannot resist being a "teacher." Teddy Roe tells of the day recently when Mr. Humphrey was giving a group of Minnesota ladies "just five minutes" of his precious time on a tour of the Senate chamber. A half hour later, with his schedule fouled up for another day, he was just winding up the most comprehensive "lecture" on the history of the Senate and the legislative process that Teddy had ever heard.

Even though he has this little "idiosyncrasy" of being late, the Vice President always makes up for it after he gets there. That was the case when the Honorable Hubert H. Humphrey spoke at the International Platform Association convention in Washington early in August. No one seemed restless about waiting for ten or fifteen minutes; there was a feeling of rapt anticipation in Sheraton Hall—and, besides, most of the members were delivering "speeches" to each other while they waited. (The IPA is a professional association of people engaged in the lecture, concert and entertainment field. The address of one of the members is listed simply as "The White House, Washington, D. C.")

There was a standing ovation when the Vice President arrived. At first glance it looked as though he had brought Drew Pearson with him. When he referred to

Pearson as "the greatest booking agent in the place," it appeared to be the other way around.

The "grand champion" of public speakers was instantly aware that this audience of speech-makers, writers and artists was "with him." He chided the IPA for working its way down from "the grand climax." The President had left him to go out to the Rose Garden, the previous morning, to talk to the IPA visitors—so, he said, "I flew down to Florida and made some speeches of my own."

Often the Vice President ignored his notes, jumping from subject to subject with rapid-fire bursts of humor, common sense and eloquent expressions of idealism. He was not making a speech—he was talking and confiding, in a stimulating atmosphere of camaraderie.

Laughing about people who speak glowingly of "the good old days," he burst out, "The best days I've had started this morning!" He told about the fellow who had accused him of being ambitious. He had fired right back, "Is that un-American?"

He says he thinks of Democracy in terms of three Ds'—Discussion, Debate, Decision. "Discussion" involves the right to be heard, and "Debate" explores the strength of an issue. "Decision" is an important characteristic of Democracy; our form of government provides leadership capable of making a decision, after discussion and debate have gone on too long or have reached a deadlock.

The Vice President noted that the Job Corps, during the late summer of 1965, was being subjected to the same blasts of critical fire as the Peace Corps had suffered during its difficult early months. The cost of training and rehabilitating the young Job Corpsmen was not worth the price, critics were saying. The dropout rate was around twenty per cent, and that was considered shocking — but not to Humphrey. He pointed out that all of those recruits from the crowded tenements and hot pavements had been dropouts in the first place. His eyes glowed with pride in the eighty per cent who are staying with the Job Corps, whose lives are being salvaged and whose futures are looking brighter every day.

Referring to it as "operation catch-up," Humphrey said that the Head Start program would keep expanding. During its first summer, nearly 560,000 preschoolers attended 13,500 Head Start Centers in 2,500 American communities. These very young people, from culturally deprived homes, are being prepared to attend good schools without feeling uncomfortable.

Humphrey gives transfusions of optimism in his speeches. In spite of all the upheavals in the modern world, he considers this an "age of miracles." The word "revolution" does not alarm him. "All change is a bit untidy," he insists, looking beneath the turbulence of restless nations to see mankind groping for freedom.

Of the prolonged American involvement in South Vietnam, he said, "We can't build peace on quicksand," and he spoke also of other enemies and impediments to progress. "We now know that the greatest enemies are disease, illiteracy, and poverty—we are finding the cures and developing the tools to fight the war that warps men's minds and bodies. Mankind is going to win."

With evangelistic fervor, the Vice President compared the building of a new world to the erecting of a magnificent cathedral. The world cannot be changed overnight; each new generation must contribute its own building blocks — its chapels and spires and stained glass windows. As he looked ahead, Humphrey also looked backward to previous accomplishments. "Why, Washington was a cow pasture one hundred and fifty years ago, and even the Capitol wasn't much of a building!"

He declared that only the strong and powerful are willing to talk about their weaknesses. "We are powerful, but our conscience bothers us," he noted. Because we are a spiritual people, we worry about our neighbors. That, Humphrey emphasized, is the difference between our democracy and other forms of government. "We have an awareness of relationship between man and man, and man and God." This, he let it be known, will be our ultimate salvation.

The distinguished speaker was still going strong when he was summoned back to the Capitol for an unexpected vote on the Dirksen amendment to the reapportionment bill.

It was a longer speech than is customary for the Vice President these days. In some instances he is not the same man—this Humphrey who used to respond to reporters with a full-length dissertation at the drop of a question, and who now sometimes answers almost brusquely, "No comment." With a straight face yet.

When the Vice President addressed the convention of the Virginia Municipal League at Virginia Beach, he received a "tremendous ovation" in a state that is looking forward to a surge of economic progress, without losing its Old Dominion charm. He said that localities must cooperate with the federal government to speed the solution of such problems as education, housing, poverty and racial discrimination. Noting that the federal government now provides more than thirteen and one-half billion dollars in funds for state and local governments, he denied that the programs resulted in "federal usurpation" of local functions.

"State and local share of all government revenues has increased more than 114 per cent in the last twenty years," he declared. "At the same time, state and local spending have increased more than 682 per cent." He pointed out that "the federal debt has jumped 20 per cent in the last twenty years, but state and local debt has increased by a whopping 420 per cent."

The Vice President always enjoys talking to young people. When he spoke to more than five thousand student-Federal employees at the first White House seminar last summer, he pleaded with them to join the fight to bring about improvements in both political parties and to retain their ideals which he said were "the hope of mankind." He told them that politics is an honorable vocation and that those who enter public life must not be afraid of criticism, and must not worry when someone picks on them.

The Vice President believes that "the right to be heard does not include the right to be taken seriously." The annual convention of the National Student Association was told that student protests against racial discrimination have "indeed been worth taking seriously." Of the morale-weakening demonstrations against American efforts in Vietnam, and the "brutal, uncontrolled, destructive hoodlumism and rioting" in some of our cities, he said that it is necessary "to differentiate between constructive and destructive protest."

As a father and an admirer of the younger generation, the Vice President often writes understandingly about the problems of modern young people, and his article in the Sunday supplement, "Parade," must have given a boost to the morale of millions of them. "What's Right With Today's Youth" is an expression of faith. He tries to fathom the reasons for the unreasonable "excesses of youth"—"rioting, violence and crime." He discusses the precariousness of life in a world which can destroy itself and where "the detonators are in the hands of the older generation."

Our young people have known nothing but hot war or cold war. Looking toward the future, they see a rat-race in which "there are more people of their age than there are jobs to go around."

The Government and private industry have become alert to the need for Youth Opportunity Centers, and the Job Corps, Community Action, and the Poverty programs; and Hubert Humphrey has had many encouraging visits with young people whose involvement in these programs have given them hope for a "second chance."

As for the majority of young people, the Vice President wrote, "I don't find them a 'beat' generation at all, and I have met them by the thousands across this country." They are "less hypocritical, more frank than we were at their age . . . they are also more intelligent and competent. For this is the age of excellence."

Of the very young men in today's armed forces, the Vice President says that "Our generals and admirals agree that they are the finest young fighting men this country has ever produced, as tough as their fathers of World War II and Korea, more alert and adaptable and so more fit to use the complex weapons of the space age."

"I have complete faith in our young generation," Mr. Humphrey declared. "Whenever I am weary or worried, I seek out young people. . . . I have found them to be a tonic; they rekindle my spirit and sharpen my wits."

Humphrey's sense of social commitment draws no color lines; it operates in terms of people who are "having a rough time" just trying to live. The Vice President has voiced his deep concern for the blind, the crippled, the mentally retarded. He has saluted those who have helped themselves, and those who have given them the faith and encouragement to rise above their handicaps. At the conclusion of a speech to the National Federation of the Blind, they made him honorary president of the organization.

"There is so much to do," Humphrey says as he looks about him. Remembering all the day-care centers during World War II, he worries about youngsters who do not have proper supervision now. Recent figures show that there are five million more working mothers than there were during World War II, but there are facilities to care for only 255,000 children. The establishment of an adequate number of day-care centers would open another wide area of employment.

Women are included in Humphrey's commitment to equal rights. Recently he told a meeting of the Governors' Commission on the Status of Women that there is a need to utilize all of the nation's skills and talents —that there should be a "smashing open of doors that have long been fastened tight or rusted because of misuse."

The Vice President fixes an analytical eye on the entire social and economic pattern. In "War On Poverty," he described the worth of the Tennessee Valley Authority, with its electric service for 311,000 rural people for the first time, its transportation, irrigation and flood control benefits, and its economic influences, highlighted by statistics of this type: ". . . by 1963, some 870 million dollars in private capital had been invested in waterfront plants and terminals. The value of recreational facilities on and along the lakes passed 150 million dollars."

He believes that cooperation is vital in economic reform. "People who are against this sort of planning are really against federal domination—and in part, they are right, because the planning needs to be done on a joint-venture basis. Planners from business, labor and farm groups need to come together with men and women in government to make policies which will encourage investments and stimulate economic activity that will be of benefit to the nation. Planning for a region must take advantage of the knowledge and experience of those who live there, work there, and plan to stay there."

He told of the Appalachia "coal ghost" town of Hazleton, Pennsylvania. With the help of the Federal government, Hazleton raised money to build an industrial park in which fifteen new industries are now located.

He was opposed to a direct subsidy of eleven billion dollars a year to lowest income groups, even though a nation with a Gross National Product of well over 600 billion dollars could afford it (1964 figures). "We can no longer afford the shortsightedness of dogma and the stupidity of inertia," he declared.

He asked in "The Cause Is Humanity," "Can we provide the kind of education that will reach out to the dropouts, the illiterates, the unskilled, the share-cropper children, the slum children, and the bewildered children caught in the pressure-cooker atmosphere of the big city?" He believes that we can, "if we explore new ideas and new proposals, and if we are not afraid to try them. . . ."

The two former teachers at the head of the United States government are not stopping with the "Head Start" program for preschool age children. In the "Upward Bound" program during the summer of 1965, high school age youngsters from slum backgrounds made one and one-half years of improvement in reading in only four weeks. Many were accepted for their freshman year of college, an upward step that could never have been envisioned by their parents.

Now the President has appointed a group to investigate a "crash plan" for world-wide education—an "outward bound" program. This is a time to recall the success of the McKinley Administration in sending one thousand American teachers to the Philippines early in the century. General Carlos P. Romulo, our great Filipino friend, has referred to the United States as an "instrument and inspiration" in the founding of an independent democracy in the Far East. Obviously we cannot ram our ideas down the throats of other proud people, but we can try to "inspire" them. Humphrey does not believe we should force our form of government on emerging nations, as the Communists seek to do. He thinks they should be allowed the freedom to make their own choices—without being "gobbled up" by large totalitarian powers. That is why he recently advocated a permanent peace-keeping force under the direction of the United Nations. "Interdependence," he declared, "is a fact of our life and times."

On August 7, 1965, President Johnson signed the Negro voting rights bill into law. He told the Negroes of the United States, "You must register. You must vote. And you must learn, so your choice advances your interest and the interest of the nation." The crusade was moving ponderously forward, with a stronger grip to each piece of legislation. In 1960, Senator Humphrey had said, "I favor a law creating federal registration of voters where voting rights are systematically denied." And there it was, in 1965.

The President also established a Cabinet-level Council on Equal Opportunity to be headed by the Vice President. The Council will serve as a coordinating agency to assist Humphrey in overseeing the implementation of the new Civil Rights Act. In a letter to the Vice President, President Johnson praised him for "the skillful and fair manner" with which he managed the 1965 bill in the Senate and for "your long-standing commitment to equal treatment and opportunity for all without regard to race, color, creed or national origin."

When he visited Jamestown on Law Day, the Vice President also delivered an address at the College of William and Mary in Williamsburg. On the day of the Watts riots, one sentence of that speech comes back to haunt us: "We cannot expect to breed respect for law and order among people who do not share the fruits of our freedom."

Humphrey has often "maneuvered" behind the scenes to pour oil on troubled waters and avert impending catastrophes in troubled racial areas. He has reasoned with key officials, and has been credited with pulling the sizzling fuses out of a number of "powder kegs." But the Watts riots caught everyone by surprise.

As the smoke began to clear above the rubble of the desolated area of Los Angeles and committees of investigators moved in, it was learned that there had been procrastination in the setting up of poverty war programs in Los Angeles. At the time of the Watts debacle, it was the only major city that had not been able to meet the poverty war standards set up by the Office of Economic Opportunity.

The "social conscience quotient" for South Dakota has reached some noteworthy levels. Diane Walta, a graduate of Brookings High, and the College of St. Catherine in St. Paul, was the only white teacher in Riis School in the Watts section of Los Angeles at the time of the riots. She had given up a teaching position in one of the "more affluent sections" of the city to help serve underprivileged humanity. "The Brookings Register," on August 25, gave front page attention to Miss Walta's "inside comments" as she reported them in letters and phone calls to her parents in South Dakota.

"Scared but determined to complete her job," Miss Walta continued to feel that someone must help the Negro cause in spite of the horror of the riots. An English teacher during the school year, Diane was a swimming instructor at the Riis pool last summer. After the arrest of a drunken driver had touched off the holocaust, the teachers were ordered to their homes, and the school was occupied by the National Guard.

When Miss Walta returned to the area on August 19, she found "block after block of my old stomping grounds leveled and burned down. . . . Fortunately, none of the schools were touched." There are some middle-class homes, but she noted that most of the "Black Channel" is a "crowded slum area of illiterate, unemployed Negroes living in dilapidated houses with thirty per cent of the children coming from broken homes." Nonracial conflict has arisen "between the Northern Negro and the great number of incoming Southern Negroes who are bringing down the Northern Negro's reputation."

Miss Walta mentioned the accusations of police brutality, but she was also deeply concerned about high illiteracy, unemployment, and crime rates among the "poor and ignorant" in Watts. She believes that education is the key solution to the problem. Dismayed but undaunted, she still was able to say, "This is my job."

When the nation was jolted by that explosion of hate-spewing humanity in Watts, Hubert Humphrey was one of those who viewed the situation with mixed emotions. He agreed that the civil rights movement had been "stabbed in the back"—that the madmen on rampage had acted with negative disregard for their own future. In a column reviewing the wanton "reign of terror" in Watts, Drew Pearson reminded violence-prone Negroes of the many crusaders and martyrs who had supported the civil rights cause, pointing out that "the Vice President of the United States was almost kicked out of the 1948 Democratic convention for championing them, and that the President of the United States has passed more legislation for them than any other President since Abraham Lincoln."

The Vice President had voiced previous apprehensions about the dismal Negro "ghetto" situation, and the post-mortem would show that he kept his sense of proportion, even as he condemned the incredible destruction and carnage in Los Angeles. In a speech at the White House conference on equal opportunity, on August 20, he warned that "nonwhites, principally Negroes, are on the verge of a major economic crisis. For the gap is widening between Negro education and training on one hand, and the requirement of the labor market on the other."

He said that no single aspect of Negro needs can be

considered separately, but "nothing is more important to the Negro in his struggle to free himself from his circle of frustration than the ability to hold a good job. What can we expect when hope is resolutely crushed from the young, when there are no jobs even for the educated, and no homes in good neighborhoods even for the hard-working?"

Recently the Vice President saluted the American advertising industry's campaign to convince Negroes that "Things are changing forever," and that "Prejudice is going out of business." After one hundred years, they must be assured that "everybody is a first-class citizen" and that business is now prepared "to open the doors of opportunity to them."

When he is concerned with security matters and certain Administration policies, Humphrey conducts himself with almost austere dignity. In most of his speeches, however, he is the same lively Humphrey who "aroused Minneapolis from a great lethargy" as a young mayor. Now he has the whole country to arouse on behalf of the Great Society program. The Humphrey political personality cannot be evaluated apart from the New Deal, the Fair Deal, the New Frontier—and above all, the Great Society.

I was thinking of all the splendid publicity Hubert Humphrey gets these days, from some of the finest writers in the nation, and I said to Humphrey's former press secretary, Robert Jensen, that it's a far cry from some of the scathing political attacks that used to be launched against Humphrey in Minnesota in the old days. And Mr. Jensen said, "Well, everything has changed." It is the age of the "new consensus."

The wisdom of Roscoe Drummond is regarded with respect all over the country. In a recent appraisal of the Vice President, he noted that, "The President is giving Humphrey the largest opportunities ever given a Vice President to be ready to take up the Presidency," and that, "Humphrey is responding to these opportunities in ways that reassure those who work with him."

Mr. Drummond commends Mr. Humphrey on continuing to do his homework. "He puts in an eighteen-hour day nearly seven days a week. The light at his bedside never goes out until he has finished studying every scrap of CIA and other intelligence. . . . The Vice President has deliberately acquainted himself not only with the Joint Chiefs of Staff but with the second and third echelons of the armed services. He respects them. They respect him. They know he is neither soft nor appeasement-minded. . . ." As for Humphrey's present relationship with the business community, Mr. Drummond says that "businessmen now have reason to know that Humphrey believes profoundly in competitive enterprise and the profit incentive, knows how important risk capital is to growth and jobs and wants no animus between Government and business."

The Vice President always speaks of the President with healthy enthusiasm. He regards Lyndon Johnson as a "born and gifted leader . . . who knows how to be President, who can use power, and who likes his job. Even with all my glands, my extrovertish nature, I know who's President."

Humphrey used to be known as a legislator who

seethed with bright new ideas. Recently Steward Alsop described "The Heir Apparent" as saying "in his humorous, staccato voice, over a quick snack in the Senate dining room: 'You're not going to get any bright ideas from Hubert Humphrey—if I have some ideas I give them to Lyndon Johnson. There's no Humphrey program, just the Johnson program, and there are no Humphrey people, just Johnson people."

There is no question that Vice President Humphrey is an "Administration man." During the uproar about Arthur Schlesinger's suggestion, in his Kennedy biography, that John F. Kennedy planned to "sack" Secretary of State Dean Rusk, Humphrey said publicly that the charge was both "harmful" and "mischievous." He again expressed his admiration for President Kennedy's judgment and said that he would not have sent Rusk to appear before Congress so often if he hadn't had implicit faith in him.

Except for some complimentary remarks about Senators Bobby and Edward Kennedy, Humphrey has usually managed to dodge any future political rivalry between himself and the late President's younger brothers.

As for his own prospects, the Vice President said he would be happy to accept renomination in 1968, ". . . if the President of the United States feels that I'm worthy of it and if the Democratic Convention will follow his advice and members of the convention feel I'm worthy of it, why, then, so be it."

Chapter Twenty

Statesman in a Fabulous Era

While he was worrying about other people's housing problems, quite a few Humphrey friends appointed themselves "mansion hunters" for the Vice President and his lady. Hubert and Muriel have fond memories of rearing their four children in that comfortable home in Chevy Chase, but it is not equipped for elaborate official entertaining. Washingtonians who were close to the situation believed that the Vice President should be provided with a home that is second only to the White House "in appearance and elegance." In October, the Senate agreed, passing a bill to authorize one million dollars for the project.

Mrs. Humphrey admits that the Chevy Chase home was rather crowded lately during visits from the "grown up" family. Some extra members have been added. The Solomonsons, who live in Burnsville, Minnesota, have their three small daughters. Hubert Horatio III—"Skip"—who was graduated from American University and is now studying law at the University of Minnesota, is married and the father of a baby daughter. The second son, Robert Andrew, who underwent surgery for cancer of the lymph gland while his father was tied up with the last hectic week of the 1964 Civil Rights Bill, has made a successful recovery and is attending college in Mankato, Minnesota. Douglas Sannes Humphrey, who was born the year his father was elected to his first term in the Senate, is in prep school at Faribault, Minnesota.

All the Humphreys have been immersed in the excitement of numerous political campaigns, and they have done their "homework" with natural aptitude. Is there any indication that a "Humphrey political dynasty" might be shaping up? Not at the present time, according to a reliable source. One other member of the family is "in government." The Vice President's sister, Frances Humphrey Howard, is an official in the State Department's Agency for International Development. Mrs. Howard has a son and daughter, William and Anne, and lives in Arlington, Virginia.

The other sister, Fern Humphrey Gosch, is now Mrs. William Baynes. Her first husband was killed in World War II when their children, Diane and Ralph, were very young. Ralph was about a year old at the time. Perhaps one of the most charming things about the South Dakota relatives is their self-consciousness about being quoted, but I was fortunate to be in touch with a good friend who has seen Ralph Gosch grow up and who likes him very much. I am exceedingly grateful to Dona Brown, a member of the South Dakota Board of Regents and an educator and youth counselor in Huron, who passed some of Ralph's recollections on to me, with his permission.

Little Ralph spent much of his young life with his Grandmother Humphrey, and apparently they "adored each other." Ralph likes to recall all the summers he spent with the Hubert Humphrey family too, and to reminisce "about how Aunt Muriel was like a second mother and how, when he looks back, Uncle Hubert had been the father image to him."

Uncle Hubert gave Ralph a sense of security because "he could mend his toys or his broken friendships with the neighborhood youngsters when he came to visit."

It was great for Ralph to have an uncle like Hubert Humphrey. He never came to visit without remembering to have a little change with him for treats and a present for Ralph. "The neighborhood kids always rallied around, because they knew that when he came to visit they would be included in the treats and they knew that—regardless of how long it was between trips—Uncle Hubert would remember their names." This, Ralph told Dona, pleased and fascinated the kids.

As the youngster grew older, the gift money grew too, and even now—when Ralph is in college—Hubert never forgets to "slip Ralph a bill" for something special. His uncle has never forgotten Ralph's birthday, and he has advised him with major decisions.

Uncle Hubert already had a well-developed "Job Corps technique" when the youngsters gathered at the Humphrey home in Minnesota in the summer. "They would have the yard and boat and everything perfect —the kids thought." Along would come Uncle Hubert and tactfully show them what to do to make the lawn look like a park—pulling weeds, straightening a grass line, giving the youngsters a lesson in landscaping as he went along. Ralph said he was a perfectionist and loved to help the young people learn about boats and yard work. It fascinated Ralph to see his uncle spending his leisure time that way, as though it "rested" him.

When Ralph was married recently, the Vice President and Mrs. Humphrey had a delightful reunion with friends and relatives at the wedding. They seemed to want to talk to everyone, and most of the time they were carrying, or holding hands with, a little great-niece or nephew. There may be occasional differences of political opinion, but the person-to-person opinion from Huron is, "They are kind people."

Both Hubert and Muriel Humphrey "identify easily" with millions of Americans in all walks of life. When Muriel was busy with four youngsters, she said, "You can't be a good mother and a social butterfly too" —a sentiment dear to the hearts of most mothers.

Above the door in one of the Vice President's offices is the motto: "Let me not judge my brother until I have walked three miles in his moccasins." After that, as Humphrey has often demonstrated, you do not judge —you begin to understand. Before he became a college instructor, there was all the mileage of those paper-boy years, and he walked in the "moccasins" of a "soda jerk," waiter, clerk and pharmacist in the drugstore, and he knew his way around the farm country. Later he learned how it felt to be a janitor, a radio newscaster, and a New Deal vocational director.

He likes to recall that he was a country boy and a

small-town businessman. He still serves as "honorary president" of Humphrey's Drugstore in Huron, and he renews his pharmacist's license every year. On the wall of his office in the New Senate Office Building—along with the Four Freedoms Foundation Award and the Stephen Wise Award—are framed certificates of honorary membership in a number of pharmaceutical societies.

Also in that office are a bronze bust of President Kennedy and a framed copy of his Inaugural Address. Among the "lighter touches," in a trophy case, is a black "Hobo Day" derby from South Dakota State University.

American statesmen are history-conscious, even in the furnishing of their offices. How does it feel to visit the Vice President's "ceremonial room" across the hall from the Senate—to sit in his comfortable tapestry-covered chair behind his desk, looking up at "Teddy" Roosevelt's chandelier? It is a thrill; it is a time to wish the walls could "talk history" and to wonder how it feels to be a Vice President of the United States.

The formality of the chamber is softened by warm colors and the polished sheen of legendary pieces of furniture. When the Vice President looks up from his desk, he sees a fine old grandfather's clock standing against the opposite wall. Above it is the mirror that Dolley Madison brought back from Europe to hang in the White House. Her protests about paying duty on that item stimulated legislation that ultimately provided for the separation of the executive and congressional branches of the government and "equalized" the tax and tariff laws for everyone.

In the corner to the left is the handsome small desk used by Supreme Court Justice John Catron of Tennessee who served in the Supreme Court from 1837 to 1865. During the past century, only three other Justices have equaled or surpassed his twenty-eight years of service.

Above the desk is the bust of one of those "unidentifiable" gentlemen—a former Vice President named Henry Wilson. In a delightfully informative column entitled "Humphrey on History," Drew Pearson told of the impromptu "speech" that the Vice President delivered to his two grandsons during a visit. They were regaled with fascinating details about other features of the room, but Henry Wilson, a "drop-out" who never had a year of schooling and was a shoemaker's apprentice as a boy, received most of the attention. Humphrey admired both the eloquence and the incorruptibility of Henry Wilson who, as a Senator, had the most polished language and perfect grammar of any speaker of his day and was finally elected Vice President during the Grant administration.

"During and after the Civil War we had one of the most corrupt governments in history," Humphrey explained. "Henry Wilson was here at a time when the railroad lobbyists sat on the Senate floor beside their favorite Senator with bottles of whisky in their desks. But not one breath of scandal touched him."

The Vice President told the boys, "Somebody wanted to take that statue away, but I wouldn't let 'em. I have kept it there as an inspiration to young people."

According to their Grandfather Pearson, the Vice President gave the teen-agers some invaluable political advice. "If you ever get into government, beware of bureaucrats. Keep your contacts with the outside world. If not, you'll find yourself just seeing government people. Tell your grandfather to keep close to some of these high officials and shake 'em up occasionally so they don't get into a rut. The State Department will try to hem Arthur Goldberg in so tight that he'll be afraid to open a letter. They won't succeed because Arthur's a stem-winder. But the bureaucrats will try."

And now back to the Vice President's desk, where he is likely to glance up once in awhile at the glittering grandeur of the chandelier hanging from the ceiling —because it's practically impossible to miss it. President Theodore Roosevelt had liked his fresh air, but the night breezes made the chandelier tinkle in his bedroom, so he sent it over to the Vice President's office "to keep him awake." There is no Vice President less likely to go to sleep than Vice President Humphrey, but he is intrigued with the historical significance of that chandelier. A lighting fixture of that type would overwhelm a housewife in more ways than one; each piece of crystal must be removed and cleaned separately with ammonia and water to keep the chandelier sparkling, and it is a four or five days' job.

Swiveling around to the left in his chair, the Vice President can admire the rich coloring of the huge portrait of George Washington which Rembrandt Peale painted from life. The handsome canvas is currently valued at half a million dollars.

In back of the Vice President's chair is a colonial fireplace with a large mirror above it. There are several mottoes on the mantel, including a favorite one from St. Francis of Assisi: "Lord, make me an instrument of your Peace."

Not long after the visit to the Vice President's office in the Senate, that quotation from St. Francis reached a position of current prominence. The word had gone out that His Holiness, Pope Paul VI, would bring a message of "Peace and Good Will" from the heart of the Vatican to the representatives of mankind in the United Nations on the twentieth anniversary of the world organization. The historic occasion was saluted with a commemorative medal bearing the likeness of the Holy Father on one side, and the words, "Lord, make me an instrument of your Peace" on the other.

Pope Paul VI, who bridged twenty centuries of history with his unprecedented pilgrimage to New York, was seen by Americans as a pontiff who blended ecclesiastical dignity with a warm, magnetic personality. Americans of all races and faiths seemed touched by the aura of his presence. It was unlike any other weekday Monday, when the concerns of the market place usually dominate the minds of New Yorkers.

Leading statesmen traveled to New York to greet Pope Paul. The President of the United States conferred with him about world problems, and the Vice President and other American notables spoke with the spiritual shepherd of a flock that numbers more than five hundred and fifty million Roman Catholics. Because it is well organized on a world-wide scale, the

Catholic Church is in an influential position to help advance the social reforms pledged by Pope John XXIII and Pope Paul VI.

That afternoon it was felt that doors had been thrown open to a new age of enlightenment as the Pope paid "cordial personal homage" to the United Nations, calling it "the last hope of concord and peace" in the world. He looked beyond his "brothers" gathered in the General Assembly and spoke a plea for the millions of neglected souls—"the poor, the disinherited, the suffering, of those who hunger and thirst for justice, for the dignity of life, for freedom, for well-being and progress." They would be the beneficiaries of peace, when wealth and scientific talent could be turned aside from the construction of vast armaments.

Speaking with awesome authority, Pope Paul hurled forth the words that are the hopeful ideal of the United Nations and of all men of good will: "War no more! War never again!" And it seemed as though all of history had come together, through thousands of years of groping for light, at the crossroads of the United Nations on that extraordinary afternoon.

One grand climax followed another, during that week of October's bright blue weather. On the very next day, October 5, President Johnson announced casually at an afternoon press conference that he was planning to have an operation at Bethesda Naval Hospital on the following Friday. He sounded as though he had the utmost faith in his doctors, in his Vice President, and in the good behavior of his fellow citizens.

After the successful removal of the Chief Executive's gall bladder, the American sense of humor bounced back to normal. "What was the last thing the doctor said before he cut into the President?" a reporter asked.

"Scalpel," replied Presidential Press Secretary Bill Moyers.

If anyone wanted to be melodramatic, it might be said that Hubert Humphrey was "close to the Presidency" for a few hours on the morning of Friday, October 8. The Vice President did everything possible to diminish his own role during that crucial period. If he were needed, he would be there. He knew that the eyes of the nation had swung toward him immediately, but he conducted himself with unobtrusive equanimity. There was no furor about his being an "Acting President," even when President Johnson was on the operating table.

The President had chosen a week that was appropriately crowded with other momentous events. The World Series started a seven-game extravaganza on Wednesday, October 6, and the Vice President was at Metropolitan Stadium in Bloomington to throw out the first ball and cheer for his state's team. As Eric Sevareid pointed out, Minnesota could now boast an American League pennant winner, a Vice President, and the Guthrie Theater. As befitted a graduate of that section of the University campus, he gave Minneapolis most of the credit.

The out-of-town speaking schedule of the "jet-age statesman"—who sometimes talks to college students, farm groups, mayors' conferences and other organizations in two or three different parts of the country in a single day—was kept purposely light immediately after the operation. He kept himself available for frequent conferences in the Presidential suite in the hospital.

Both the Vice President and Mrs. Humphrey were happy to relieve the President and Mrs. Johnson of any public engagements during the convalescent period. On October 12, Muriel Humphrey was "pinch hitting" for Lady Bird Johnson at the first Dolley Madison award ceremony honoring Anna Freud, the daughter of Sigmund Freud, for her outstanding service to children.

The Vice President must have been feeling restless that day, because he went out and found himself an audience. He dropped in at the Convention of the National Association of Retail Druggists in Washington. In an impromptu speech lasting almost forty minutes, the nation's "most prominent pharmacist" told his "fellow druggists" to take a constructive, healthy look at Medicare. Humphrey recalled that he had begun attending the Association conventions with his father when he was a small boy in South Dakota. He brought first-hand news from the Presidential bedside that the Chief Executive was "well on the road to full and complete and happy recovery," and he beamed as he spoke also of the health of the nation's pocketbook at a time when it is "not fantastic to speak of a trillion-dollar economy."

When he referred to the record of the 89th Congress as "the greatest, most outstanding legislative achievement in the history of this Republic," he was among those who search for adequate adjectives to describe the legislative avalanche of 1965.

The record of the first session of the 89th Congress has been called "remarkable," "incredible," and "fabulous." Above all, it was unexpected, because President Johnson was something of an "unknown quantity" when tragedy summoned him to the highest office in the land. His first references to a "Great Society" were greeted with indulgent skepticism.

Early in 1964, President Johnson began telling Congress in effect that "Those things which are good for the people are necessary." He brought a broad range of neglected social reforms up to date as a foundation for the Great Society, and then he began to surge ahead in a manner that has dazzled his contemporaries. By his side, both as a Senator and as Vice President, was a man who had often fought for the same principles of human justice and a better life "for the least of these my brethren"—often in the face of ridicule.

Among the panoramic array of bills designed to advance the mental and physical standards of the nation are those dealing with voting rights—Medicare and increased social security benefits—immigration reforms—all the broad vistas of regional development — urban improvements — agricultural benefits — the war on poverty and educational enrichment programs all along the line—beautification, flood control, and air and water pollution control—transportation expansion plans—new hospital centers and medical research —military pay raises—and grants for the cultural arts.

The excise tax cut is contributing to the health of the economy. The political health of the country will be assured by the Presidential succession bill. No one can possibly resort to the old political tactic of referring to the 1965 session as a "do-nothing Congress."

Is the Great Society economically healthy for the country? It would be difficult to argue against prosperity. The stock exchange — the barometer of economic weather—barely wavered at the news of the President's scheduled operation before it headed upward again. He had taken the people into his confidence as though it were an "American family affair." The matter-of-fact reaction on Wall Street, where millions of average Americans exercise their capitalistic prerogatives, was an endorsement of Hubert Humphrey by investment-minded Americans, an indication of respect.

They had seen the Vice President's eyes sparkle during his speeches as he lauded the country's phenomenal record of almost sixty months of accelerated economic growth. At the rate we are progressing, he said jubilantly, the Gross National Product—which represents the measure of the volume of goods and services produced by the American economy—will soar above $667,000,000,000 in 1965.

For the sake of "comparative figures," the Gross National Product should sometimes be weighed in terms of the national debt, which was estimated at close to $319,000,000,000 at the end of 1965. When I was discussing these figures with John Stewart, one of the Vice President's well-informed assistants, he mentioned that the national debt has been well above half of the G.N.P. in some previous years. A check revealed that in 1955, for instance, the Treasury Department listed the national debt at $274,374,222,802. The Commerce Department figure for the Gross National Product that year was $397,469,000,000.

Are the Great Society social reforms good for the country? They are designed as a vast pattern for human progress. Currently they are being "tried for size" —with tucks and seams to provide for present adjustments and plenty of material for future expansion.

To put it another way, there is now more "science" in political and social science than there ever was before. The scientist in his laboratory usually knows his goal, but he needs to allow for a multitude of factors that might need to be taken into consideration as he goes along. Sometimes there are weary months and years of recalculation, of malfunction, of asking, "What has gone wrong? And why?" The conscientious scientist doesn't just crash his test tubes to the floor and walk away; he analyzes the situation and searches for missing ingredients.

The experiments in human progress go on in Washington, too, in what one commentator called President Johnson's "economy-minded New Deal." The civil rights movement has been making remarkable headway in the last few years, but the big city riots were reason enough to ask, "What has gone wrong? And why?"

In the Great Society program—where the "wrongs" may include the threat of inflation, sudden racial outbursts, exploitation of poverty programs by political "eager beavers," and misunderstanding of our international good intentions—patience and vision are demanded, day after day. As the Vice President says, "There are no pat formulas," but the goals are obvious. The Great Society is searching diligently for answers to the human problem in areas where it was once considered proper to let nature take its course.

There would be no Gemini program if space scientists were satisfied just to "coast along." We would still be back with the coaster wagon.

When Hubert Horatio Humphrey went into the Senate in 1948, he was dedicated to the belief that many of President Roosevelt's New Deal policies could ultimately be the salvation of millions of "neglected" Americans. With him, compassion was always in fashion, and he made no bones about saying so.

In surveying the bountiful harvest of humanity-enriching legislation in 1965, it was apparent that the President and Vice President had even more in common than the fact that they had both been country boys who had come up "the hard way" and respected each other's integrity of purpose. Above all, both men had shared the impact of the New Deal ideal. Undoubtedly that was the reason why Senator Humphrey supported Senator Johnson for majority leader in 1952 against the opposition of some of his liberal friends. The Vice President likes to point out that it was Vice President Johnson who backed him for majority whip in 1960 and that he "owes everything to him."

Even though his voting record may sometimes have

indicated otherwise, the tall Texan's sentiments must have been as closely allied with the New Deal as Humphrey's were, with some allowances for regional latitude. Humphrey likes to recall that in their Senate days, "I would tell him he was much more liberal than he realized, and he would reply that I was much more conservative than I thought I was."

In pointing out that Humphrey was publicly in favor of an up-dated New Deal type of program all along, there is no attempt to take any of the credit or glory away from the President. Obviously Lyndon Johnson is the most remarkable "fairy godfather" who ever waved an executive wand in the interests of a Great Society.

As the Vice President prepared to rap the Senate gavel for the second session of the 89th Congress, the President was still casting a reproachful eye at some leftover business—including the repeal of 14(b) of the Taft-Hartley Act, reapportionment of state legislatures, funds for the teachers corps and urban housing improvement, and additional minimum wage measures. Toward the end of the first session, certain blocs in Congress looked almost aghast at the wonders they had wrought. Had they been too cooperative? As long as they were passing the Administration's bills, it looked as though they would never get home. The first session of the 89th Congress adjourned in a spirit of belated balkiness, but nothing could dim the historic blaze of "faith, hope and charity" that was already illuminating the Great Society sky.

The opening days of the first and second sessions of the 89th Congress were notable for their contrast-

ing moods. That January day in 1965 had been devoted
to bursts of laudatory and seriocomical eloquence in
honor of Hubert Humphrey. His former colleagues
pointed out that their most loquacious member had
been promoted to a position in which he would be muz-
zled by the rule of "constitutional silence" imposed
upon the presiding officer of the Senate. Gone were the
days of lengthy, lively Humphrey speeches on the Senate floor! Senator Russell Long underscored the irony
of it all when he recalled, "It was Lyndon Johnson who
made the statement in this chamber that Hubert Humphrey was the greatest coordinator of mind and tongue
of any man in the world. The time it took him to pre-
pare a speech was the length of time it took to draw
a deep breath."

The first day of the second session, in 1966, was
somber by comparison. There were smiles and congratulations after the Vice President administered the
oath of office to the newest Senator, Harry F. Byrd Jr.
of Virginia, who had succeeded his father by appointment. However, the shadow of the heightening conflict
in South Vietnam was reflected in the prayer of Bishop
W. Earl Leddon of Washington's Wesley Theological
Seminary, as he spoke over the bowed heads of the
members of the powerful United States Senate: ". . .
We pray that in these days of mortal peril America may
be privileged to lift a brave, clear voice in the council
of the nations in defiance of terror and all tyranny,
and in defense of the things that make for peace."

At the turn of the new year, the President of the
United States sent his "Spokesman for the Great Society" on a Far Eastern tour to the friendly nations of

the Philippines, Taiwan, Japan and South Korea. While he was in Manila, he attended the inauguration of Philippine President Ferdinand Marcos. Manila is the home city of General Carlos P. Romulo—the internationally famous diplomat, military officer, author, and President of the University of the Philippines— who has recently been appointed Philippine Minister of Education. When General Romulo learned that I would be writing about Vice President Humphrey, he congratulated me, and added, "Humphrey is an intellectual more than a politician. I hold him in the highest esteem and he is one of my best friends in America."

Behind the ceremonial pomp of that tour to the Far East, the Vice President was conferring on a policy level about the increasingly critical situation in the neighboring country of Vietnam. Even though North Vietnamese PT boats had fired on American destroyers in the Gulf of Tonkin in 1964 and accelerated Viet Cong activity was noted, it had seemed as though "the freedom line" in South Vietnam could be held without large-scale American involvement.

Suddenly the citizens of the United States were aware that the Viet Cong menace to South Vietnam was no longer a "brush fire." American soldiers by the tens of thousands were being sent to fight an undeclared war on the other side of the world—in a small, unstable nation that had been part of French Indo-China until 1954. Americans were sharply divided in their opinions. The most militant "war hawks" called for saturation bombing of Communist North Vietnam, the power behind the Viet Cong, even at the risk of precipitating the United States into a war with Red

China. The "doves" argued with undove-like fierce-
ness that the conflict in South Vietnam was a civil war
and that the United States had no business trying to
control it. Many anxious civil rights leaders joined the
"doves" because they remembered that Negroes—no
matter how heroically they had fought on the battle-
fields—had usually been shoved back into the ghettos
after previous wars.

The moderates, which included the Administration
leaders, could not take refuge in "easy answers."
Theirs was the burden of anguish and soul-searching,
because it is not easy to send young American men out
to kill or be killed. They heard people say that South
Vietnam was a small, faraway country—that it was
ridiculous for American blood to be shed there. But
Czechoslovakia had seemed a small, faraway nation in
1938; at Munich, it had been considered prudent for
Prime Minister Chamberlain to concede Czechoslovakia to Hitler for the sake of "peace in our time."
After World War II, the Russians had pounced upon
one country after another in eastern Europe. The Chinese Reds have already outlined their expansion plans,
and Vietnam and the rest of the Indo-Chinese penin-
sula are high on the list.

Young Americans in 1965 and 1966 were demonstrating in a variety of ways. A small, conspicuous percentage picketed for withdrawal from Vietnam. A
much larger percentage signed petitions saluting and
supporting the troops in South Vietnam. The young
men who "demonstrated" in induction centers made
the most significant impact—one recent draft call was
cut more than 10,000 because of voluntary enlistments.

The sons of men who had frozen in Korea were step-
ping forward to "sweat it out" in South Vietnam. Were
these the "pampered young capitalists" of the Red
Chinese propaganda dispatches?

God willing that the world survives and prospers,
the history of the undeclared war in Vietnam will some
day fill many books. Usually the battlefront engagements were more sensible and orderly than some of
the grisly "human torch" spectacles on the home front.

While Americans anxiously pondered the grim
horror of guerrilla warfare in South Vietnam, they
were sometimes distracted by the fury of the "peace
doves" on the Senate Foreign Relations Committee
who were investigating the "validity" of the conflict.
Although it undoubtedly gave comfort to Hanoi, it
was a triumph for free democracy at home. Two Russians had just been sentenced to long terms at hard
labor for writing books that were critical of the Soviet
system. In the United States, when Senator Wayne
Morse disagreed most disagreeably about United States
policy, no one tried to ship him off to "Siberia." There
was some disapproval, but the patriotism and sincerity
of the "opposition Senators" was not questioned.

Chapter Twenty-one

Masters of the Future

With his startling talent for "springing surprises," President Johnson flew to Honolulu on the first week-end in February to confer with South Vietnamese leaders about the progress of the conflict and to give personal recognition to Saigon's ties with Washington. It was much more than a military conference. Humanitarian problems, involving specific plans "to defeat social misery" in South Vietnam, received a major share of attention.

The President capped the climax, on February 8, with the announcement that he would meet Vice President Humphrey in Los Angeles on his way home. After a briefing on the Honolulu conference, the Vice President was scheduled to join the South Vietnamese chief of state, Lieut. Gen. Nguyen Van Thieu, and Prime Minister Nguyen Cao Ky, and fly with them to Saigon on February 9.

At least one "fight promoter" immediately suggested that the Asian "social reform plan" was primarily a Humphrey project and that he had been chaffing to get at it. It was a splendid compliment, but it ignored the fact that President Johnson had often coupled his own peace pleas with pledges of huge sums for reconstruction and development of free nations in Southeast Asia. On the positive side, progressive commentators noted that Humphrey's trip could be interpreted as heralding a great new age of American foreign policy—of a "Marshall Plan" for underdeveloped Asian nations.

It is quite possible that President Johnson wanted to give the Humphrey personality extensive national and international exposure. When the Vice President scored disappointingly low in a recent Gallup "popularity poll," it indicated that most Americans were unfamiliar with his people-meeting qualities and his impressive record of legislative achievement.

Ahead of Humphrey on February 9 was the vast doorway to Asia and the South Pacific, and he and his party soared through it by jet toward the small, war-ravaged land on which the entire world was focusing its attention.

Although they had scarcely noticed its name in their classroom history books, South Vietnam had become the battleground base for more than 200,000 young American men. Almost immediately after his arrival in Saigon, the Vice President set out to visit military areas where he saluted the courage of American servicemen and thanked them for their sacrifices in the cause of world freedom. In a short-sleeved shirt, with a "baseball cap" on his head, he roamed about in a Jeep and told American GI's that the folks back home

were proud of them. Sometimes the smoke and roar of
battle were not far distant, but he kept his air of alert
respect and good humor as he awarded medals to combat heroes, toured the bases of allied units, and inspected military hospital facilities.

At First Infantry Division headquarters, where he
awarded nine Silver Star medals for heroism, he said,
"I want you to know that the American people are very
proud of this army and of what you are doing. We are
waging a war against aggressors and killers and against
the conditions which bring about communism. We are
going to win both."

Unmindful of personal danger in a country where
there are no guaranteed safety zones, Humphrey set
out eagerly by helicopter to see the countryside. He
visited schools, farms, and a village construction project which had been developed by young Vietnamese
students. As an example of promising reform measures
that the Saigon government had been sponsoring,
Prime Minister Ky took pride in showing Vice President Humphrey the large-scale rural housing project
at Phuthohoa.

Life Scout Humphrey demonstrated that Scouting
is international when he exchanged the Boy Scout
oath and salute with Vietnamese youngsters. An Associated Press reporter caught the "Humphrey spirit"
in a report about his visit to a village in the Saigon
area: "The exuberant Vice President talked with village elders and local chiefs, inspected a variety of improvements, shook hands, voiced a greeting in Vietnamese and joined in group singing."

When one little girl hung back bashfully from the songfest, Humphrey knelt beside her, took her tiny hands in his and brought her into the circle of Vietnamese toddlers. "One, two, three . . . one, two, three," he chanted, clapping his hands and bobbing his head.

On February 11, Humphrey sent back this word from Saigon: "I think the American people ought to know that there are two wars going on here, one military and one against poverty, disease and illiteracy." He found glimmers of hope in the reforms that had already been introduced, and in the attitudes of the people. "These people are magnificent. They are breaking away from old things and finding new ways."

During conferences with American military and AID teams from three provinces, Humphrey received optimistic assurances that the construction programs would be more successful in the future. Because of constant enemy harassment, stabilization had been difficult at the village level. The Secretary of Agriculture, Orville Freeman, was also in South Vietnam, examining crop prospects and possibilities for massive land reform programs.

The Vice President found the visit to Vietnam "reassuring." He said that "in the midst of human suffering I have seen the indomitable spirit of hope . . . I have felt the surging determination of the Vietnamese people." Out in the provinces, Humphrey noticed that some significant progress had been made in the social revolution. He knows that there is still so much to be done, but he is no stranger to miracles of human betterment in the United States—and he has the faith, optimism and imagination to picture a better world for all of mankind. To those who would say it can't be done, it should be remembered that Humphrey is a past master at pioneering bright ideas and "trying them for size."

Humphrey could see that South Vietnam needed immediate military, social and political assistance. "Every free country which cherishes freedom for itself should be making a contribution to the Vietnamese people," he declared. He asserted that he would have "no hesitancy in asking each country I visit and every ambassador I meet to help in meeting the humanitarian needs of this country."

From the sweltering heat of South Vietnam, to temperate climates, to snowy Seoul—the Vice President visited South Vietnam, Thailand, Laos, Pakistan, India, Australia, New Zealand, the Philippines and Korea during his two-week inspection trip. In all the deprived areas he toured, Humphrey carried the "Great Society" message of hope to people whose families had known nothing but bare subsistence survival for centuries.

While Southeast Asia was wondering whether the United States would adhere to its commitments there, Humphrey made it clear that Southeast Asia must bear its share of the determination and responsibility. He firmly outlined the desperate need for evidence of "partnership" policies—of an honest approach to a future in which freedom from tyranny must be built on a solid foundation of social-consciousness, of each man's concern for the welfare of his neighbor as well as himself. This philosophy must extend from free nation to free nation, if individual freedom is to be achieved and preserved.

The Vice President had not been sent to Asia with empty hands. He made specific pledges of economic and military aid to several nations, always emphasizing that plans for specific results must be forthcoming. Often he referred hopefully to the time when the roar of guns and the horrors of human slaughter would end. In Karachi, Pakistan, he told an audience, "My government has been and continues to be engaged in a most searching and intensive effort to bring about an honorable peace in Southeast Asia."

At the airport in Canberra, Australia, he told Prime Minister Harold Holt, "I see the United States, Australia and New Zealand working together with other nations of this area to build a better society for millions and millions of people of Asia."

Roving Ambassador W. Averill Harriman, who was with the Humphrey party throughout the trip, spoke of the "stimulating" impression the Vice President made in Australia and New Zealand and "his useful influence on each of the countries we visited." Both Australia and New Zealand have contributed to the war effort in South Vietnam.

Humphrey was good-natured about hecklers who demonstrated in some of the cities he visited—he said they reminded him of home.

Back in Washington, the "doves" were still arguing fiercely, and out of the confusion came a suggestion from Senator Robert Kennedy that the Viet Cong be included in a future coalition government in South Vietnam. This, Kennedy believed, might be the only possible compromise. With the sights and sounds of the conflict still desperately clear in his mind, Humphrey shot back the "quote of the month" from the other side of the world. The Kennedy proposal he retorted, would be equivalent to "putting a fox in the chicken coop."

Aside from its international implications, commentators interpreted the exchange as an inevitable political confrontation between two future presidential contenders.

Before returning home, Humphrey held meaningful conferences with government leaders in the Philippines and Korea. In the small, brave democracy of the Philippines, where the pro-Communist Huk uprising of the 1950's had threatened to become another Korea or Vietnam, President Ferdinand Marcos did not wait for Vice President Humphrey to ask for more cooperation in the present Asian conflict. He announced confidently that he expected the Philippine Congress to approve sending 2,000 engineering troops to South Vietnam, and he even spoke of sending combat troops. The Philippines, which is not a wealthy country, would foot the bill themselves. Korea, with American financing, volunteered to add more than 20,000 troops, which would double the number of South Koreans serving in South Vietnam.

On the evening of February 23, the Vice President arrived back in Washington after his 43,000-mile, nine-nation Asian tour. The President met him as he stepped off the helicopter that had brought him to the White House, and they hugged each other like a couple of long-lost brothers.

During a short outdoor ceremony, President Johnson assured the Vice President that "we think you performed a most useful and constructive service." Humphrey declared that he had returned to Washington "with a deep sense of confidence in our cause, and its ultimate triumph." He also said in effect that Hanoi was sustained by the conviction that Americans at home might grow "weary" of the war, but he knew that the troops in South Vietnam had the "force and determination to win." Afterward, Humphrey spent an hour privately briefing the President on the trip.

The next morning the returning diplomat conferred with several large groups of Congressmen at the White House. Afterward he told reporters that we cannot expect "any quick and easy solutions," but he said that plans to "defeat the Viet Cong" were strengthened by Saigon's new emphasis on "fulfillment of the goals of the social revolution." In the afternoon he held another briefing with about seventy-five members of the liberal Democratic Study Group, many of whom were "doves."

A key to Administration policy could be found in one paragraph of President Johnson's speech at the Freedom Award dinner in New York that night: "Washington will not impose upon the people of South Vietnam a government not of their choice. Nor," he continued, "will North Vietnam impose upon the people of South Vietnam a government not of their choice."

On the humanitarian side, he continued to leave the "peace and prosperity door" wide open with pledges of reconstruction and economic aid to North Vietnam as well as South Vietnam. Never before in history have the motives of a country been so good—and often so little understood by the people who could benefit most. Many underdeveloped nations have swung toward Communism in the belief that the United States wants to overpower them with what Vice President Humphrey has called "economic imperialism"—a modern form of "ugly colonialism" in which "greedy American businessmen" try to take over the industries and resources of a country with no consideration for the education or living standards of the people. There have been some instances of that type of activity and some "greedy native leaders" have compounded the sin, but there is evidence today that most of the free world is trying to close the door on that dark period of history and emerge into an era of humanitarian enlightenment.

The fierce and furious Vietnam debate, featuring an all-star cast of strange bedfellows, was still raging on Capitol Hill when the Ambassador for the Great Society returned home. In an outrageously funny column, Art Buchwald announced a "guessing contest" to determine the words with which the Vice President might have greeted the President during that homecoming embrace. Included among the possible entries was this one: "Please don't make me testify in front of the Senate Foreign Relations Committee."

On his first day at home, the "doves" held their fire and treated the Vice President with special congeniality considering that he disagreed with them

about the good-neighborly intentions of North Vietnam. Even Senator Morse delivered himself of only one
mild rebuke. It became obvio₠ that Humphrey was
being "saved" for a formal appearance before the Senate Foreign Relations Committee, but he politely declined to lower himself into the hot-seat at that time.

The Humphrey-Kennedy debate flared up again
when Senator Robert Kennedy suggested on "Meet the
Press" that the Communists "might end up in some
way or another within the government structure of
Vietnam either in the interim period or the final period." This, he believed, was the conclusion we must
reach if we were "honest and realistic" about nego-
tiating a peace in Vietnam.

On the same afternoon, Vice President Humphrey
answered the proposal on another TV interview. "If
we are really honest with ourselves, we would not
want a group to be able to shoot itself or shoot its way
into power. . . . The United States of America should
not be dictating to the peoples of South Vietnam that
their mortal enemy, that has killed their people,
burned their homes, destroyed their villages, assas-
sinated their village chiefs, should be a part of the
government."

The Vice President had just been in close touch
with scores of young servicemen in a terror-ridden
country in which the enemy murders civilians in their
beds, plants hideous booby traps, uses helpless women
and children as "camouflage," and is not even sickened
by its own colossal death toll. It would be difficult to
find an American serviceman in South Vietnam who

would use gentlemanly language at the prospect of letting the Viet Cong dictate peace terms.

On February 24 the House voted 350 to 7 to authorize $415 million in supplemental economic aid, $275 million of it for South Vietnam. There was no criticism of Administration policy during the House debate, but everyone knew that the "opposition" in the Senate would be waiting with a volley of protests.

The $4.8 billion Vietnam military authorization had been causing an uproar in the Senate for two weeks. On February 28, when the "doves" and "hawks" clashed heatedly, it was necessary for Senator "Mike" Mansfield to appeal for orderly debate. Considering the sound and fury—and the threat of further delay— the opposition vote proved to be negligible as the bill sped through Congress on the afternoon of March 1. The House vote was 392 to 4, and the Senate vote was 93 to 2. Many members made it clear, however, that they did not favor an enlargement of the war. This approach kept putting the Administration in a peculiar position. Nobody had ever wanted a war in the first place, not even a small one. To his critics, President Johnson kept asking, "What would you do?" Only the most fiery-eyed "doves" were in favor of deserting South Vietnam.

When the occasion might no longer be used for procrastination purposes in delaying vital funds for the soldiers in South Vietnam, Vice President Humphrey was agreeable about entering the Senate Foreign Relations "lions' den" for a private session which lasted more than three hours. This was "home territory" for him—as a Senator, he had been a member of the Committee for eleven years. The reports that emerged reflected much sweetness and light. Committee Chairman J. William Fulbright, a leading "dove," voiced his respect for the Vice President's vigorous answers and referred to Humphrey as "a very nice fellow—we all like him very much." The Vice President returned the compliment with a smiling assertion that the Committee had treated him "with fairness and respect and, at times, with kindness." However, the opposition members on the Committee still held reservations about government policy in Vietnam.

The Humphrey who came back from Southeast Asia was not a "dove" who had sprouted "hawk feathers" of indignation overnight. Vietnam did not appear to be a threat when he wrote in "The Cause Is Humanity": "Only force itself — and willingness to use it swiftly, powerfully and courageously—can maintain a free government in power when subversion and terrorism are used against it."

When he appeared before the liberal Democratic Study Group and other audiences of Congressmen after his return from Vietnam, he recalled some of his problems as mayor of Minneapolis. Gangsterism and Murder, Inc., had infiltrated the city. "But in cleaning them up, I did not invite them to participate in the police department." He declared pointedly, "The Viet Cong is not an Asian ADA. It's a well-organized terrorist outfit."

From his attitude about the Vietnam problem, it was apparent that the Vice President believes we must honor our commitments to humanity by protecting freedom and dignity, in South Vietnam as well as in the United States. As an ardent crusader for world disarmament and the pursuit of peace in the United Nations, he considers war a miserable business—but he believes that human degradation and enslavement of men's minds are even more intolerable in a civilized, progressive world.

As a political scientist, Humphrey is familiar with all our commitments, including SEATO. When Secretary of State Dean Rusk was interrogated by the Senate Foreign Relations Committee, he spoke at length about SEATO. The Southeast Asian Treaty Organization pact, which was signed in Manila in 1954 by representatives of the United States, Britain, Australia, New Zealand, France, Thailand, Pakistan and the Philippines, was considered an Asian counterpart of the Atlantic Charter. It was designed to protect the forces of democracy against aggression. For many dreary, hopeless centuries, native leaders had sought Western recognition of their rights to govern themselves as free people. General Carlos Romulo wrote of SEATO: "What a triumph for freedom this Charter!" The power status of some of the signatory nations has changed in the interim, but the important question for today and tomorrow is, "Has the threat of aggression changed?" As of today, Vice President Humphrey does not believe that it has. He has emphasized that Peking, rather than Hanoi or Moscow, is the principal culprit and that nations in Asia must join in planned unprovocative containment.

It has been a precarious time in history, with contradictions to the right and left. A number of authorities, who are now insisting that Red China should have been admitted to the United Nations long ago, are ignoring Red China's previous ultimatum—that Chiang Kai-shek's Republic of China must be ousted because there can be only one China in the U.N. So much for "simple solutions."

In Indonesia, where Communist educators in the government were instrumental in raising the deplorable colonial literacy rate, Communists have suddenly been liquidated by the tens of thousands. It could be said, "Let the Communists educate the people of Asia and Africa—as soon as they learn to think for themselves, they will insist on free elections, free speech, and perhaps even free enterprise." But it hasn't quite turned out that way in Russia and China.

In the former Gold Coast State of Ghana, the "lifetime presidency" of Kwame Nkrumah was suddenly interrupted, and demonstrators were quoting Abraham Lincoln and carrying banners ordering the Communists to go home. It is entirely possible that the determination of the United States to "hold the freedom line" in a distant small nation has sparked "freedom rebellions" in other parts of the world. Such developments are momentarily reassuring, but "practical liberals" are looking forward to the day when the rebellious youth of the world will devote more energy to working and building instead of demonstrating— when the Family of Man will live together in a spirit of peace and mutual progress, with no one needing to tell anyone else to go home.

In Washington, the poverty war and other areas of

improvement are not being neglected. The Administration believes that our thriving economy can afford both guns and a reasonable amount of "butter." Vice President Humphrey is giving much of his attention to domestic problems again, but he will also continue to remind Americans that they must become more "Asian-minded" in an age when people can get so far so fast.

At a period in history when the world demands men who have the courage of their vision, American leaders realize that scores of tomorrow's vital problems must be solved today. When he signed a measure for additional research facilities at universities and hospitals last year, President Johnson spoke of continuing to set up ambitious, realistic goals, declaring that, "We must advance daily, or we will fail eternally."

In "War On Poverty," Vice President Humphrey endorsed those sentiments with a challenge that sums up the stature of the man and the quality of his statesmanship:

"Only if we wait passively for the future to come will we be its victims rather than its masters."

Credits

Acknowledgments

The Vice President is famed as a statesman who has always done his "homework" conscientiously. A biographer, seeking to do likewise, will be awed at the vast quantities of material dealing with this man's life and activities. Feature writers and columnists find him a fascinating subject; they capture his personality in phrases ranging from sincere solemnity to the most rollicking rhetoric.

For a public figure who is considered an extrovert, the Vice President shows no inclination to influence the people who write about him. Biographers usually need to get jobs on his staff to study him close up—at a sometimes breathless pace. I thank my predecessors for the occasional loan of their "track shoes."

In addition to the books listed on the credit page, grateful appreciation is extended to those commentators and syndicated journalists whom I have been permitted to quote at length: Roscoe Drummond, Harry Golden, Drew Pearson, Fletcher Knebel, Mary Tinley Daly, William S. White, and the Rev. Fr. Geno C.

Baroni. I would also like to thank numerous reporters and authors whose brief quotations have added color and zest.

Among the magazines and newspapers that have made the compilation of this book possible are Look, Life, Saturday Review, The Saturday Evening Post, Newsweek, Time, The Catholic Virginian, the Twin Cities and Washington, D. C. newspapers, New York Times, Brookings (S. D.) Register, Peoria Journal Star, The Carolina Israelite, Los Angeles Times, Parade Sunday supplement, Huron (S. D.) Plainsman, Winchester (Va.) Evening Star, and Northern Virginia Daily. The Congressional Record and other authoritative sources have also been consulted.

People of both major parties have responded generously to requests for reminiscences and anecdotes. I am especially grateful to two friends, Mrs. R. C. Lee of Peoria, Illinois, and Dona Brown of Huron, South Dakota. In addition to personal recollections, their connections with Ralph Gosch and Mrs. Harry Steed have provided some superb human interest material for this biography. Topping the list of other friends who have alerted me to Humphrey news are Lee and Harry Lovett. In various ways, my membership in The International Platform Association gave me access to valuable "exclusive" information.

A rich biographical harvest was reaped on Capitol Hill. There was Grace Tully, a great lady Democrat who makes other humans feel better for knowing her. It was through Grace that I met perspicacious young Teddy Roe, Senator "Mike" Mansfield's assistant, to whom the intricate operations of the Senate are no mystery. I shall always be grateful for Teddy's sage editorial advice and delightful anecdotes — and for keeping me from making several "boo-boos."

It was a pleasure and a political education to talk with three dedicated members of the Vice President's "brain trust"—Julius Cahn, John Stewart, and former press secretary Robert Jensen. I thank them for taking time out from their exceedingly busy schedules to answer my questions. Other members of the Vice President's office staff have been most courteous.

Again I offer an appreciative salute to the Handley Library staff in Winchester, Virginia, where I can always count on a gracious, heartwarming response to requests for assistance.

A detailed account of my researching experiences in the Library of Congress would resemble a "grand tour." My sincere thanks to everyone—Mr. Hunt of the Stack and Reader Division in the main building, the study room and periodical personnel in the annex, and the guards who registered my typewriter in and out. During the hours that were spent with films and files of the Minneapolis Tribune and Star Journal, and the St. Paul Dispatch and Pioneer Press, I felt as though I were reliving many of my years in Minnesota.

Among other rewarding experiences was a lengthy session in the manuscript division where the doctoral thesis of Charles E. Gilbert—"Problems of a Senator: A Study in Legislative Behavior"—is on microflim. Dr. Gilbert's thesis is a valuable political science document, and I thank him and the Library of Congress for making it available.

Gladys Zehnpfennig